SIMPLICIUS

On Aristotle's

"On the Heavens 1.1-4"

SIMPLICIUS

On Aristotle's "On the Heavens 1.1-4"

Translated by
R. J. Hankinson

Cornell University Press

Ithaca, New York

First published 2002 by Cornell University Press.

ISBN 0-8014-3907-8

Acknowledgments

The present translations have been made possible by generous and imaginative funding from the following sources: the National Endowment for the Humanities, Division of Research Programs, an independent federal agency of the USA; the Leverhulme Trust; the British Academy; the Jowett Copyright Trustees; the Royal Society (UK); Centro Internazionale A. Beltrame di Storia dello Spazio e del Tempo (Padua); Mario Mignucci; Liverpool University; the Leventis Foundation; the Arts and Humanities Research Board of the British Academy; the Esmée Fairbairn Charitable Trust; the Henry Brown Trust; Mr and Mrs N. Egon; the Netherlands Organisation for Scientific Research (NWO/GW). The editor wishes to thank Catherine Dalimier, Edward Hussey, Ian Mueller, David Robinson and David Sider for their comments, and Ian Crystal and Han Baltussen for preparing the volume for press.

Printed in Great Britain

Librarians: Library of Congress Cataloging-in-Publication Data are available

Contents

Conventions

[…] Square brackets enclose words or phrases that have been added to the translation or the lemmata for purposes of clarity, as well as those portions of the lemmata which are not quoted by Simplicius.

<…> Angle brackets enclose conjectures relating to the Greek text, i.e. additions to the transmitted text deriving from parallel sources and editorial conjecture, and transposition of words or phrases. Accompanying notes provide further details.

(…) Round brackets, besides being used for ordinary parentheses, contain transliterated Greek words and Bekker page references to the Aristotelian text.

Preface

Richard Sorabji

Aristotle thinks of the stars, sun, moon and planets as rotating round the earth at the centre on transparent spheres. Like most Greeks, he takes the rotation to be real not apparent. In chapter 1 of *On the Heavens* he defines body, and then notoriously introduces a fifth element, beyond Plato's four, to explain the rotation of the celestial spheres. This decision created a rupture in dynamics, separating celestial rotation from the rectilinear motion beneath the heavens. Even a member of Aristotle's school, Xenarchus, we are told by Simplicius, pp. 13-14; 20-6; 42; 50-1; 55-6, rejected his fifth element. He did so with the help of the powerful objection (21,32-22,17) that Aristotle admits, on the basis of comets and meteors, that the spherical belt of fire, in its natural place just below the heavens, rotates (Aristotle *Meteor.* 1.4; 1.7; *On the Heavens* 1.2), and further holds that an element acquires its pure form only when in its natural place (*On the Heavens* 4.3, 310a33-4). In that case, Xenarchus objects, the natural state of truly actual fire is not one of upward motion to its place, but one of rotation in its place, so that it becomes superfluous to postulate a fifth element, separate from fire, to account for celestial rotation. The same result follows, he holds, if rotation is only one of two natural motions of fire (23,31-27,7).

The Neoplatonist Simplicius, like some other late Neoplatonists, treats the rotation of the spherical fire-belt differently. It is not, after all, in the nature of fire to rotate as it is in the nature of the fifth element. Rather, fire's motion, influenced by the higher nature of the fifth element, can be called supernatural (*huper phusin*), *above* its nature, 21,22-5, a concept first used by Origen in the third century AD in relation to the resurrection, but reminiscent of Plato *Timaeus* 41A-B.

Simplicius further seeks to harmonise Plato and Aristotle. Plato, he says, anticipated the need for the fifth element. What Plato believed was that the heavens were composed of all four elements but with the purest kind of fire, namely light, predominating, 66,33-67,5; 85,7-15. That Plato would not mind this being called a fifth element is shown by his associating with the heavens (*Timaeus* 55C) the fifth of the five convex regular solids recognized by geometry, 12,16-27. This last argument had earlier been produced by Proclus *in Tim.* 1.6,29-7,2; 2.49,29-50,2 Diehl, but in very different spirit. In his preface, Proclus wanted to show that everything said by Aristotle had been anticipated by Plato. On the other hand, in 85,31-86,7 Simplicius argues in the opposite direction that Aristotle didn't mean there to be a fifth element quite literally, but spoke of the mixture as if it were an extra element, to emphasise its divinity, which Simplicius' Christian contemporaries denied.

Simplicius reveals (32,1-11) that the Aristotelian Alexander of Aphrodisias knew of a very serious objection to Aristotle's celestial system, and that the objection was also expounded (504,17-506,3) by Alexander's teacher Sosigenes. The planets were seen to be closer at some times of the year than at others, and so the transparent spheres on which they were said to revolve could not all rotate, in Aristotle's way, around the same centre. The standard solutions were circles on circles (epicycles), or eccentrics. We are not told how Alexander accommodated these in his system. But we do know from Alexander *Quaestiones* 1.25 that Alexander reduced Aristotle's system of up to fifty-five transparent spheres (Aristotle *Metaph.* 12.8) down to a mere seven.

Aristotle's philosopher-god is turned by Simplicius, following his teacher Ammonius, into a creator-god, like Plato's. Ammonius wrote a whole book on the subject whose arguments Simplicius summarises in another work, *in Phys.* 1361,11-1363,12. But the creation is beginningless, as shown by the argument that, if you try to imagine a time when it began, you cannot answer the question, 'Why not sooner?', *in Cael.* 138,2-16. Once again, the contrast with Proclus is striking. Proclus had complained (*in Tim.* 1.266,28-268,24) that Aristotle ought to have accepted a creator-god, but failed to do so.

In explaining the Creation, Simplicius follows the Neoplatonist expansion of Aristotle's four 'causes', or types of explanatory factors, to a set of six. Besides Aristotle's formal, final, efficient and material causes, there is the Platonic paradigmatic cause already known to Seneca *Ep.* 65,4-16, and based on the idea that Platonic Forms are paradigms. And then there is the instrumental cause. Aristotle had regarded his material cause as instrumental (e.g. *On Generation of Animals* 5.9), but the instrumental had been treated as a distinct cause by Galen, *On Antecedent Causes* 6.63-6, as explained by Jim Hankinson, 'Galen's theory of causation', *Aufstieg und Niedergang der römischen Welt* 2.37.2. The first to ascribe all six causes to Plato had been Proclus, *in Tim.* 263,19-30.

The manoeuvres behind Simplicius' account finish up by giving us a cosmology significantly different from Aristotle's original conception. I have been describing Simplicius' commentary *On Aristotle On the Heavens* Book 1, Chapters 1-4 as a whole. But in fact the translation of these chapters will be divided into two volumes in this series. The second volume (*Simplicius: Against Philoponus on the Eternity of the World*, translated by I. Mueller *et al.*, forthcoming) will cover the controversy between

Simplicius and Philoponus and will therefore partly overlap with an earlier volume in this series, *Philoponus: On Aristotle on the Eternity of the World*, translated by Christian Wildberg, 1987.

Introduction

(i) Simplicius' times

Simplicius stands at the very end of the ancient Greek tradition, at least as it is usually conceived. His life coincided with the closure of the pagan philosophical schools of Athens and the exile of their members by the Christian emperor Justinian in AD 529, with which Greek philosophy is traditionally supposed to have come to an end. History does not of course parcel itself out thus neatly around a few critical dates learned in school – but this conventional *terminus* serves a useful purpose in fixing our attention on what was undoubtedly a turning-point in the history of Western civilisation.

The Athenian pagan Neoplatonists, who had flourished in relative tranquillity and freedom for more than a century, at least since the time of Plutarch of Athens (*fl. c.* AD 400), at any rate by comparison with their persecuted brethren in Alexandria, were unceremoniously shut down and kicked out. They moved first apparently to Ctesiphon in Mesopotamia, and thence scattered to other places; some may have returned at length to Athens[1] – although I think the evidence tells against this[2] – but if they did it was never again to teach the old philosophy with an official *imprimatur* of an established school behind them. For the last time, pagan philosophy was ousted from official acceptance in Athens. The Athenian school continued for the rest of the century, but when it came to an end, the long ideological battle for hegemony that had been fought at least since the time of Constantine was finally settled, in the Greco-Roman world at least, in favour of Christianity – although in truth that ultimate victory had been secure for some time.

Simplicius was part of this school, and of its forced upheaval and exile. And it was in this exile[3] that he composed the bulk of his commentaries on Aristotle in the pious hope (he was a deeply religious man) of keeping the flame of the old rationality alive against the encroaching darkness (as he saw it) of Christian dogma. For his commentaries are not merely dry expositions and exegeses of Aristotle's difficult and elliptical texts – they are part of a lively and frequently acerbic philosophical debate between pagan Neoplatonism and its Christian usurper, the foremost representative of which was the Alexandrian John Philoponus, Simplicius' contemporary and arch intellectual enemy.[4]

Much of what Simplicius writes in his commentary on *de Caelo* is animated by a bitter rejection of the views of Philoponus, expressed in his treatise *Against Aristotle on the Eternity of the World* (written at some time in the 530s) in which he had upheld, against Aristotle, the thesis of the world's creation in time.[5]

Philoponus had originally endorsed Aristotle's view that the world had no beginning, in the course of editing the lectures of his pagan master in Alexandria, Ammonius. But in his additions to these texts, and above all in the sequence of three polemics *On the Eternity of the World*, of which the first, directed against the 5th-century Neoplatonist systematizer Proclus, was composed in 529 (*Against Aristotle* was the second of the series), Philoponus showed himself a man of the new wave, boldly rejecting the central tenets of Aristotelian physical theory in favour of a new dynamics and a cosmology of original generation.

His Platonism was much more closely allied to a literal reading of the *Timaeus*, according to which the Demiurge (i.e. God) really had created the world and its contents, as opposed to the figurative interpretation common in syncretistic Neoplatonist circles and endorsed by Simplicius (but which was familiar to Aristotle, and stretched back to Plato's earliest successors in the Academy) to the effect that Plato simply meant to give a graphic illustration of the metaphysical composition of the world, not of any actual temporal origination of it.[6]

Simplicius treats both Philoponus and the doctrine he represents as upstart and intellectually disreputable: indeed the very fact that he considers Philoponus so evidently his intellectual inferior argues for the view[7] that he does not deliberately distort his position (although he may well on occasion misunderstand it)[8] – one does not misrepresent a position that one is in any case confident of demolishing.

Simplicius' *in de Caelo* indeed preserves by far the bulk of the surviving fragments of Philoponus' anti-Aristotelian treatise (ably collated and translated by Christian Wildberg elsewhere in this series: op. cit., n. 7). Large sections of Simplicius' commentary on Chapters 2-4 of Book 1 of *de Caelo* are devoted to the exposition and refutation of Philoponus' views – and these have been omitted from this volume. As Wildberg (op. cit., n. 27) remarks:

> one can distinguish four long and clearly separated sections which Simplicius, digressing from the commentary proper, dedicates to the refutation of 'the Grammarian': (1) *in de Caelo* 26-59;[9] (2) *in de Caelo* 66-91; (3) *in de Caelo* 119-42; (4) *in de Caelo* 156-99.

Large parts of these sections, since they are self-contained, and since their Philoponan content has already been translated in Wildberg's book, are omitted from this volume. Simplicius' replies to Philoponus are due to be translated in the series by Ian Mueller.

According to Simplicius (*in Cael.* 119,7), Philoponus arrogated to himself the title of 'Grammarian'; and Simplicius regularly refers to him thus (e.g. at 49,10; 56,26; 70,34; 73,10; 156,26; 162,20) not without a discernible tinge of irony. Indeed, when he deals with Philoponus, Simplicius' normally dry style becomes greatly enlivened with the characteristic Greek relish for personal abuse. He accuses Philoponus of plagiarizing Xenarchus (ibid. 25,22-5), of pandering to an uneducated Christian public (ibid. 26,2-12), and of an unlovely combination of arrogance, self-aggrandizement, and ignorance (ibid. 26,25-31).

He calls him, after the ironic fashion of Greek invective, 'this man of noble birth' (ibid. 48,14), 'this estimable man' (ibid. 45,27; 83,25; 170,11; 176,13; 188,2), 'excellent fellow' (ibid. 58,4; 78,9), and more in the same vein. At ibid. 66,10 (and *in Phys.* 1117,15) he refers to Philoponus as 'the Telchin'. The Telchines were originally a tribe of legendary Cretan metalworkers; for some reason the epithet became associated with maliciousness and back-biting, and perhaps also philistinism (Callimachus directs the prologue of his *Aitia* 'Against the Telchines', in this case opponents of his own refined and delicate aesthetic).

Simplicius' bitterness at the Christians' success is tangible – and he consoles himself with the conviction that this triumph (and the fame of Philoponus' writings) is temporary and will be short-lived, like the brief, deceptive blooms of the gardens of Adonis (ibid. 25,34-6). That belief may now seem, with the benefit of hindsight, to have been mere wishful thinking; but there was no reason at the time to think that the issue had been finally settled by the imperial edict of 529, the same year as saw the publication of Philoponus' first great blast against pagan Neoplatonism, *Against Proclus*. It is only in retrospect that we can see Simplicius not as fighting a strategic and temporary retreat against a temporarily dominant adversary, but as mounting a final and doomed last-ditch stand against the Christian tide. The expulsion of 529 might have seemed but a temporary set-back at the time – we can now see it as the crux of history that it was.

(ii) Simplicius' life and works

About Simplicius' life we know remarkably little, although we can date that of his rival with some accuracy. Philoponus' life spanned the period roughly from 490 to the 570s. He produced at least some of his first major Aristotelian commentary (*in Phys.*) in 517, although there is dispute as to its precise order of composition.[10] As I noted above, the appearance of his *Against Proclus on the Eternity of the World* in Alexandria coincided with Justinian's expulsion; and the *Against Aristotle*, against which Simplicius rails in our text, followed shortly thereafter.

That gives us a *terminus post quem* for *in Cael.*; but it is a vague one. On the not unreasonable (although clearly not unexceptionable) assumption that Simplicius composed at least the anti-Philoponan passages of *in*

Cael. shortly after reading Philoponus' treatise, that would place them in the 530s, and on other grounds this seems the likeliest date for the composition of our text. However, it is apparent that he would have needed access to a relatively well-stocked library in order to produce work of such detailed scholarship (he evidently had access to texts of Alexander, Iamblichus, Syrianus, Ammonius, and Philoponus, as well as those of Plato,[11] Aristotle, Plotinus, and, most famously, Parmenides; he may also have had texts of Nicholas of Damascus and Xenarchus to hand as well) and it is indeed partly this fact which has induced some to postulate a return to Athens after a brief Persian exile.[12]

We know from the historian Agathias (*Hist.* 2.30.3ff.) that 'Damascius of Syria, Simplicius of Cilicia, Eulamius of Phrygia, Priscian of Lydia, Hermias and Diogenes from Phoenicia, and Isidore of Gaza, the finest flower ... of our time' had abandoned the Byzantine empire of Justinian because of the increasing persecution of non-Christians there; they sought refuge with the Persian king Chosroes, perhaps led there, as Ilsetraut Hadot suggests,[13] by the prospect of the relative ideological freedom of the Nestorian university of Nisibis.

Chosroes had a codicil added to the peace treaty he concluded with Justinian in 532 providing safe passage and freedom of thought for the exiles in their homeland, a fact which has also encouraged some to believe in their ultimate peaceful return to Athens. But as Hadot[14] notes, it is hard to believe that such treaty-clauses would inspire much confidence in religious refugees in a time rife with intolerance and pogrom, and in a town as volatile as Athens. After all, the Persian king could not guarantee their safety hundreds of miles away on the other side of the Byzantine empire. Moreover, there is no other indication of a return to Athens.

It now seems increasingly likely, in my view, on the basis of evidence painstakingly collected by Michel Tardieu,[15] that Simplicius in fact decamped to the city of Harrân (the Roman Carrhae, scene of Crassus' catastrophic defeat by the Parthians in 53 BC), only a few miles over the Byzantine frontier in a fluid border region, where there was a flourishing tradition of religious dissent that was to survive for another five centuries. There was also there, in later years, a school of Neoplatonism – and it is conjectured that this was the remote descendant of one established there by some at least of the exiled Hellenic philosophers, under the protection of the Persian king, who was committed to supporting any ideological bulwark against the encroaching tide of Christianity.[16]

That Simplicius did indeed remain in this remote but flourishing border-town is further suggested by a tantalizing remark in a recently-reconstituted passage of Simplicius' commentary on Epictetus' *Handbook*. The new text of Hadot[17] has Simplicius in direct communication with a Manichaean, and Tardieu claims,[18] perhaps a trifle exaggeratedly, that Harrân was just about the only place in the entire empire where this would have been possible. Moreover there is no reason to doubt that it could have possessed library resources sufficient to meet Simplicius' considerable needs.

Thus we can hypothesize that, sometime after 532 when the philosophical exiles re-crossed the Persian-Byzantine border with Chosroes' safe-conduct (Agathias, *Hist.* 2.31.5ff.), Simplicius settled down to a life of relative quiet, comfort, and safety (Agathias claims that the exiles 'took advantage of their exile in no small and insignificant manner, but in order to pass the remainder of their lives in the most pleasant and agreeable fashion': *Hist.* 2.31.3) to write his great commentaries.[19]

On the basis of internal cross-references, *in Cael.* seems to be the earliest of the authentic Simplician commentaries on Aristotle, antedating both *in Physica*[20] and *in Categorias*. *In Phys.* must have been written at least after 532, and very probably after 538, since it speaks of Damascius, the last head of the school in Athens and Simplicius' co-exile and teacher, as though he were already dead, while he is known to have been alive at the earlier date and is likely to have lived until the later.[21]

Further evidence for the date of *in Cael.* is to be derived from a first-hand reference (525,13) to an observation of the strength of the wind made near the river Aboras in Mesopotamia; as Hadot says, since the river in question passes close to Harrân, it now seems plausible to date the commentary to the period after Simplicius had settled there. Thus a date in the mid-530s seems on balance most probable for the composition of our text. But more than that we cannot, as yet at least, say with certainty.

In addition to Damascius, Simplicius had also studied with the Neoplatonist Ammonius ('our leader Ammonius', Simplicius calls him: *in Cael.* 271,19), who happened also to be the teacher of Philoponus, in Alexandria. Ammonius' teaching career spanned the fifty years around the turn of the sixth century, and so the simple fact that the two great antagonists were each at some time pupils of the same master does not of itself cast doubt on Simplicius' insistence that he has never met 'the Grammarian' (*in Cael.* 26,18-19), and hence that he is not motivated by personal animosity.

At some point, then, in the early decades of the sixth century, Simplicius moved from Alexandria to Athens, from where he was expelled by the edict of 529. He made his home at least for a while in the Persian empire and may – or more likely may not – at some time have returned to Athens. And that is all we know.

(iii) Simplicius' methods and style

Like many of his contemporaries, Simplicius wrote voluminously; and his works (those that survive at least) all take the form of commentaries on Aristotle (although they contain various digressions and divagations from the form of commentary proper). They are wordy to the point of windiness, and precise to the point of pedantry. They are enormously detailed, and heavily repetitious. With the exception of the flashes of brilliance to be found in the personal invective, as noted above, their dryness of style is largely unenlivened by wit, or indeed anything else. No one, I think, would read Simplicius for fun; and like most late antique writers he would have benefited greatly from a good and ruthless editor.

The commentary on *de Caelo* is typically (perhaps even excessively) long-winded. It runs to 731 largish printed pages of Greek in Heiberg's 1894 edition for the *Commentaria in Aristotelem Graeca*, which makes it more than ten times the length of Aristotle's original text; and much of that length is taken up with what appears, to the modern eye at least, to be mere, trivial, scholastic quibbling.

Yet it would be rash and premature to conclude that Simplicius contains nothing of interest for the modern reader. Apart from his controversies with Philoponus which have been noted above, Simplicius reports a wealth of detail regarding other authorities now lost to us. In particular, he had at his side Alexander of Aphrodisias' commentary on *de Caelo* (now lost), from which he quotes extensively and upon which he comments, sometimes agreeing, sometimes disagreeing with the conclusions of his exegetic predecessor, an engagement which allows us to reconstruct the general outlines of Alexander's interpretation in some detail.

Moreover, the nature of these disagreements is itself instructive. Alexander saw himself as an orthodox Aristotelian defending the true Peripatetic way; and his Aristotle is, for the most part, one fully recognizable, indeed familiar, to modern eyes. Simplicius, on the other hand, is a highly religious, albeit pagan, Neoplatonist, and moreover one who stands at the end of a five-hundred-year long tradition of Platonist syncretism: his Aristotle is the Aristotle of the Platonist revival, more of an extender and codifier of the doctrines of his master than a radical and original thinker.

Equally, his Plato is a Plato read in the light of later systematic developments. Simplicius is quite happy to credit Plato with positing six types of cause (the standard Neoplatonic six causes in fact), three in a primary sense (the Creator, the exemplar, and the end), along with three 'co-operative causes' (*sunaitia*):[22] matter, form, and the instrument; while Alexander (reported by Simplicius in the same passage) holds that Plato speaks only of 'three principles', matter, the Creator, and the paradigm (*in Phys.* 1.2, 26,5-25).

The two commentators disagree deeply in their interpretation of Plato's writing, in particular as regards the *Timaeus*, a text which, for obvious reasons, both of them frequently compare with *de Caelo*. While Alexander sticks closely to a literal reading of the text, Simplicius insists that behind it one may readily discern the extra categories, including the Aristotelian final cause, and the immanent enmattered form.

Alexander, in line with Aristotelian orthodoxy, interprets the *Timaeus* as offering an account of a creation of the universe in time; Plato's universe, then, was generated, but is indestructible, a combination which Aristotle himself holds to be impossible (*Cael.* 1.10-12); his *Timaeus*, then, is a text to be refuted from a Peripatetic standpoint. Simplicius, as was noted above (n. 7), takes the 'generation' to be a matter of ongoing, and everlasting, metaphysical dependency, a move which allows him to re-integrate the views of Plato and Aristotle into a suitably syncretistic whole: this, indeed, is the express purpose of the long digression on generation and the metaphysical structure of reality, which takes up *in Cael.* 1.3, 92,32-107,24.

Precisely congruent disagreements may be found in their respective treatments of Aristotle. In his exegesis of *Metaph.* 5.2, Alexander insists (surely rightly) that only four fundamental types of cause are to be found there. By contrast, when Simplicius comments on the (virtually identical) *Phys.* 2.3, he once more discovers the six causes of Neoplatonist orthodoxy, picking up on Aristotle's remark that there are a number of 'intermediates', which function as instruments (*Phys.* 2.3, 194b35ff.), in order to attribute an instrumental cause to him (*in Phys.* 2.3, 316,3-11), taking issue with Alexander's contention (again surely a reasonable one) that these should be characterized as intermediate efficient causes.

Moreover, he also contrives to discover in Aristotle not only enmattered, immanent forms, but separated, paradigmatic Forms as well (*in Phys.* 2.3, 314,9-23), bringing the number up to the canonical six, interpreting Aristotle's remark to the effect that four is 'pretty much' the number of the causes (*Phys.* 2.3, 195a3), to mean that really he thought that there were six of them (*in Phys.* 2.3, 316,22-9).

Characteristic of this divergence in interpretative strategy and method is Simplicius' disagreement with Alexander over the role of Aristotle's Prime Mover. Alexander takes it to function simply as a final cause for all motion (*in Cael.* 1.8, 271,11-27); Simplicius, in best Neoplatonizing fashion, seeks to make the Prime Mover an efficient cause of the existence of the universe as well (*in Cael.* 87,3-11; 143,9-144,4; 154,6-156,24; 271,5-21, *in Phys.* 256,16-25; 1360,25.28-31; 1362,8.16.32). Moreover, he summarises the arguments from a whole book by Ammonius to this effect, at *in Phys.* 1361,11-1363,12. (See Sorabji, *Matter, Space and Motion*, ch. 15.) This view harmonised Aristotle with Plato's belief in a Creator God.

Equally, in the one substantial digression translated in this volume (*in Cael.* 92,32-107,24), we learn a good deal about the Neoplatonic treatment of causation and generation standard in Simplicius' time; and Simplicius apparently feels no tension in transferring these concepts to Aristotle. Yet Simplicius is not simply an unintelligent syncretist: he is, in fact, a careful and sympathetic reader of Aristotle, concerned to acquit him of the grosser fallacies and stupidities attributed to him by his opponents, principally of course Philoponus.

This fact, in conjunction with the palpable strangeness, to a modern philosophical sensibility, of Simplicius' syncretizing interpretations of Aristotle, is in itself interesting. The Neoplatonist interpreters of Aristotle lived in an intellectual world which is in many ways utterly foreign to our own. Their readings of their texts were coloured, indeed dictated, by the necessity of finding within them the appropriate, synthetic truth. Their understandings of the authors in the Greek philosophical tradition were derived from what was, by Simplicius' day, a centuries-old tradition of Platonist hermeneutics. It is startling, as well as stimulating and refreshing, to see Aristotle through such an unfamiliar lens; and it may help serve as a valuable correction to the tendency to suppose that the Aristotle of the modern analytically-trained historian is the only intellectually respectable one.

Finally, Simplicius' commentaries are an invaluable source for the views of other ancient philosophers whose works are now lost. As is relatively well known, we owe most of what we know of Parmenides' Way of Truth to Simplicius' conscientiousness in transcribing it 'since copies of it are now difficult to come by' (*in Phys.* 1.3, 144,25-9). In our text (*in Cael.* 1.10, 294,33-295,24) a substantial fragment of Aristotle's lost *On Democritus* is preserved, as well as reports of the views of otherwise little-known Peripatetics, such as Xenarchus (1.2; 13,22-14,21; 21,33-25,23; 42,6-16; 55,23-56,25) and Nicholas of Damascus (1.1, 3,28-9). His commentary on *Cael.* 1.8 (264,25-265,6) contains a fascinating (if controversial)[23] glimpse of the great astronomer Hipparchus' account of weight, lightness, and motion. And these are not isolated nuggets.

The surviving fragments of Xenarchus' *Against the Fifth Substance*, almost all of which are preserved in the commentary on *Cael.* 1.2, are of particular importance, and not only for their intrinsic interest, which is considerable. Little is known about Xenarchus, or about the early Imperial Aristotelianism, of which he is a representative (see Ch. 2, n. 83); but it is evident from what Simplicius reports that he was an Aristotelian who was quite prepared to take issue with his Master on a number of topics. In particular, as the title of his treatise suggests, he rejected the Aristotelian arguments for a separate fifth element, and argued that the heavenly bodies were composed of fire, producing ingenious objections to Aristotle's reasonings in favour of the ether, and his account of natural motions and places, which Simplicius accuses Philoponus of plagiarizing.

What emerges from this is the extent to which one could disagree with Aristotle at the end of the first century BC and yet still count oneself an Aristotelian. Indeed ever since Theophrastus took over the Lyceum on Aristotle's death, subsequent Peripatetics were not chary about adapting, even rejecting, key elements in his philosophy. The most radical in this regard was Strato of Lampsacus, the third head of the Lyceum, who can barely be counted as Aristotelian at all (he abandoned teleology and the theory of natural place, as well as the doctrine of the ether), but as the example of Xenarchus shows, to be an Aristotelian in this period was very far from being a slavish adherent to the words of the *maestro di color che sanno*.

This free approach was halted by Alexander, who saw his role as one of expounding an orthodoxy, and of extending it into domains that Aristotle himself had not touched (this too was a practice inaugurated by Theophrastus). We may thus, with Simplicius' help, distinguish three very broadly-drawn phases in post-Aristotelian Aristotelian philosophy: first comes the period of free adaptation and re-evaluation begun by Theophrastus, carried to an extreme by Strato, and exemplified by Xenarchus; then comes the era of orthodox interpretation most closely associated with Alexander; and finally we have the age of the Neoplatonist commentators like Simplicius himself, whose interpretative goals are both more ambitious and more nuanced.

So Simplicius' work is, in a variety of different ways, a rich trove for the historian of ideas attempting to reconstruct the intellectual history of some of the murkier periods in ancient philosophy. But it would be a mistake to think that Simplicius' commentaries are valuable only for the information they contain about other thinkers. Simplicius' own discussions are sometimes tedious and unilluminating; but from time to time he will cast genuine light on a difficult passage, and introduce interesting and original ideas of his own. And if he is often ploddingly pedestrian, he is rarely simply silly. Readers who take the trouble to re-read Aristotle's text carefully against the background of Simplicius' exegesis will find their own interpretations and understandings of its arguments deepened and enriched.

Simplicius was not a philosopher of the first rank. But he had an able philosophical intelligence, albeit one which may seem, to modern sensibilities at any rate, to be excessively scholastic in temper. His work is not worthy of the immortal fame of an Aristotle. But nor does it merit the obscurity into which it has sunk, until very recent times at any rate, in the modern philosophical community.

(iv) *De Caelo* and *In de Caelo* 1.1-4

De Caelo is one of the most important and influential of Aristotle's treatises, and if its bright reputation has been somewhat dimmed in recent years, there are now encouraging signs that this eclipse is coming to an end. Historically, its claim to serious attention is unchallengeable; it formed the intellectual foundation for the cosmology of the Arabic schools of the early middle ages, and as such was much commented upon by the Arabic masters, in particular Averroes and Avicenna. Thomas Aquinas, following the Latin version of William of Moerbeke, elevated it to an equally canonical status in the Christian west from the thirteenth century onwards.

As we have seen, his defence of the uncreated and indestructible nature of the world drew fire from the Christian Philoponus, who is the true originator of an alternative, anti-Aristotelian cosmology and dynamics which gained adherents in the later middle ages.

But in spite of a series of attacks on Aristotle's positions on these issues undertaken by Bonaventure and Buridan among others, under the authority of Aquinas they remained the orthodoxy until the seventeenth century, when Galileo began to mount his heroic and ultimately successful – albeit personally disastrous – assault on the Aristotelian world-picture. In Galileo's *magnum opus* of cosmological revisionism, the *Dialogues concerning the Two Principal World-Systems* of 1632, the publication of which led to his final arraignment, trial, and sentencing to house-arrest in perpetuity, the text of *de Caelo* lies constantly in the background of the discussion.

Moreover, Galileo's hostility to Aristotle has often been misrepresented as denigration of the Stagirite's intellectual abilities, which is very far from being the case. Galileo had the greatest respect for Aristotle – so much so that he was quite convinced that he would, if presented with the evidence for heliocentricity (or at any rate that against geocentricity), have abandoned his original views. Like Newton, Galileo was quite happy to admit that he stood upon the shoulders of giants. His disagreement was with the Aristotelians, particularly the scholastic practitioners of the art he regularly crossed in the universities of Northern Italy (in particular those of Pisa and Padua, where he taught at the beginning of his career), whom he caricatured as hidebound, intellectually-sclerotic adherents of authority and book-learning as opposed to careful observation and rigorous empirically-based argument.

In this context, it is significant, if perhaps a trifle unfair (the name was obviously *ben trovato* for other reasons), that he names the exponent of ossified orthodoxy in his *Dialogues* 'Simplicio'.

This volume is the first of three, which together translate the commentary sections of Simplicius' commentary on the first book of *de Caelo* (the second and third will contain his commentary on Chapters 5-9 and 10-12 respectively). This division was necessitated by the length of Simplicius' text – but it is not an entirely arbitrary one. At the end of his *Prologue* (6,7-27), where Simplicius himself offers a résumé of the contents of Book 1 of *de Caelo*, which suggests, *inter alia*, the naturalness of the breaks between Chapters 4 and 5, and 9 and 10. Thus the resulting three volumes deal with the basic subject-matter of the inquiry into nature, and the argument for the existence of a separate element for the heavenly bodies (*Cael.* 1.1-4), the finitude and uniqueness of the cosmos (*Cael.* 1.5-9), and its ungenerability, indestructibility, and eternity (*Cael.* 1.10-12).

In the part of the text dealt with in this volume, Chapter 1 proposes that physical science is concerned with bodies and magnitudes and their properties, and establishes the completeness of three-dimensional extension. Chapter 2 derives the existence of five elements on the basis of a consideration of the three natural directions of motion which the elements must exhibit, and infers that the celestial element, whose natural motion is circular, is distinct from any of the terrestrial elements, which naturally move in straight lines.[24] Chapters 3-4 prove that the celestial element is ungenerated and indestructible, on the grounds that it has no contrary.

Simplicius begins his work with a short *Prologue*, in which he addresses the question of the overall aim or intention of the treatise, its *skopos* or subject-matter. Assigning the correct *skopos* to a work was a matter of some importance to the commentators; it was a matter of determining the principle of unity behind the work ('each treatise demands a single subject dealing with one thing', Simplicius writes at 3,15). This poses something of a problem in the case of *de Caelo*, which seems to range over a variety of different topics, and Simplicius reports much divergence of views among his predecessors. Is it about 'the world and the five bodies in it' (as Alexander said: 1,10-12)? Or is it really only about the 'divine and heavenly body', with the discussion of the other elements included only insofar as they depend upon it (the view of Iamblichus: 1,24-2,5)? Or is it solely about the heavens, with the other elements mentioned 'only insofar as it contributes to the study of the heavenly bodies' (Syrianus and his followers: 2,5-12)? Simplicius' own contention is that the treatise concerns the five elements and their properties, and not the whole world as such (4,25-5,13).

In truth, *de Caelo* is something of a rag-bag, and as such resistant to the imposition of any artificial unity upon it. Moreover, knowing what we know about the composition and transmission of Aristotle's surviving works, this should occasion no surprise: what we have of Aristotle was put together out of notes for lecture-courses by later editors. Yet if one had to opt for a unifying theme, that of the elements and their fundamental properties and what can be deduced about the world on the basis of those properties would be better than most.

The search for the *skopos*, then, turns out to be characteristic of Simplicius' approach, and neatly encapsulates his strengths and his weaknesses. He is hamstrung by the late antique desire to see form and system in everything; he reports the views of others at what some might consider to be needless length; but his conclusions are, given the constraints within which he is working, for the most part intelligent and judicious. The project may be misconceived – but if you are going to carry it out at all, you could do it very much worse.

After the *Prologue*, Simplicius treats Aristotle's text line by line, lemma by lemma, chapter by chapter. The MSS of Simplicius reproduce only the opening and closing words of each lemma, the supposition presumably being that anyone using the commentary would also have a text of Aristotle to hand. In common with some of the translators in this series, I have chosen to include the whole of the texts that Simplicius comments upon: the parts of each lemma that do not appear in the MSS are enclosed within square brackets.

Thus this volume contains, *inter alia*, a translation of the first book of *de Caelo*. The basis for this translation is the version prepared by Mohan Matthen and myself for our forthcoming collaborative contribution to the Clarendon Aristotle Series, but it is not identical with it. I have standardized the technical terminology to conform to the translations I prefer in the case of Simplicius; and additionally there are several places where the text of Aristotle that Simplicius had before him clearly differs in some way (usually fairly insignificantly) from the preferred modern versions: D.J. Allan in the *OCT*, Guthrie in the Loeb Classical Library (*Aristotle*: in twenty-three volumes; VI: *On the Heavens*, London, 1939), or Moraux in the Budé (*Aristote: du Ciel*, Paris, 1965). I have indicated these divergences in notes as they occur.

The Greek text used is that of I.L. Heiberg in the *Commentaria in Aristotelem Graeca* (*CAG*: under the general editorship of H. Diels), vol. VII, Berlin, 1894. In a few places where I have departed from that text, I have noted the fact ad loc., and a full list of preferred readings appears on pp. 15-16.

I am very much in the debt of several anonymous 'vetters', as a result of whose skills my translation is much healthier than it would otherwise have been, in terms of both accuracy and felicity. On the occasions where I have rejected their advice, I have not done so lightly nor without careful consideration. In addition, Kirk Sanders read considerable portions of the earlier sections, and offered many useful suggestions relating to both form and content. The Project's various assistants (Han Baltussen, Sylvia Berryman, Eleni Vambouli, Ian Crystal) have, at various times, rendered assistance with exemplary skill and tact. Finally, I would also like to thank Richard Sorabji, for inviting me to contribute to his series, for his unfailing enthusiasm and encouragement, for several particular suggestions for improvement which I have gratefully adopted, and above all for his patience in awaiting the results of a project that took me much longer than I had originally expected it to.

Notes

1. This position is adopted by A. Cameron, 'The last days of the Academy at Athens', *Proceedings of the Cambridge Philological Society* 195, n.s. 15 (1969), 7-29.

2. See A. Frantz, 'Pagan philosophers in Christian Athens', *Proceedings of the American Philological Society* 119 (1975), 29-38 and P. Athanassiadi, *Damascius: The Philosophical History*, text, translation and notes (Athens, 1999).

3. I incline to the view, *pace* Cameron (art. cit., n. 1 above), that Simplicius did not return to live in Athens (see further below); but even if he did, his position there, cut off from an organized school and from formal teaching may without hyperbole be described as a form of exile.

4. The revival of interest in Philoponus, and appreciation of his importance as a pivotal figure in the (albeit long drawn-out and delayed) movement from Aristotelianism to the rise of impetus-theory, has been engineered (in the Anglophone world at least) largely by the efforts of Richard Sorabji: see his (ed.) *Philoponus and the Rejection of Aristotelian Science* (London, 1987); see also Sorabji, *Time,*

Creation and the Continuum (London, 1982), and *Matter, Space and Motion* (London, 1988).

5. On the dating of Philoponus' treatise, see R. Sorabji, 'Introduction: purpose, content and significance', in C. Wildberg, *Philoponus: Against Aristotle on the Eternity of the World* (London, 1987), 23-4.

6. For Aristotle's familiarity with (and rejection of) the figurative interpretation, see *Cael.* 1.10, 279b32-280a11; Simplicius discusses the issue at *in Cael.* 1.10, 296,1-301,28 and 303,33-307,11; see also *in Cael.* 1.3, 103,1-107,19.

7. Expressed by C. Wildberg, *Philoponus: Against Aristotle on the Eternity of the World* (London 1987), 30-1.

8. As he does on at least one occasion in the case of Alexander of Aphrodisias' commentary on the *Physics*: see M. Rashad, 'New Fragments of Alexander in Simplicius', in R.R.K. Sorabji (ed.) *Aristotle and After*, BICS supp. vol. 68 (1997).

9. The numbering given refers to the edition of I.L. Heiberg, *Simplicii in Aristotelis de Caelo Commentaria* (Berlin 1894), vol. VII of *Commentaria in Aristotelem Graeca* [*CAG*].

10. See K. Verrycken, 'The development of Philoponus' thought and its chronology', in R. Sorabji (ed.) *Aristotle Transformed* (London 1990), esp. 244-54. See also Frans de Haas, *Philoponus' New Definition of Prime Matter: Aspects of its background in Neoplatonism and the Ancient Commentary Tradition* (Leiden 1997) and Wildberg's review in *Hermathena* of Clemens Scholten, *Antike Naturphilosophie und christliche Kosmologie in der Schrift de Opificio Mundi des Johannes Philoponus*.

11. In spite of the fact that he sometimes seems to be quoting from memory (e.g. at 104,32-105,2: a passage from the *Statesman*), it is unreasonable to imagine that all his lengthy citations from other sources were memorized.

12. The best case for this has been made out by A. Cameron, op. cit. n. 1.

13. I. Hadot, 'The life and works of Simplicius in Greek and Arabic sources', in Sorabji, op. cit. n. 10, 278-80. Also see I. Hadot, Introduction, *Simplicius Commentaire sur le Manuel d' Epictète* (Leiden 1996).

14. Op. cit., n. 12, 280.

15. See M. Tardieu, 'Sâbiens coraniques et "Sâbiens" de Harrân', *Journal Asiatique* 127 (1986); id., 'Les calendriers en usage à Harrân d'après les sources arabes et le commentaire de Simplicius à la *Physique* d'Aristote', in I. Hadot (ed.), *Simplicius – sa vie, son oeuvre, sa survie* (Berlin 1987) and I. Hadot, Introduction, *Simplicius. Commentaire sur le Manuel d'Epictète* (Leiden 1996). But see also the doubts expressed by Paul Foulkes, 'Where was Simplicius?' *JHS* 112 (1992), 143, S. van Riet, 'A propos de la biographie de Simplicius', *Rev. Phil. de Louv.* 89 (1991), 506-14; H.J. Blumenthal, '529 and its sequel: what happened to the Academy?' *Byzantium* 48 (1978), 369-85 and reprinted in his *Soul and the Intellect* (Aldershot 1993); and most recently J. Lameer, 'From Alexandria to Baghdad: Reflections on the genesis of a problematical tradition', in G. Endress and R. Kruk (eds.) *The Ancient Traditions in Christian and Islamic Hellenism* (Leiden 1997), 181-91.

16. Procopius, the official (and unofficial) historian of Justinian's reign, records that Chosroes exempted Harrân from tribute payments on the grounds that the citizens had retained their paganism: *Bella* 2.13.7.

17. First noted in I. Hadot, 'Die Widerlegung des Manichäismus im Epiktetkommentar des Simplikios', *Archiv für Geschichte der Philosophie* 50 (1969), 46.

18. Art. cit. (1986), n. 15.

19. I am less convinced than I was when I first wrote these pages of the thesis of Simplicius' sojourn in Harrân – but I am far from persuaded that he never resided there, at any rate during the 530s when he was composing *in Cael.* Lameer (art. cit., n. 15) undermines the case for the existence of an actual Neoplatonist institution in Harrân at the time of Simplicius' exile; but that in itself does not show that Simplicius did not live and work there. The whole issue needs (and is currently receiving) further investigation.

20. But this is not entirely certain, and our text appears to contain at least one reference to the *Physics* commentary: *in Cael.* 1.3, 108,20: see n. 362 ad loc.

21. For the evidence for this, deriving from an epitaph for a dead slave attributed to 'the philosopher Damascius' on a funeral stele now in Emesa dated to 538, see Hadot, op. cit., 290.

22. Plato does indeed speak of *sunaitia* (*Tim.* 46C, *Politicus* 281D-E); but he never parcels them out thus neatly into the standard Neoplatonist categories; on these issues, see R.J. Hankinson, *Cause and Explanation in Ancient Greek Thought* (Oxford 1998), chs. 3 and 12.

23. See M. Wolff, 'Philoponus and the rise of pre-classical dynamics', in Sorabji (ed.) *Philoponus and the Rejection of Aristotelian Science* (London 1988), 100-4.

24. A conclusion fiercely resisted by Philoponus; this forms the core of his disagreement with Aristotle (and Simplicius) on cosmology: see Wildberg (1987).

Textual Emendations

5,21	Reading *to auto* with D
5,27	Reading *en toutois hoti*, with bc
7,9-10	Perhaps deleting *te kai poiousi*
13,2	Perhaps reading *apophainein* in place of *apophaskein*
19,9-10	Reading *haplê* in the lemma (1.2, 269a16), with Simplicius' exemplar, rather than *allê*, with the MSS of Aristotle
21,26	Reading *erôtêsei*, with BEb, against Heiberg's *erôtêsoi* <*an*>
22,19	Adding a comma after *Aristotelous*
23,26	Perhaps reading *sunthetou* for *haplou*
24,7	Reading *prosupethemetha* for the MSS *pröupethemetha*
24,15	Reading *einai hêtton* with E in place of *hêtton einai*
24,15-16	Perhaps adding *ou monon* before *erei* and *kai* before *kineisthai*
38,11,12	Retaining *oude kata phusin*, omitted by Heiberg
41,21	Perhaps deleting *alla kata phusin*
50,25	Reading *lithinês* with D for *plinthinês*
51,15	Reading *parapheromenon* with E^2; or perhaps reading *auto* [with E^2b] *peripheron*: 'which carries it around'
52,26	Adding a full-stop after *aphukton*
53,4	Marking *thaumaston kai pantelôs alogon* as a quotation from Aristotle
55,11	Deleting *kai* after *eipein*; or, if it is retained, reading *dioti* with Bc for *dêlon, hoti* as printed by Heiberg; or alternatively reading *dêlonoti*: 'and <because> clearly, insofar as …'
56,14	Reading *êtoi* for *têi* with D
64,1-2	Reading *hoion pasa gê kai mikra*, with Dc, and *bôlos* for *bôlon*, and marking the text as a quotation from Aristotle
65,1	Marking *tên pasan gên kai mikran bôlon* as a quotation from Aristotle
94,5	Reading *apo tou ontos* (cf. 94,2); the MSS simply have *tou ontos*, or *hupo tou ontos* (c)
94,13	Perhaps reading *kai tên kata to einai paratasin*
96,11	Reading *oude to einai*, with c, for *oude tôi einai*
97,15	Reading *proskeitai en allois genesiourgôs*, from the margin of D
98,22	Perhaps reading *hupo* before *tôn poiountôn*

100,4	*ê posotêtas* should probably be deleted
102,9-10	Reading *ek mê toioutou, pephukotos de <ginesthai toioutou>, pasin*, etc., paralleling 102,3-4 above. Possibly also supply *kai tais ousiais* before *kai tois ex enantiôn*
106,4	Placing a question mark instead of full stop after *moiras*
108,13	Perhaps supplying *enantion ti* after *oude ara*
115,1	Punctuating with a semi-colon after *akousteon*
116,31	Reading *theiou* (as in the equivalent clause at 117,18-19), as against *theou*, printed by Heiberg
147,1	Reading *periphereias*, with D, against *periphereis* of the other MSS, printed by Heiberg
149,15-16	Reading *antiparastasin*, with BE^2bc, against *antiperistasin*, with ADE
152,12-15	Marking *plên hoti … allas antitheseis* as a quotation from Alexander
153,10	Reading *hôs* for *pôs* of the MSS

Simplicius
On Aristotle
On the Heavens 1.1-4

Translation

Simplicius' Commentary on Book One of Aristotle's 'On the Heavens'

[PROLOGUE]

Alexander[1] says that the subject[2] of Aristotle's treatise *On the Heav-* 1,2
ens is the world.[3] He says that 'heaven' is used in three senses by Aristotle in this work, to mean both the sphere of the fixed stars and the whole of the divine revolving body, which in this book he also calls the 'furthest heaven' (with the adjective),[4] and additionally 'the world', as Plato called it when he said 'the whole heaven, or the world or whatever else it might care to be called'.[5] And he adduces Theophrastus as witness, since he talks in his *On the Heavens* not only of the divine body but also about things which come to be and about their principles.[6] Thus Alexander says [the treatise] is about the world and the five bodies[7] in it, that of the heaven and the four of the sublunary world, fire, air, water, earth.

He is led to this conjecture by the first book's discussion of the whole world (whether there is one world or many, and whether it is finite or infinite, ungenerated and indestructible or not), and by the fact that, having spoken of the heaven in the strict sense in the first two books of this treatise, he went on to develop the argument concerning the four elements in the third and fourth books as a sequel to that about the first body.[8] For this reason [Aristotle] makes a fresh start in the third book and explains that a physical treatise concerns bodies, and summarizing what has gone before he writes as follows: 'thus we have spoken of the first of the elements, both saying what kind of nature it has and saying that it is ungenerated and indestructible; it remains to speak of the other two'[9] (by 'two' he means the two groupings, that of the light, comprising fire and air, and that of the heavy, comprising water and earth).

The divine Iamblichus,[10] on the other hand, says that, having set
up the heavenly and divine body as the subject of this work, Aristotle 2,1
in fact includes the study of the whole world, since it is substantially contained in it and under its control in regard to the production of generation; although it is also concerned with the elements and the powers that inhere in them, since all of these things depend upon the heaven and the things which revolve with it.

The great Syrianus[11] and his followers say that the treatise concerns the heaven proper, i.e. the eternal, revolving body, relying, so it seems, on the title, and not accepting Alexander's claim that its subject is the world and the world's simple bodies. For, so they say, whatever is said about the four elements here is not said in its own right, but [only insofar as] it contributes to the study of the heavenly bodies. For it is in order to show that the heavenly body is not made of the four elements but is simple, and that it is not one of the four[12] but is something else besides them, having neither lightness nor weight as they do, that he goes through the whole of the preceding argument, saying that some of the elements are light, others heavy, and subsumes the four under two headings, the light and the heavy.

Each of the aforementioned [scholars], in my view, gives his own account of the subject-matter in the light of his division of Aristotle's physical works. For some of them concern the natural principles which are common to every natural object, such as matter and form, motion and place, and time, and nature itself, and the productive causes[13] which arise as subsidiaries of it, as well as those things which natural scientists have thought to exist (although in fact they do not), such as void and the infinite, things the books of the treatise entitled the *Physics* explain. And after the principles of the real natural bodies it was necessary further to discuss the bodies themselves.

Of the bodies, as Alexander would say, some are simple, some compound, and of the simples, one is eternal and moves in a circle while the others are subject to generation and rectilinear motion. And he says that our treatise has all of these as its subject, as well as the world which is composed of all of them. However, the others say that of the natural bodies one is eternal (with which the present treatise is concerned), while the rest partake of generation and destruction. Seeking to explain these, he first produced a general account called *On Generation and Destruction*, and then, of generable and destructible things, those in the atmosphere he treated of in the *Meteorology*, while of terrestrial composite things, some are animate, others inanimate; and he explained the inanimate in the writings on minerals.

And of animate things, some have the capacity for sensation and locomotion, namely animals, while others are insensate and rooted, namely plants. And he wrote both about plants and animals, offering general remarks regarding their generation, the differentiation and function of their parts, and their motion and activity, in texts such as *On the Motion of Animals* and *On Sleep and Waking*, making particular comments about each species of animal in *The History of Animals*. Such being the division, then, according to all the exegetes of Aristotle's works, this treatise should clearly be taken up after the *Physics*, whether it is concerned with the world and the five simple bodies in it, or with the eternal and revolving body [only].

However, we must perhaps take issue with Alexander's contention that Aristotle's argument in this treatise clearly concerns the whole world and all of the simple bodies, in the first place because each treatise demands a single subject dealing with one thing, in relation to which it weaves together its individual parts;[14] and secondly because [Aristotle] clearly does not explain the world in this treatise as Plato did in the *Timaeus*, where he treated both of the principles of natural objects, matter and form, motion and time, and of the general composition of the world, and gave a particular account both of the heavenly bodies and of those below the moon, in the latter case occupying himself both with atmospheric phenomena and with the minerals, plants, and animals on the earth up to and including the composition of man and of his parts.

Here, however, very little is said about the world as a whole, and only such things as it has in common with the heaven, i.e. that it is eternal, limited in size, and single, and that it has these features because the heaven is eternal, limited and single. But if anyone wishes to inspect Aristotle's theory of the world, it must be said that he presents his account of the world in all of his physical treatises taken together.

As a matter of fact, Nicholas the Peripatetic,[15] if I remember aright, constructed the account, which he had entitled *On the Universe*, of everything in the world by species. But Aristotle himself does not say, either when setting out in summary in the third book of this treatise what is said in it, or in the prologue to the *Meteorology*, that he has discussed the world, or the heaven in the sense of the world, even if 'heaven' is sometimes used by him to mean the whole world. But I will more appropriately set out his remarks on the subject a little later on.[16]

Against the other exegetes, it should be said that the discussion of the four elements in these texts does not appear merely adventitious, and nor do they seem to be treated for the sake of the study of the heavenly bodies in themselves, but rather he discusses them in their own right. For not to mention the fact that the account of them takes up almost half of the whole treatise, it is also the fact that after the exposition concerning the heavenly bodies which he offers in the first two books of the treatise, at the beginning of the third book he once again uses the prologue from the first,[17] thus emphasizing the coherence of the work and showing that physical enquiry is concerned with the [simple] bodies, so that the two final books have the same subject as well.

And he immediately adduces the following argument: 'since we have dealt with the first of the elements, what it is by nature, and that it is indestructible and ungenerated, it remains to speak of the other two',[18] meaning by 'two' the two groupings of the light and the heavy. In the prologue to the *Meteorology*, he writes as follows: 'we have already dealt with the primary natural causes and with each natural motion, and with the ordered movements of the stars in the heavens and with the bodily elements, how many they are and of what kind, and what their mutual transformations are, and concerning generation and decay in general'.[19]

So in these passages, after the treatment of the physical principles,[20] that is to say in the present treatise, he says that he has spoken neither of the world, as Alexander thinks, nor solely of the divine and eternal body, as the more modern exegetes have it, but rather about the elementary bodies in their own right, how many they are and of what kind.

Thus it seems to me clearly to be the case that in these books[21] Aristotle treats of both the heavens and the sublunary four elements. So that the subject not be diffuse but be shown to be focused on one thing, it should be said that after the treatment of the natural principles (i.e. whatever the principles of natural bodies may be), he speaks of the simple bodies, those which are put together immediately from the natural principles, and which are the parts of the whole.

Of these the first is the heavenly body, which gives its title to the treatise as being more worthy of honour [sc. than the others], and after that the four sublunary elements which become the composite bodies. He constructs his account about everything as being one concerning the primary and simple bodies (which is why they are all called elements), and not only the sublunary ones but the heaven too, when he says 'concerning the first of the elements', insofar as it too is a simple body even though the heaven would not strictly be called an element, since nothing is constructed out of it,[22] while an element is that primary thing out of which something is constructed and into which it is ultimately resolved.

If indeed Alexander had said its subject was only the simple bodies, and not the world, I would not have taken issue with him. Moreover, if he were to say that it is about the world in the sense of being about the simple elements which are in the world, or insofar as the whole world is contained within the heaven, as Iamblichus says, but not about both the entire cosmos and all of the simple bodies, as he himself has written, I will not dispute with him; nor indeed with those who say that its subject is the heaven, at least if they are of Iamblichus' mind, insofar as the four sublunary elements depend upon the heaven and the bodies which rotate in the heaven.

But Alexander, in interpreting the passage shortly after the beginning which begins 'so concerning the nature of the Universe',[23] says that the argument which concerns the world as a whole is clearly primary in his mind in the first book, while the second contains the arguments dealing with the heaven, the third and fourth dealing with the four elements. That the treatise following the *Physics* (which dealt with the natural principles) is concerned with the simple and primary bodies is made clear by the opening to the first two books in which he speaks of the body of the heaven, and by the fact that he has made the same thing[24] the prologue to the final books as well, namely that 'natural science ... is concerned with bodies ..., their affections and motions',[25] thus making the argument primarily concern the primary bodies.

And that is why he begins his exposition in these books immediately with the continuous, which is precisely the genus of body, and makes the most complete exposition of the nature of body, insofar as it is body, right at the outset.[26] What is said concerning the world as a whole in these books,[27] namely that it is ungenerated and indestructible, that it is unique, finite, and spherical with nothing remaining outside of it in the form of either body or void; these things, which belong primarily to the heaven (and to the world as a whole [only] as a result of the heaven), are reasonably said in the books *On the Heavens* to belong pre-eminently to the heaven, but sometimes they gain a mention as belonging to the whole world. And it is not necessary on account of this to imagine the world to be the subject, but rather the simple bodies of which the most primary is the heaven which gives a share of its goods to the whole world.

So this would be the subject of the present treatise, being named after its most important part, which is that on which the rest depend. Both Aristotle and his exegetes reasonably determine its position in the order of reading as being after the treatise on *Physics*. For whether its subject is the simple bodies or whether it is the eternal and divine body which is simple, it is right for it to precede the others which deal with the composite things which are generated and destroyed, and to follow the exposition of natural principles. And the treatment is divided into that concerning the revolving and divine body which is dealt with in the first two books, and that concerning the sublunary elements, about which the remaining two are written.

In the first book he shows, on the basis of the simple motions, that there are five simple bodies, that which moves in a circle and the four which have rectilinear motion; and that the body that moves in a circle is neither one of the four, nor compounded out of them, but a fifth substance exalted above and exceeding the other four.[28] And he also shows it to be ungenerated and indestructible, on the grounds that generations and decays are from contraries into contraries, while nothing is contrary to the body that moves in a circle;[29] and he shows this from the fact that of contrary [elements] the motions too are contrary, while for circular motion there is no contrary.[30]

Next he shows that the heaven is limited in size, and generally that an infinite body, in particular one that moves,[31] cannot be infinite, and that it is unique and that there is neither a plurality nor a numerical infinity of heavens. It follows from this that the whole world is ungenerated, indestructible, finite in size, and one in number, since it is composed of all the natural and perceptible body that there is, and there remains neither a body nor even a void outside the heaven.[32]

After this, picking up the argument concerning the ungenerated and indestructible, he shows that the heaven is ungenerated and indestructible, and because of it the world is too, and that it is not generated yet indestructible, as some think,[33] nor yet ungenerated and destructible.[34] And finally, generalizing the argument, he shows that generability and destructibility are mutually entailing, as too are ungenerability and indestructibility.[35]

[CHAPTER 1]

268a1-6 Natural science [seems for the most part principally concerned with bodies and magnitudes, with their affections and their motions, as well as with those causal principles (*arkhai*) which are to do with that type of substance, since of those things which are naturally constituted some are bodies and magnitudes, while others are what have body and magnitude,] and others still are the causal principles of the things which have them.

The prologue sets out the subject of the treatise and its position, i.e. that it is continuous with the *Physics*. Since the latter was concerned with the natural principles, it is necessary next to speak of what derives from the principles, and these things are in the first place bodies.

He reasons as follows: natural science is concerned with naturally-constituted things; naturally-constituted things are either bodies, like fire, water, stone, and wood, or things which have bodies, like plants and animals, or the principles of things which have bodies, such as matter, form, motion,[36] and suchlike. Moreover, soul is the principle of things which have bodies, such as animals and plants. So after the treatment of the physical principles it is necessary to treat of bodies and the things which have bodies, and it is clear that in their case there are more bodies and that the study of them is larger.[37] And the things which have bodies and their principles are mainly known to natural scientists on the basis of the bodies.

Consequently 'natural science seems for the most part principally'[38] concerned with bodies and the affections of bodies (that is their passive qualities, in virtue of which they both are affected and act),[39] and also with their motions. There are different forms of motion, one being in respect of place, another in respect of alteration, another in respect of growth and diminution. For the moment let 'motion' include both generation and destruction.

He seems to have ascended from affections to motions as though in the direction of the more general; for the affections too are motions of a sort, at least if he does not distinguish motions from affections by limiting the former to actions. That he draws the conclusion of the argument by the mediation of the naturally-constituted things is made clear by the reason-giving connective 'since' in the clause 'since of those things which are naturally constituted some are bodies',[40] and so on.

But it is 'for the most part principally concerned with bodies'[41] either because it also concerns the things which have body, which he appends later on, or, if these too are to be counted along with bodies, because it is also about the principles, as he explicitly adds. And if one says that all these too are included in the [category of] bodies, nevertheless the discussion of place, time, and void would still be beyond their scope, as indeed would [the discussion] which is concerned not with natural science, but with things which create difficulties for natural science, about which he dealt in the first book of the *Physics*, in the arguments he propounded against Parmenides and Melissus.[42] But of course since it happened that they talked about nature, but not about natural problems, discussion of them is thus somewhat beyond the scope of [that of] bodies. 'For the most part' would then be added because of philosophical caution; and perhaps he appended 'it seems' for the same reason too.

'Concerned with bodies and magnitudes' is pleonastic, in that both signify the same thing, unless it is indicative of the fact that every body has magnitude, and that there are no indivisible and partless bodies, as some say there are.[43] Or perhaps it is there because the natural scientist does not discourse solely about bodies, but also about length and breadth,[44] insofar as they are the limits of bodies. Or perhaps indeed because he is concerned with time and place: for insofar as they are continuous and divisible these things too have magnitude, although they are not bodies. In general, if he speaks of the naturally continuous, and not everything continuous is body, as he himself will say a little further on,[45] he rightly mentions both body and magnitude.

However Alexander adds that the fact that there is nothing else naturally constituted which has magnitude besides body is a sign that this is pleonasm. But as I see it both time, place, and motion, as well as lines and surfaces, since they are continuous and always divisible, are physical magnitudes, although they are not bodies.

268a6-28 Thus the continuous is [what is divisible into what is divisible without limit; body is what is divisible in every way. Magnitude divisible in one direction is a line, that in two a plane, that in three a body: there is no other magnitude over and above these, for the three are all there are, and threefold is every way there is. For it is as the Pythagoreans say: the totality and everything in it are made determinate in threes, since end, middle and beginning give the number of the totality, and their number is the triad. Thus we have taken it from nature, from her ordinances as it were, and we employ this number too in the worship of the gods. We also assign predicates in this way; for we say of two things 'both', and of two people 'both of them', but we do not say 'all', employing rather this predicate first of all in the case of threes – and we follow these courses because, as I have said, nature herself leads us thus. And so since 'everything', 'the totality' and 'the complete' do not differ from one another in form, but if they do so only in their matter and in the things of which they are said, body will be the only complete magnitude, since it is the only one that is determined in three ways (that is, in every way). And as it is divisible in three ways, it is divisible in every way. Of the others, some are in one way, some in two, since whatever number is appropriate for them is also the number of their continuity and divisibility: one is continuous in one direction, another in two,] while that of this type is so in every way.

After having shown that the natural scientist is concerned with bodies, and evidently primarily with the simple ones (since these are primarily natural and have in themselves the principle of natural motion), and seeking to define 'body', he first defines the continuous, in terms of which body and the other magnitudes [will be defined], because the continuous is everything which 'is divisible into what is divisible without limit', whether it be divisible in one [dimension] or in two or in three. For line and plane are continuous even though they are not yet bodies, for the former is continuous and divisible in one [dimension only], the latter in two, while body is in every way.

And he shows that body is in every way divisible and in every way continuous and extended from its three-dimensionality and its threefold divisibility: for 'three are all there are, and threefold is every way there is'. He shows that a body's being three-dimensional is its being omni-dimensional from there being no magnitude possessing more than three dimensions; so what has three dimensions has them all.

This is also given credibility by the property of threeness, since three both is and is said to be all, and 'threefold every way there is'. And that we are right to say this the Pythagoreans briefly showed as follows: the totality has beginning, middle, and end, and as such is delimited by the triad. And perhaps we say of the totality that it is complete on account of its having beginning, middle, and end. For what is not a totality lacks something by comparison with the totality, and is incomplete.

But if this is right, one might say that Alexander did not validly argue from the totality's completeness to its having beginning, middle, and end: for perhaps this belongs to the complete on account of its being the totality, and perhaps these things should be contraposed with one another, the totality, and the complete, and the having beginning, middle, and end, so that it is said to be complete on account of its having an end.[46] But what has an end clearly also has a beginning and a middle. So Alexander rightly argued from completeness: for in fact in what follows Aristotle infers its totality from its completeness.

He also shows that three is everything and complete from the holy rituals which employ this number, and this, namely that 'three are all there are, and threefold every way there is', gains credibility above all from the usage of words. He shows once more on the basis of what has been said that body alone of magnitudes is extended in every dimension, as he said earlier, adding that it is the only complete thing because 'everything', 'total', and 'complete' are all the same in form even if they may on occasion differ in subject-matter since, as Alexander says, 'everything' is predicated in respect of divisible quantity, 'total' in respect of the continuous, and both in respect of completeness.[47] He argues as follows: body alone among magnitudes is three-dimensional and defined by threes; and something of this kind is complete and extended in every dimension. It is worth noting that Aristotle has uncharacteristically made use of Pythagorean proofs in the service of demonstration.[48]

Perhaps someone might wonder how the three-dimensional can be the omni-dimensional on the grounds that three is complete. For let a complete number be one which has beginning and middle and end; how can that which is bounded by three be all and complete in virtue of that, given that sometimes it will require others? For will a man who has three fingers have all his fingers since he has three of them, and will three elements of bodies or of speech be all the elements there are? Or because three are all the dimensions there are, and that which is three-dimensional is omni-dimensional, so that there is no other dimension? So perhaps, having demonstrated that it [sc. the three-dimensional] is dimensional in every way there is on the grounds that there is no other dimension, he employs the arguments from threes as well on grounds of their general acceptance.

The estimable Ptolemy beautifully demonstrated in his single volume *On Dimension*[49] that there are no more than three dimensions from the fact that dimensions must be bounded, and dimensions are bounded in respect of the taking of straight perpendiculars, while it is only possible to take three straight lines at right-angles to each other, two according to which the plane is defined, the third measuring depth. Consequently, if there were another dimension after the third it would be utterly unmeasured and indeterminate. Thus Aristotle seems to have established that there is no transference to another dimension by enumeration of instances, while Ptolemy demonstrated it.[50]

> **268a28-b5** So whichever magnitudes are divisible [are also continuous; but whether in addition everything continuous is also divisible is not yet clear from the current investigation. On the other hand it is clear that there is no progression to some other type, as there is from length to plane, and to body from plane, for in that case this kind of magnitude would not be complete, since necessarily every advance is in respect of some defect, and it is not possible for the complete to be defective:] for it is in every way.

Having defined as continuous things which are 'divisible into what is divisible without limit', and saying that body is that which is 'divisible in every way', he stops, since it was demonstrated in the *Physics*[51] that continuous things were divisible on the grounds that magnitudes cannot be composed of partless things, while here this has not yet been shown, but will be.

That divisible things are continuous is self-evident. For if non-continuous things which have already been divided are not divisible, it is clear that divisible things will be continuous.[52] Consequently the position that body, being divisible, is continuous is not shaken.[53] Neither [is the claim] that it is divisible in every way: for this was shown not on the grounds of its continuousness, but because it is not possible to progress to another type; for if it were, it would not be complete, since progression is in respect of some deficiency.[54]

> **268b5-10** So each body which has the form of a part [is of such a kind according to this definition,[55] since it has all the dimensions. But each is determined by contact with what is close to it (and hence in a way each of these bodies is many). But the totality of which these things are parts is necessarily complete, and totally so, as the name indicates,] and not in one way but not in another.

Having said that body, *qua* body, is complete in its dimensionality because it has all the dimensions, since the whole world as a totality is also complete, in order that no one might think that the same thing is referred to in both cases by completeness and totality, he plausibly distinguishes between them, saying that of bodies on the one hand some are parts and have retained the form of a part (i.e. the heaven,[56] fire, air, water, and earth), while on the other hand there is also the whole[57] of which these are parts.

Furthermore, in respect of the bodies considered as parts, 'total' and 'complete' are predicated in respect of the formula and definition of body (because body is three- and omni-dimensional), but because it is a part and does not comprise everything, and there are many things outside of it, and it is delimited from many things by touching them, which entails that each thing is many, since it is partitioned by its contacts with the many other things, for this reason it is not total and complete in its existence, since it has in this respect a progression to something else, and so for this reason it is incomplete.[58]

But the totality and the whole of which these are parts are complete not only in terms of the definition of body, but also in respect of its containing everything, and there being nothing outside of it, and its not being delimited by contact with anything; consequently this is in every way complete.

[CHAPTER 2]

> **268b11-14** Concerning the nature of the totality, then, [we may inquire later on whether it is infinite in respect of magnitude or whether the whole mass is finite. Let us now speak of the parts it has in virtue of form,] taking this as our starting-point.

Having said that each body, whether part or whole, was in a way complete, and that it is whole insofar as it has nothing outside of itself, he realised that he needed a demonstration of this, and of whether it was as something infinite or finite that it had nothing outside of itself. Perhaps it seemed logical, after the discussion of the nature of the simple[59] body, to speak of the nature of the totality and then of its parts. But since, as I see it, he includes the discussion of the totality in that of the heaven (for in showing that the heaven is finite he has shown that the totality is finite), for this reason he postpones the discussion of the totality, first of all undertaking to speak of what parts it has, and how many they are. He is right to say 'whether it is infinite in respect of magnitude', since it is infinite in respect of both spatial and temporal extension.

Alexander also says that the discussion of the entire cosmos was pre-eminent for him [sc. Aristotle], but that this entailed the [discussion] of the eternal revolving body, which is brought to a conclusion in the second book, while in addition to these things he gives the account of the four elements in the two final books. But since he sought to complete the treatment of the revolving body with a view to the discussion of the entire cosmos (that it is not infinite, that it is spherical, that it is ungenerated and indestructible), he first shows that there is such a body, and then turns to the exposition of things to do with the totality. And one must attend to the things which are said about the totality (that it is not infinite, that it is spherical, that it is ungenerated and indestructible), [to see] if they are said of the entire cosmos in its own right, or if, rather, the totality is not said to have these things in virtue of the heaven.

For at the beginning of the second book, in concluding that the heaven as a whole neither came to be nor is destroyed, he himself makes it clear that even if he speaks of the whole cosmos he is claiming that it has these properties in virtue of the heaven, when he writes shortly after the beginning that 'for this reason it would be right to persuade oneself that the statements of the ancients, and more particularly those of our ancestors, were true: that there is something immortal and divine among things which not only have motion, but which have it in such a way that it has no limit',[60] and so on, lest I copy out more.

By 'parts of the totality in virtue of form', he means those which differ from one another in virtue of their form:[61] heaven, fire, air, water, earth, since these are the primary parts of the totality. For the parts of earth and of each of the other [elements] are uniform, and so they too are parts of the totality, but not directly but rather as parts of parts. And these are not parts properly so-called, but pieces.[62] So the primary parts of the totality are the ones which differ in virtue of form.

> **268b14-20** For all the natural bodies [and magnitudes are of themselves, we say, moveable in respect of place, since we say that their nature is a source of motion for them. All change in respect of place (which we call movement) is either straight, or circular, or a mixture of the two, since these are the only two simple motions.] The reason for this is that these, namely the straight and the circular, are the only simple magnitudes.

Beginning the discussion of the heavenly body, and wishing to show 12,1 that it is eternal, he first establishes that it is distinct from the four elements. He establishes this on the basis of the natural motions. For if what it is to be natural for natural objects consists in their having a nature, and nature is a source of motion, demonstration from natural motions will immediately proceed from a clearer basis, since [it will proceed] from activities: for activities are more evident than substances. But at the same time [it will proceed] from more authoritative sources, since [it will proceed] from causes.

With a view to establishing this on the basis of motions, he adopts these six hypotheses:[63] [1] that there are two simple motions (circular and rectilinear); [2] that simple motion is of a simple body; [3] that the motion of a simple body is simple;[64] [4] that there is one natural motion for each body; [5] that for one thing there is <at most>[65] one contrary; and [6] that the heavens move in a circle, as perception confirms. Plotinus recalled these hypotheses in his *On the Cosmos*: for, wishing to prove the eternity of the heavens in the Platonic manner, he says: 'Aristotle would have no trouble, if one were to accept his hypotheses concerning the fifth body',[66] meaning these ones, since the numerical eternity[67] [of the heaven] follows from their being the case.

Plato also seems to assign another substance to the heavens: for if he thinks that the five shapes of the five bodies are form-producing,[68] and if he says that the totality was delineated, in respect of its being a determinate heaven, by the dodecahedron, which is something distinct from the pyramid, octahedron, icosahedron, and cube, it is clear that according to him it is distinct in respect of substance as well.

And that Plato did indeed think that there were five simple bodies corresponding to the five shapes is sufficiently shown by Xenocrates, his most faithful pupil, when he wrote the following in his *Life of Plato*: 'thus he divided up living things, dividing them into forms and parts in every way, until he arrived at the five elements of living things, which indeed he specified as the five shapes and bodies, namely ether, fire, water, earth, and air'.[69] And so the dodecahedron was according to him the shape of a simple body, namely that of the heaven, which he called 'ether'.

And if he says that heaven [comes] from fire,[70] he means that it [comes] from light, for he says too that light is a form of fire;[71] and the stars are made of the four [elements], but not those involved in generation, but rather of fire *qua* light-bearer and earth *qua* resistant to perception, and of those in between *qua* intermediates.[72] So if Aristotle too accepts that they are visible and tangible, not even he will be able to avoid constructing the heavenly bodies from these extremes, in which there is the perfection of the elements. [But this is problematic.][73] For he wants it [sc. the heavenly body] to be in every way exalted above the incomplete and rectilinearly-moving sublunary four. Equally, if in fact he says that it is simple, it is probable 13,1
that he will deny that it is a composite of these things. [But this is problematic.] For we shall learn that he says that it is ensouled[74] and a living thing, and that he claims that living things have composite bodies.[75]

That the natural bodies are not only movable, but particularly movable with respect to place, is clear from the fact that the primary [type of] motion is that in respect of place in all of the senses of 'primary', as he showed in the final book of the *Physics*,[76] and [from the fact] that, since nature is a source of motion, it will be most particularly a source and a cause for the first of the natural motions. Dividing the natural motions, he says that some are simple, others non-simple. And having shown that there are simple motions, he will be able to prove immediately that they belong to simple bodies, that the motions of simple bodies are simple, and that the simple [motions] are the circular and the rectilinear. For neither of them can be composed from different ones.

That these are the only simple motions, he shows by consideration of lines. For each motion occurs along some linear interval, so if there are only two simple types of line, there will only be two simple motions. He does not consider magnitudes to be productive causes[77] of motion, but as material causes, and as having the status of prerequisites,[78] as Alexander says. For if there is motion it is impossible for there not to be magnitude, but if there is magnitude it is not necessary that there be motion; and this is appropriate to matter.[79] And one must consider the possibility whether perhaps the configuration of the underlying[80] magnitude is in a way a cause for the configuration of the motion and whether the configuration of the motion is a cause[81] for the configuration of the underlying magnitude.

Xenarchus, taking issue with much of what is said here in his writings *Against the Fifth Substance*,[82] also takes issue with [the claim that] 'the reason for this is that these, namely the straight and the circular, are the only simple magnitudes', for he says that:

> the helix drawn on a cylinder is also a simple line, since each part of it is congruent with every equal part; and so if there is another simple magnitude besides the two, there will be another simple motion besides the two [simple motions] and another simple body besides the five, namely that which moves with this motion.

Alexander, however, answers Xenarchus in two ways, first by means of a counter-objection. For while agreeing that the cylindrical helix is simple, he says that Aristotle did not consider the simple magnitudes to be productive causes of the motions.[83] For it is not the case, if a
14,1 simple body moves with a simple motion along a simple line, that it immediately follows that a simple natural body will move with a simple motion along *every* simple line, which is what Xenarchus assumes. For Aristotle did not suppose this.[84]

But perhaps a more powerful rejoinder is to be found in Aristotle's clear statement that the reason is that these (i.e. the straight and the circular) are the only simple magnitudes. For even though he says that they function as material causes,[85] and for this reason itself it is not necessary that if there is another simple magnitude there will be another simple motion as well, nevertheless the claim that these are the only simple magnitudes would be falsified if in fact there is another one.

Better was Alexander's [second] response to the objection when he said that the helix on the cylinder is not in any case a simple line, since it can be generated out of two dissimilar motions, namely the circular and the rectilinear. For when a straight line is traced in a circle on the surface of the cylinder, and a point is moved smoothly in a straight line, a helix is generated, as Xenarchus himself agrees when he writes:

> let there be a rectangle, and let this be moved in a circle about one of its sides, which remains stationary and which is the axis of the cylinder; on the side which is parallel to it and which is rotating let a point be moved, and in the same time let this point traverse this line and let the quadrilateral be brought back to the same place again from which it started moving. Thus the quadrilateral produces a cylinder, and the point moving along the straight line [produces] a helix, one moreover which is simple, [so he says,] since it is uniform.[86]

But even though it is uniform, it is not simple. For every simple line is certainly uniform, but not every uniform line is simple, unless it is single in form and unless also, if it is generated by motion, the motion itself is single in form, or rather one. For in fact the helix of the solar motion[87] is generated by two circular motions, that of the sun through the zodiac, and that of the fixed [sphere], and since each is generated around different poles the helix too will have a mixed nature. Moreover, Alexander says, the simple motions have their simplicity in virtue of their orientation to the centre of the totality; for one of them is around the centre, while the others are away from and towards the centre. But the helix is not of such a kind.

> **268b20-6** Circular motion, then, is [that around the centre, while straight is that upwards and downwards. By 'upwards', I mean away from the centre, by 'downwards' towards the centre. Consequently all simple movement must either be away from the centre, towards the centre, or around the centre. And it seems that this accords logically with what we said at the outset: since body is completed in the number three,] so too is its motion.

Having said that there are two simple motions, rectilinear and circular, he defines the circular motion by saying that it is that around 15,1 the centre of the totality, which, as Alexander says, was what he indicated with the article, when he said around *the* centre. Consequently the motion of wheels in general, since it does not occur around the centre of the totality, is not simple circular motion. For it has in a way an up and a down in each part, [since any given part is] at one time going up, at another down. And he says that of the simple rectilinear motions one is upward the other downward; and he clarifies each of these by saying that 'upward' means away from the centre, 'downward' towards the centre. And that he makes the centre for both the circular and rectilinear motions the same he shows by saying 'consequently all simple movement must', etc.: he sought to construct all of them in respect of a single orientation towards the centre.

Moreover, [motion] rightwards and leftwards, forwards and backwards, whenever they are simple, occur either upwards or towards the centre. For the movements of animals are no longer simple since they occur by way of flexing and extension of the limbs. Consequently even lateral movements are rectilinear upward and downward ones:[88] so says Alexander. But perhaps movement leftwards and rightwards, forwards and backwards is not natural for the simple bodies, but [it is] for animals which possess right and left, front and back. Earth, fire, and the others do not move with this type of motion except forcibly, by being thrown, or extruded, or struck by others.

Having first assumed as self-evident [the premisses] that there are two types of simple lines, the rectilinear and that around a circumference, and that simple motions occur along simple lines, he reasoned effectively as follows: simple motions occur along simple lines; motions that occur along simple lines occur either along a straight line or along a circle. And the conclusion is clear.[89]

Then further, as I see it, he took it to be self-evident that the most particularly-defined straight line within a sphere is that which extends from the centre to the circumference. Consequently there are two motions along a straight line within a sphere, one upwards and away from the centre, the other downwards and towards the centre. There are therefore three simple motions which have their orientation in relation to the centre: that away from the centre, that towards the centre, and that around the centre. The connection, which is said to 'accord logically', between there being three motions and the three-dimensionality of body seems to me to depart from Aristotle's rigour, unless some argument can establish some affinity between motions and dimensions.[90]

268b26-269a2 Since of bodies [some are simple while others are compounded of them (by 'simple' I mean those which have a natural source of motion, such as fire and earth, and their kinds, and things akin to them), it is necessary that some of their motions will be simple while others will be in a way mixed, and that those of the simple bodies will be simple, while those of the compounds will be mixed,] and that they will move in respect of whatever predominates. 16,1

Having established the first hypothesis,[91] namely that there are three simple motions, that away from the middle, that towards the middle, and that around the middle, he moves on to the second and third [hypotheses], showing [3] that the motion of a simple body is simple, and [2] that simple motion is of a simple body.

He shows these things by dividing bodies into simple and composite just as previously [he had divided] motions into simple and mixed. Having defined simple bodies, he then properly assigns the simple motions to the simple bodies, and the mixed to the composite. And each motion is a motion of some body in respect of place. Simple bodies, he says, are those which possess a source of natural motion only; for animals and plants too possess a source of motion, but not however of natural motion (at least insofar as they are such),[92] but rather of animate motion, for which reason they move differently and in different ways. For the composite things do not consist solely of uniform parts, but are also equipped with organic parts, since they possess in addition a soul which uses the body as a tool.

Nature is the source of simple motion, which is why natural things[93] possess simple motion only. And in saying which these things are he adds 'such as fire and earth, and their kinds, and things akin to them', meaning by 'kinds of earth' the sandy, stony, earthy, pale, dark, and so on. Kinds of fire are coals, flame, and light, as Plato said.[94] Alexander explained this well: 'For having said', he says, ' "such as fire and earth", he adds the phrase "and their kinds", signifying all fire in general and not this fire only, and all earth in general and not this only, but rather the form of fire and earth insofar as they are fire and earth.' And air is 'akin to' fire, water to earth, even if there is some other simple body, as the fifth will be shown to be – for this too is natural.

'And if,' Alexander says, 'natural bodies have their being in their having within themselves a source of motion, while of these some are simple and others are composed of them, it will follow that the motions of simple bodies will be simple, of composite bodies composite.' But perhaps Aristotle put it more precisely, saying that simple bodies are those which possess a natural source of motion, while composite bodies, insofar as they are composite, possess not a natural source of motion, but rather an animate one, for which reason they are equipped with organic parts.

There is only one simple motion; for simple motion is of a simple body. And a simple body, given that it is simple, has the source of only one motion within itself. For if it were to have a source of many motions, even if they were simple, it would no longer be simple, but would be [composed] of as many bodies as had the sources of motion. For the composite [body] differs from the simple in this way, namely in its having within itself sources of many simple motions.

A single motion is not invariably simple;[95] nor, as I see it, is that motion of animals which occurs by way of the extension and flexing of the limbs genuinely single, while oblique motion, such as that of shooting-stars, is a single motion, but is not simple, since it is composed of the upward and the downward, as is the helical motion of the straight and the circular.

Alexander said that these motions have been called 'in a way mixed', 'because motion is not mixed in the same way as bodies are. For the simple bodies subsist and exist at the same time together with one another in the mixture, whereas in the case of motion the first does not persist along with the second so as to enable us to say that this was mixed with that'.[96] But perhaps it is true in the case of motions which are serially mixed, for example in the case of the expansion and flexing of the limbs, that the former motion does not persist; but in the case of oblique motions, in which the upward and the downward are mixed into one form, it is no longer in my view true, and similarly in the case of helical motions. But 'in a way' should rather be understood in regard to what is appropriate to motion.[97]

The natural motion of composite bodies occurs in respect of that which predominates; for the human body, if someone hurls it, is carried downwards because of the predomination of the earthy in it. As I see it, when he added 'they will move in respect of whatever predominates', Aristotle was thinking of those four things which are called by us 'elements' but which are not properly simple, moving rather in respect of the predominant among the simple motions. For there would not be simple [bodies] separated by place given that the totality is constructed by composition.[98]

But perhaps even the heaven is a composition of the extremes of the four elements,[99] given that it is visible and tangible, but since the extreme of fire predominates in it, it too is said to be [composed] of a simple [body], just as the four [elements are said to be] simple in relation to the putting together of the complex [bodies]. And every body that moves with a simple motion is either simple or it moves with this motion in virtue of the predominance of one of the simple [bodies] within it; for a composite body does not move with a simple motion insofar as it is composite.

269a2-7 So given that there is simple motion, [and circular motion is simple, and if it is both the case that of a simple body the motion is simple and that simple motion is of a simple body[100] (since if it were of a compound, it would be in respect of what predominates), necessarily there is some simple body which naturally moves with a circular motion] in accordance with its own nature. 18,1

Having shown that circular motion is simple on the grounds that the magnitude along which it occurs is simple too, and having shown that of a simple body the motion is simple and that simple motion is of a simple body, he reasons out the rest as follows: since circular motion is simple, and since of a simple body the motion is simple and that simple motion is of a simple body, 'necessarily there is some simple body which naturally moves in a circular motion in accordance with its own nature'; but the antecedent [is true], as has been established: therefore the consequent [is true].[101]

Alexander says: 'he reasonably propounded this not as hypothetical ('if … circular motion is simple'), but rather employed the factual connective 'given that' (*eiper*), since he has previously demonstrated all the propositions'. But perhaps *eiper* is still hypothetical, and not identical in force to *epeidêper* ('in view of the fact that'). The *per* added to the hypothetical *ei* ('if') does not alter its force, just as it does not [alter the force] of *epeidê*, ('since'), which is a factual connective. Perhaps he propounds it hypothetically because of philosophical caution. But it is clear that he could have propounded the hypothetical propositions which have been demonstrated categorically, in the following manner: circular motion is simple; simple motion is of a simple body; therefore there is a simple body which moves naturally in a circle.

269a7-9 For while it might by force [move with the motion of another, distinct body, it could not do so naturally, given that there is only one such motion for each of the simple bodies, namely that] in accordance with its nature.

Having shown that 'necessarily there is some simple body which naturally moves with a circular motion in accordance with its own nature', he proceeds to show that none of the four elements moves in a circle either naturally or unnaturally.

That they do not do so naturally he shows as follows: if there is one natural motion for each of the simple bodies (since of simple bodies it is simple, and simple motion is single), it is clear that for each of the four elements, being simple, there will be a simple and single natural motion. So if their natural motion is rectilinear, it is clear that circular

motion would not be natural for them, but must (if indeed there is any) be forcible for them. For it might move with the same motion as
19,1 another, distinct body by force, or it might be moved by force in some way by the motion of another, and not of one only but of some other as well;[102] for fire can be moved by force either downwards or in a circle.

But it is impossible that it be moved naturally with the motion of another, given that for each of them there is one natural [motion]. Just as he established earlier that even if the body that moves with a circular motion is composite, since that [motion] is simple it will move with the motion appropriate to the one simple [body] which predominates in it, he now shows that even if something moves with a circular motion by force, since that [motion] is simple there will at all events be something that moves with that [motion] naturally.

> **269a9-18** Furthermore, if unnatural [motion] is contrary [to natural [motion], and for one thing there is one contrary, then since circular motion is simple, if it is not the natural motion of the moving body then it must be unnatural for it. So if fire, or something else of this kind, moves in a circle, then its natural motion will be contrary to the circular. But for one thing there is one contrary <at most>;[103] and upwards and downwards are contraries of one another. But if it is some other body which moves in a circle, there will be some simple[104] motion natural to it. But this is impossible, since if it is upwards it would be fire or air,] and if downwards water or earth.

Next he shows that, if circular motion does not belong by nature to one of the four, but nevertheless it is posited as belonging [to one of them], necessarily it must be unnatural for it. So when it has been established that it does not belong to it unnaturally either (it having already been established that it does not do so naturally), he concludes that it does not belong to it at all. And that if it does not do so naturally it must do so unnaturally, he showed from the fact that the unnatural is the opposite[105] of the natural. So if the natural is not present, the unnatural must be, then this, and nor something else, must be its contrary, given that 'for one thing there is one contrary'; for nature does not unjustly range many things against one.[106] So if the natural is not present, its contrary, namely the unnatural, will be present, given that the unnatural is the contrary of the natural and that 'for one thing there is one contrary'.

Ingeniously he says that the reason why, if circular motion is not natural then it is unnatural, is that it is simple. For if it were not simple, it would be possible for it to be neither contrary nor unnatural, but simply non-natural.[107] But something moving with a simple motion must move, if it moves at all, either with a natural or an unnatural motion. (Or with one of the intermediates which is not simple[108] – but circular [motion] is simple). That none of the four elements is carried around in a circle unnaturally, he shows by once again relying on the fact that 'for one thing there is one contrary'. For if upward motion is natural for fire, and downward [motion] is the contrary of upward, and for one thing there is one contrary, circular motion would not be unnatural for fire, and for the same reasons neither would it be for any of the other three.

20,1 That circular motion is not unnatural for any other simple body he shows from the necessity of there being some simple motion for it, since it is simple; but the only simple motions are upwards and downwards, and if it moved with one of these this would be one of the four and nothing else.[109] And while there are two simple rectilinear motions, namely the upward and the downward, there are not two rectilinearly-moving elements only, but four. He will state the reason for this in the discussions of the heavy and the light:[110] earth is unqualifiedly heavy, fire unqualifiedly light, since the one settles to the bottom of everything and the other rises to the top of everything, while air and water share in the characteristics of both, since they are both heavy and light, although not related to the same thing.[111] For this reason there are two genuinely simple elements, fire and earth.

One ought to know that Ptolemy in his *On the Elements* and his *Optics*,[112] the great Plotinus,[113] and Xenarchus in his objections *Against the Fifth Substance*, say that there is rectilinear motion of the elements only when they are in an unnatural place, but not when they have reached their natural place. And Aristotle appears to agree with this when he says in the fourth book of this treatise that 'in moving towards its proper place each thing moves towards its proper form',[114] and so too Alexander, along with these people, in his *On Generation*,[115] as will be said.[116]

For in reality if they move seeking their proper places and their proper entire masses from some other place and some unnatural disposition, clearly they will not move when they are in their perfectly natural condition, but as the aforementioned gentlemen (Ptolemy, Xenarchus, Plotinus) say, when they are in their natural condition and in their proper places the elements will either remain at rest or move in a circle. Clearly the earth, the water, and the watery part of the air remain at rest, while the fire and the bright part of the air move in a circle, revolving along with the heaven according to its proper character.[117]

So if this is true (and Aristotle himself says in the *Meteorology*[118] that the rotation of the fire-sphere is evidenced by comets and the other phenomena which coalesce within it and rise and set with the stars), how can Aristotle in this treatise first of all attempt in a way to establish, on the basis of the unnatural motion of things below the moon, that the motion of the heavenly body is superior and special by comparison with them? I shall dispose of this difficulty, which was brought up by Xenarchus, in a little while.[119] Now we must explain how he can say that neither fire nor any other of the four can move in a circle, either naturally (if there is a single natural motion for each [body], which for them is rectilinear), or unnaturally (if for one thing there is one contrary and the contrary of the upward is the downward and not the circular).

21,1 It is worth considering, however, that perhaps Aristotle does not mean this, namely that none of the four elements can move in a circle at all, but only that they can do so neither naturally nor unnaturally. He has established that there is something which moves naturally in a circle, and which is neither fire nor any of the other elements. Take fire for example: it would not have this motion naturally (since that of fire is rectilinear, and there is a single natural motion for each); nor yet unnaturally (since the unnatural motion of fire is downwards, and for one thing there is one contrary).

And that this circular motion belongs to none of the four elements he showed as follows: he shows that this circular motion, being simple, does not belong to any other body which moves contrary to its nature, [arguing] from the necessity of its [i.e. the body] having some simple natural motion too which would clearly have to be rectilinear. For there is no other simple motion, apart from the circular. Consequently it would again be one of the four elements, which is impossible.

Allow, then, that these contentions have a certain reasonableness: but given that even according to Aristotle fire moves in a circle, does it move with that motion naturally or unnaturally? If it does so naturally, there will no longer be a single natural motion for each thing, given that it moves upwards naturally. But if it does so unnaturally, there will no longer be one opposite for each thing, since for fire [motion] downwards is unnatural.

Perhaps, then, circular motion cannot be natural for fire in the sense of being a property of it, even if it rotates with an unwavering[120] [motion]: for neither is motion from the east natural to the planets.[121] But nor yet is it unnatural, in the sense of being the contrary of the natural, since [motion] of this kind is harmful and unstable. But it must be something other than natural, since it is [the motion] of something greater which controls it. And perhaps it was for this reason that Aristotle did not say that it was possible for the [motion] of the other, distinct body to be unnatural, but rather by force. For there is such a thing as beneficial force which is not unnatural, but which might be called 'preternatural'.

But someone will reasonably ask us,[122] if the entire mass of the fire moves with a visible motion foreign to it and preternatural, does it have some natural eternal motion, or do the upper elements come to rest having attained their proper place, just as earth and water do insofar as they are at rest with themselves? I reply that the inclination of the whole fire towards the heaven is just like that of the earth towards the centre, as will be more completely explained in what follows, where Aristotle says that both whole and part move towards the same place.[123]

Xenarchus, in his difficulties raised *Against the Fifth Substance*, after the one concerned with simple lines,[124] raises a second difficulty against the natural motion of a simple body's being simple. 'For rectilinear motion', he says,

> is natural to none of the four elements when they are actual,[125] but only when they are coming to be so. But something which is coming to be is not so unqualifiedly, but is between being and non-being, like a moving object:[126] and in fact this is between the place it aims at and that which it occupied before, and generation is akin to motion, since it too is a change. And for this reason we say that the fire which moves upwards is not properly called fire, but is coming to be fire; and that when it has come to its proper place, and risen above everything else and come to rest, then it will have come to be fire genuinely. For it achieves its form, insofar as it is light, in this position. And earth is genuinely earth when it settles beneath everything else and occupies the middle place.[127] So too for water and air, water when it rises above the earth and settles beneath the air, and air when it rises above the water and settles beneath the fire. So [he says] it is false that of a simple body there is a simple natural motion. For it has been shown that motion is a property not of that which is, but of that which is coming to be. Therefore if one must assign a motion also to things that already are, and for it to be simple, one must assign them circular motion, given that these are the two simple motions, namely circular and rectilinear, while rectilinear motion is for the four [elements] when they are coming to be, not when they are, then one might without absurdity assign circular motion to fire, and rest to the other three.

In resolving this difficulty, Alexander allows that rectilinear [motion] does not belong to things which are in every way complete (as Aristotle had allowed) in his writings *On Generation*,[128] when he clearly says that they would not be able to move unless there was something in them potentially: for motion is the actuality of the thing in potentiality;[129] and this is then complete in every way whenever they are in their natural places.[130] For he says that the upward-moving body is not deficient in respect of its being fire, but in respect of its being really fire in the natural place towards which it moves, and similarly with the others. But he says that it is clear that the aforementioned motions are natural even for things already complete in respect of form from the fact that whenever something has lifted the earth by contact from the bottom, where earth is already earth in actuality, it moves downwards in the same way; for it does not cease being what it is as a result of being removed from its proper place.[131]

Furthermore, he says, if earth is heavy and fire is light, and motions of this kind are natural for them, the argument is not shaken unless one defines the light not as that which moves upwards but rather that which rises above everything, and heavy not as that which moves downwards but rather that which settles below everything. Moreover, Plato's *Timaeus* demonstrates that 'up' and 'down' are relative rather than absolute terms.[132]

For if Aristotle allows that what moves towards its proper place moves towards its form, while Alexander [allows] that what is in its proper place is complete in every way,[133] they must surely offer definitions of these things. But someone who wishes to argue on the basis of their motions has no need of these definitions. Perhaps then even Aristotle knows that rectilinear motion belongs to elements which are incomplete and deficient and which are involved in generation and destruction, but wishing to distinguish them from the heavenly bodies he argued on the basis of their motion, showing that there belongs to them motion appropriate for generation and destruction, while to the heavenly body [there belongs] that [motion] receptive of everlastingness.

Xenarchus raises a further difficulty, saying that it is not necessary that, if nature assigns to the naturally simple bodies simple, proper, and kindred motions, it must already for this reason also have assigned simple natural bodies to the simple motions; for it does not assign a composite [body] to composite [motion], otherwise there would be an infinite number of them; for the composite motions are infinite.

Against this difficulty, I think, it should be said that composite bodies which are assigned to composite motions are not infinite; for the composite motions are not infinite in form, but rather by recurrence, as bodies are; for even if each composite body moved with many composite motions, they would not be infinite in form but only, if at all, infinite in number; so the moving things are not compelled to be infinite in number, unless these things too are infinite.[134]

Alexander seems to me either to have been reacting to this objection of Xenarchus differently, or to have been recording his response to another of the following kind: if the generated composite is single, and if of single things there is a single motion, the same motion will belong both to the simple and the composite [body], since the motion of the simple[135] body is single.

Accordingly, Alexander resolves this by saying that even if the motion of the composite [body] is single, it is not simple; for while what is simple is single, what is single is not invariably simple.[136] For just because a body is single, it is not necessarily simple too. Consequently the [motion] of the composite [body] will be single, but not simple. And even if it is simple, it will not be so as being of a composite [body], but rather in respect of what predominates;[137] for in a composite [body] the sources of motion are many, which is why it is composite.

These too are Xenarchus' words:

> grant that there are two simple lines, the circular and the straight, and that each of the four [elements], earth, water, air, and fire, whenever they exist, genuinely have as a natural motion that along a straight line. But what is to prevent one, or some, or all of these basic subjects from being naturally inclined to move in a circle as well? For surely we did not also make the additional assumption that there is only a single natural [motion] for each of them. Indeed such an additional assumption would not even be possible, since it is quite evidently false: for each of the [elements] in the middle has two natural motions. For water moves naturally upward from earth but the opposite from fire and air, while air moves downward from fire and upward from water.

But that we have indeed made the additional assumption[138] that there is a single natural motion for the simple <bodies> is clear from Aristotle's saying 'for while it might move with the motion of another, distinct body by force, it could not do so naturally, given that there is only one natural motion for each of the simple bodies.'[139] Moreover, that the intermediate elements do not have two sources of motion in themselves is clear from the following: air is light, but less so than fire, while water is heavy, but less so than earth. [Motion] downwards for air and upwards for water belongs to them by force and not naturally, and the more and the less do not alter their forms.[140]

And if someone wants to say that with a mixture of its opposite the one [i.e. air] is less light[141] [sc. than fire] and the other [i.e. water] less heavy [sc. than earth], he will be saying <not only> that these things are not genuinely simple, as even Aristotle holds, but that they move generally in respect of what predominates, and sometimes even share in both forms.[142] For simple bodies are distinguished from those which are not simply by the fact that they have the principle of a single nature, and perhaps for this reason Aristotle frequently discusses the simple <bodies> as though they were two.[143] Thus Alexander both poses and resolves the objections of Xenarchus in this context.

But Xenarchus enunciates another one of the same kind as follows:

> it is impossible for a simple body to have natural circular motion given that all the parts in simple bodies, which are uniform, should move at the same speed. In a circle the parts near the centre move more slowly than those at the periphery, given that they move a shorter distance in the same time. Moreover, in a sphere the circles around the poles move more slowly than those further away, while the largest of the parallels[144] moves most swiftly of all.

Against this difficulty it should be said, I think, that Aristotle says that the simple circular motion which occurs for a single [body] along a circular line is single. On the other hand, the reasoning which creates the difficulty, in assuming there to be many circles of unequal speeds in the sphere (while equally in a plane circle there are those [circles] near the centre and those at the periphery), tries to show that there is a single non-simple motion composed of all of them. For he[145] did not refute [the claim] that there is at least a simple motion for each of the circles in the sphere as well as for each of the ones in the circular plane.

25,1 And in fact both the motion which occurs along the circle which is always visible[146] and that along the celestial equator are similarly simple, even though one is the slowest, the other the fastest; and the motion of each of the inscribed circles of the circles in the planes is similarly simple and is of a simple body, namely that part of it. For in fact Aristotle did not say that the many circular motions are a single simple motion, or of a simple body, but rather that simple motion, which is also single, is invariably of a simple body, and that of a simple and single body the motion is simple and single.[147] Consequently the reasoning applies both to the whole heaven as being a single indivisible thing, and to each part of it, if someone were to divide it into parts. For the assumption was made only in regard to a single motion occurring along a single circle.

Finally in this context Xenarchus finds fault with us for making use of mathematical demonstrations when dealing with physical matters, relying on the forms of lines whenever we make the causes of the simple motions depend upon the simple lines. Well, if we were indeed employing the lines mathematically, we would really have departed from our subject. But if, since each motion occurs along a linear interval, simple [motion] along a simple [interval], composite along a composite, we have adduced the forms of the intervals by way of illustration of the difference between the motions, how can we be said to be establishing physical things mathematically? For if both the physicist and the mathematician make use of lines both as in surfaces and as in bodies, simply employing lines is not mathematical, but rather employing them mathematically is. These are the things that Xenarchus had to say against the hypotheses adopted by Aristotle.

[Here begins the first major digression from straightforward commentary into anti-Philoponan polemic. Wildberg's fragments 1 and 4-17 of Philoponus' *Against Aristotle on the Eternity of the World* are to be found in these pages (25,23-38,5), which I omit. See Wildberg (1987), 41-50]

> **269a18-30** Furthermore, this type of movement must necessarily be primary[, since what is complete is prior by nature to what is incomplete, and a circle is one of the complete things, while no straight line is so. For an infinite line cannot be (since then it would have a limit and an end); but neither can any of the finite lines be (for there is always something beyond each of them, since all of them can be extended). Consequently, given that the prior motion will be that of the body which is prior by nature, and that motion in a circle is prior to that in a straight line, and that motion in a straight line belongs to the simple bodies (since fire moves upwards in a straight line, while earthy things move downwards towards the centre), circular motion too must belong to one of the simple bodies: for of the mixed bodies we have said[148] that the movement occurs in respect of whichever of the simple bodies predominates in the mixture.][149] 38,6

Having shown that there is another natural simple motion besides the rectilinear, namely that in a circle, and that simple motions are of simple bodies, he concludes from these [premisses] that there is another simple body, besides the four rectilinearly-moving elements, for which circular motion is natural.[150] And having shown too that none of the four elements can move with circular motion either naturally[151] or unnaturally, he proceeds to show that the revolving [body] is prior to and more divine than the rectilinearly-moving bodies. And he shows this by showing that circular motion is naturally first of all motions; and this [he shows] by showing that a circular line is prior by nature to a straight line, and this by showing that it is complete, while a straight line is incomplete, just as he established that there was a simple body which moved with a natural circular motion on the grounds that circular motion was simple, and that circular motion was simple on the grounds that a circular line was simple.

Simplicity is established at the same time as primacy, since primary things are invariably simple, because simple things are prior by nature to composite ones. Moreover, he showed in the eighth book of the *Physics*[152] that circular motion is prior to rectilinear. There he showed it on the grounds of its being complete, simple, and perfectly continuous; while here the demonstration is generated by way of completeness. For it is self-evident that the complete is prior by nature to the incomplete, given that incomplete things come from complete ones.

That circular motion is complete he showed from the completeness of the circle, and this from its being limited and having an end, as befits complete things, and further from its not being capable of being added to in any way while still retaining its form: for addition takes place in respect of some deficiency. But he did not show these things [directly] of the circle, but rather having shown the incompleteness of rectilinear [line] on the basis of certain things, since these things are not present in the circle but their opposites are, he showed that the circle is complete.

39,1 That every rectilinear [line] is incomplete he shows first of all by distinguishing between finite and infinite [lines]. For every [line] is either infinite or finite (not that there actually is, according to him, any rectilinear [line] which is in itself infinite, since the totality is finite;[153] but some people think that there is, and even if there is not, the disjunction takes care of any counter-example, since it includes any [line] that is indefinitely augmented in the imagination). So if an infinite [line] is that which possesses neither end nor boundary, but is indefinite, it would not be complete; for the complete is that which is already finite and bounded, and is not deficient in any of its own [parts]. But a finite [line] has something beyond it so that it can be added to; and since what is increasing does not yet comprehend all of itself, it would be incomplete. But the circle, on the other hand, is both finite and has an end, and has nothing beyond [itself], nor can it be added to and yet retain its form.[154]

Alexander shows the circle to be complete from its having beginning, middle, and end, if at least, he says, its beginning is the centre, its limit the outermost line,[155] and its middle the plane between them; I think it should be noted, however, that perhaps Aristotle has here taken the thing in accordance with which the motion is accomplished to be a linear circle and not a plane. For this reason he did not see fit to demonstrate it in the same way as Alexander, but rather from [the fact that] even though it is finite it does not admit of any addition. And it would have beginning, middle, and end, except that each of them is everywhere: for whichever part of it you take is capable of being beginning, middle, and end. And this, I think, should be an indication of the utter completeness of the circle, given that it manifests completeness in every respect.[156]

But how will there be 'something beyond'[157] every finite line? For since the diameter of the totality is finite too, what could be beyond it, given that there is nothing beyond the cosmos? And how can it not be absurd for every straight line to be incomplete, given that there is a particular form belonging to the straight, which itself ought to have a share of completeness as the other forms do, so that, even if there are some incomplete straight [lines], there must at any rate be a complete one as well?[158]

But Alexander interprets [the claim] that we can increase conceptually any given line not as meaning [that we can do so] by increasing the straight line but rather by increasing a straight line of some particular size.[159] Consequently, while the form of the straight line, insofar as it is straight, is complete in every way both in small and in large [lines], the magnitude is complete only in the one which cuts off the whole measure of the cosmic straight line.[160] Its formal completeness too is deficient in comparison with the circular form and its completeness, in that it does not converge upon itself, but flows out insofar as its own form is concerned to unmeasurability and infinity, while limits are put upon its extension by the measures of the Demiurge.[161] This then indicates that there is something beyond each finite line just insofar as, in regard to its own form and indeterminate flow, it always has something which is deficient and capable of being 40,1 added to.[162]

So, having assumed that the more complete motion is prior (since, he says, the complete is prior by nature to the incomplete); and having demonstrated that the circle is prior in nature to the straight line because it is more complete, and that what holds for the lines along which the motions [take place] holds for the motions as well, he [sc. Aristotle] has his conclusion, namely that circular motion is prior to that in a straight line. To this premiss he added another evident one asserting that the prior motion is of the body that is prior by nature. Again he has his conclusion: that circular motion is of a body prior by nature to those which [move] in straight lines, which follows as a clear conclusion derived from the two conjoined premisses.

Then, wishing to show that the body that is prior by nature is that which moves in a circle, and that it is simple and distinct from the four elements, he does so, I believe, as follows. If there are two simple motions of simple bodies, namely the rectilinear and the circular, and rectilinear motion belongs to the simple sublunary bodies which move up and down, it is necessary that circular motion will belong to some simple body distinct from the sublunary ones: for motion is always of a moved body, and simple [motion] of a simple [body].[163] For even if some mixed body moves with a simple motion, as a man falling from a roof moves towards the middle, he still moves with the motion appropriate to the predominant simple [body] in the mixture, in this case the earthy one.

Alexander, however, says that he [sc. Aristotle] shows that this body which is primary by nature is simple by means of the following argument from the lesser and greater, which may be briefly expressed: if, in the case of the motions for which it is less reasonable that the moving bodies are simple they are simple, then in the case of circular motion, for which it is more reasonable that the moving [body] be simple, all the more will this be simple. But perhaps it is not clear that it is more reasonable that the thing which moves simply in a circle be simple, rather than that which has the [motion] which is prior by nature, if there is such a thing: for simple things are prior to composites. So perhaps the issue should rather be posed as follows: if, in the case of those things of which, being posterior by nature (i.e. the rectilinear ones: for this has been shown), it is less reasonable [to assume] the substance to be simple, [the motion] of these is simple, then in the case of those things of which, being prior by nature (i.e. the circular ones) it is more reasonable [to assume] the substance to be simple, of these all the more would [the motion] be simple. Let these things then be said by way of clarifying Aristotle's remarks. But as Alexander says, some object to the stated doctrine that the more complete is prior by nature and what is prior is simpler. For if the cosmos is more complete than each of the things from which it is made, while what is more complete is prior and what is primary is also simple, then the cosmos will be both prior to the things from which it is made and simpler than them.

But as Alexander says, the cosmos does not precede its parts, even though what is composed of them seems simpler. Conceding as much, Alexander attempts to resolve the difficulty by saying that the cosmos is more complete in the sense of being more all-encompassing, while circular motion and the circle [are more complete] than rectilinear motion and the straight line not because they contain them, but rather in respect of their form. So, in the case of these treated separately,[164] he says, it is true that the more complete is both prior and simpler, but not in the case of wholes and parts (for, he says, the whole is more complete than its parts, and is primary both in nature and substance, but not in time): for in addition to its being simple and complete, this[165] is also primary in time. But that circular motion is prior to rectilinear not only in substance but also in time Aristotle shows in the eighth book of the *Physics*.[166] So at any rate says Alexander.

But perhaps 'prior' was not meant temporally, since there was never any time when there was circular but not rectilinear motion, even if the former is the cause of the latter, and much less [was there a time] when there was a circle but no straight line; [but this is natural].[167] At any rate, Aristotle clearly says 'since what is complete is prior by nature to what is incomplete' and again 'given that the prior motion will be that of the body which is prior by nature'. Thus the cosmos, being more complete than its parts will be prior by nature to them, as Alexander too agrees I believe, and simpler. For if it is prior by nature it will be more unified, and what is more unified is more akin to the unit, and what is of such a kind is simpler. But we do not pay attention to the unified wholeness of the cosmos, in respect of which a single animal represents the intelligible animal,[168] but to its diverse multiplicity, and talking of this world we think that the part is simpler than the whole and that the parts are prior. But the whole produces its own diversity in itself and from its own unity.[169]

And having demonstrated that circular motion is not only of a more complete and primary [body], but also at the same time [that it is] of a simple body, since it is simple,[170] with a view to making the argument more general, whether or not the heavenly body is simple or mixed, he goes on to argue 'for of the mixed bodies we have said 42,1
that the movement occurs in respect of whichever of the simple bodies predominates in the mixture', as if he had said 'since in fact of the mixed bodies', etc.[171] So even if the heaven which moves in a circle is something composite, there would still at any rate be something simple within it, in accordance with the predominance of which it would move in a circle.

Here too Xenarchus raises the same difficulties once again, first of all that the argument employs mathematical notions, namely [those of] the straight and the circular;[172] secondly that what is moved around the periphery is not a naturally simple body on account of the differences in the velocities of the parts at the centre, those at the periphery, and those in between;[173] and thirdly that even if something does move in a circle, it is not distinct from the four [elements], given that some of them too remain at rest, while others move in a circle when they are complete,[174] particularly fire.[175] For the things which move in a straight line are incomplete and do so with an incomplete [motion], as Aristotle himself thought. Alexander did not think it worthwhile to deal with these objections, on the grounds that they had already been posed and resolved; and I will try in the remainder to avoid [dealing with] ones of this kind.

[Here again Simplicius digresses into anti-Philoponan polemic. I omit 42,17-49,25, containing Philoponus fragments 18-32 (Wildberg, 50-5)]

269a30-2 From these things then it is evident that there must by nature be some substance of a body [apart from those compositions around here, more divine] and prior to all of them. 49,26

He draws a common conclusion from what has gone before; for when these [premisses] have been posited it is clear what arises from them, namely that there is another simple circular body besides the four elements, more divine than them, and prior [to them] by nature. For if it has been shown that circular motion is simple and prior by nature to rectilinear, the [motion] which is simple and prior to the rectilinear will be of a simple body which is prior by nature to those which travel in a straight line. That what is simple and naturally prior is also more divine is clear, since this conclusion follows on the basis of what has been established.[176]

> **269a32-b2** And [it would evident] also if one were to assume further that all motion [is either natural or unnatural, and that what is unnatural for one is natural for another, as is the case for upwards and downwards. For the latter is unnatural for fire, the former for earth – and vice versa in the case of the natural. Consequently it is necessary that the circular motion too, since it is unnatural for these,] is natural of some other body.

He draws the parallel conclusion that there is another revolving body besides the four elements not only from what has already been said, but also from arguments which he now appends, of which the first is, I believe, such as Alexander says [it is]: every simple natural motion is either natural for the simple body which moves in accordance with it, or it is unnatural [for it]. What is an unnatural [motion for one body] will be natural for some other [body]. For this is what it is to be moved unnaturally in respect of a natural motion, to move with a motion which accords with the nature of something else and not according to one's own nature. For each natural motion is natural for some moving thing. So if circular motion is natural, while if a natural [motion] is unnatural [for something], it must be natural for something else, it is clear that even if circular motion is assumed to be unnatural for the four elements, there will none the less be some body besides these for which it is natural to move in a circle.

Alexander raises difficulties about this, instancing the case of the fire-sphere and Aristotle's claim that the body adjacent to the revolving body is always carried around in a circle by it,[177] and the objection of Xenarchus.[178] 'The question should be raised', he says, 'whether circular motion is unnatural or natural for it; if one holds it to be unnatural, there will be one which is natural for it, namely that upwards. Then since downward [motion] would be unnatural for it, there will be two opposites for one thing.[179] Consequently both air and fire are naturally circular-movers.'[180]

He raises difficulties first about a sphere of wood or stone;[181] for if someone moving it in a circle[182] were to ask whether this circular motion is unnatural for it, it will be shown that it is not unnatural; for there will be some natural [motion] for it, either that upwards or that downwards, since there are no other simple [motions] besides these. So whichever one says, the other will be opposite. But unnatural circular [motion] is also opposite; therefore one thing will have two opposites. In order for this result not to occur, it is necessary to say that circular motion is natural for such a sphere as well.[183] 51,1

However, I believe that he hypothesized this sphere unnecessarily. For Aristotle does not construct the argument thus far on the basis of the heaven's being spherical, but rather he argues from circular motion. And a cube (and non-circular objects in general) can move in a circle.[184]

Alexander resolves this difficulty by saying that the body dragged around by the heaven does not move circularly, since its motion is not simple; for even while it is being carried around it is necessary that whatever is light within it be borne upwards, and whatever heavy downwards. Thus its motion is mixed. But, he says, neither the wooden nor the stone sphere move in a circle, but up and down, given that what is away from the middle of the totality is up, while what is towards the middle is down.[185] But he would more readily have resolved it, I believe, by saying that this type of motion was neither natural nor of a simple [body] but created and of a composite [body],[186] and so neither natural for it nor for anything else, and consequently not unnatural, given that it is not natural for something else.[187]

In addition to the resolution [of the problem] concerning the fire-sphere, difficulties about the wandering [sphere][188] which is carried beside[189] it must be confronted, since this is also carried round by the fixed [sphere], and it is clear that nothing in this is either heavy or light, rising or falling. And it would not be natural for it (even if it has another natural [motion], namely that from the settings),[190] and there is one natural motion for each of the natural [bodies].

Nor will Aristotle allow it to be unnatural, rightly saying a little later[191] that it would be 'bizarre and downright absurd' for a motion that was continuous and eternal to be unnatural, since unnatural things are most swiftly destroyed. But it was said earlier[192] that this type of motion is neither natural nor unnatural, either for the fire-sphere or the wandering [sphere], but rather preternatural, or unnatural in that it is in accordance with the nature of something else more powerful that provides living motion [for it] in accordance with the highest degrees of life. And something unnatural in such a way is not a contrary; for it obtains neither in respect of contrary qualities (as the upward and downward do), nor do [such motions] conflict with one another, since the natural is rather preserved by the preternatural.

But this Aristotelian account requires scrutiny: how can he say that circular motion is unnatural for the sublunary elements, among which he enumerates earth and fire? For the unnatural circular motion does not obtain for the earth or the water, or anything under the air. Moreover, Alexander says, 'circular [motion] is unnatural for the four elements, and the argument seems to have this force when it says 'that what is unnatural for one is natural for another', and by giving the examples of up and down and fire and earth, and saying that of these two motions one is unnatural for fire, the other for earth, and vice versa in the case of the natural'.

So perhaps the phrase 'since it is unnatural for these, it is natural for another'[193] is not said on the grounds that the earth and the other sublunary elements move in a circle, albeit unnaturally; but rather because he treats 'unnatural' as the negation of 'natural', as if he had said 'since circular motion, although it is natural and simple, is not natural for the four elements, either because they never move in respect of it [sc. circular motion] at all (since in fact for such things it is not true to say that [they do so] naturally), or because they do move in respect of it, albeit not in accordance with their own nature but rather with that of another, it must be natural for something else: for motion is of something moved'.

And thus we resolve the apparent objection which asked how he could say earlier that the circular motion of the four elements was neither natural nor unnatural, while here he says that it is unnatural, given that 'unnatural' was there intended as the privative[194] opposite of 'natural', and for this reason it followed that there were two opposites for a single thing, while in this case [it was intended as] the negation.

> **269b2-10** In addition to these things, if movement in a circle is natural for anything,[it is clear that it would be one of the simple and primary bodies which moves naturally in a circle, just as fire does upwards and earth downwards. But if the things that move in a circle by circular movement do so unnaturally, it would be bizarre and downright absurd for this to be the only continuous and eternal motion, seeing that it is unnatural. For it is evident in other contexts that] the unnatural things are the most swiftly destroyed.

He shows the same thing, namely that the body which moves with circular motion is distinct from the four elements, once again by division. He says, in effect, that circular motion, since it is a natural and simple motion, belongs at all events to some natural and simple body either naturally or unnaturally, using the disjunctive method by way of super-addition – since it is clear that being natural [the motion] will at any rate belong to something naturally – on account of the inescapability of the disjunction.

And in order to construct the problem in many forms at the same time, he adds the following argument too, saying that if circular movement, being simple and primary, is natural (which has been proved), while every motion is at all events of some moved body, there must be some body among the simple and primary bodies which naturally moves with this motion, apart from those which move in 53,1
straight lines. For as they move with rectilinear [motion], so this moves with circular motion.

And if circular movement belongs unnaturally to what it belongs to (this is equivalent to saying if the things which move in a circle move with a circular movement unnaturally), then it is 'bizarre and downright absurd' for circular motion to be the only unnatural thing which is continuous and everlasting, as is shown in the eighth book of the *Physics*.[195] It is 'bizarre' that it should go so far beyond the accustomed nature of things; and it is 'downright absurd' if something unnatural is the cause of continuous and everlasting motion, 'for it is evident in other contexts that the unnatural things are the most swiftly destroyed': for every nature grows weary when acting not in accordance with its own form.

Things that move naturally move as a result of the actualization of their innate capacity, which exists along with their essence, and for this reason they act without wearying, while things which move unnaturally and not as a result of their natural capacity are affected rather than acting, and are propelled by external force. For this reason natural bodies have no need of rest because they act according to their own nature, while animals' bodies invariably need rest because animals' natural motions do not belong to the bodies themselves; rather they are moved by their souls, which use them as tools, since they are moved by something else.

> **269b10-13** Consequently if it were fire that moved [thus, as some say, this motion would be no less unnatural for it than that downwards, since we observe the motion of fire in a straight line from the centre.][196]

Alexander says that this claim follows from what has been shown above, since it follows for those who say that if fire is moved in a circle that this motion is no less unnatural for it than that downwards, given that upward [motion] is natural for it, and there is only one natural [motion] for each thing. Perhaps, however, this, namely that circular motion is unnatural for fire, is not what is said here: for this has been frequently remarked. Rather, having shown that circular motion is not unnatural for the body which moves in a circle, given that it is continuous and everlasting, he next shows, making use of the previously-demonstrated proposition that circular motion is not unnatural for the body which moves in a circle, that the body which moves in a circle is not fire. And he shows it as follows: If the revolving body is fire it follows that circular motion is no less unnatural for it than downwards motion. Yet circular motion is not unnatural for the revolving [body], given that it is continuous and everlasting. Therefore the revolving body is not fire.

It is possible to syllogize categorically in the second figure[197] thus: circular motion is not unnatural for the revolving body; circular motion is unnatural for fire; therefore the revolving body is not fire. If we interpret what is said in this way, we will not say that the passage is missing something, as Alexander says; and he also adds, of those who say that, being emaciated and undernourished, it moves in a circle around its nourishment because the nourishment, being stretched to the limit in a straight line, no longer reaches it,[198] that even they also agree that it is moved unnaturally, since it is forcibly driven by nourishment. And forced motion is unnatural, and unnatural [motion] posterior to natural, so that motion in a circle would not be primary if the revolving body were fire.

Here Alexander, employing many dense arguments, shows that circular motion is not natural for fire. 'For it is not reasonable,' he says, 'that it alone of the natural bodies be moved with two natural motions' (although in fact they say that not only fire but the clear part of air as well is moved in a circle). 'It is absurd' he says, 'for fire, as a simple body, to have two natural principles of motion: for it is clear that it retains its upward [motion] as well, since if it were to be scattered downwards, it would move in this way [i.e. upwards] once more'.

Perhaps, however, if it were scattered downwards, it would, in becoming incomplete, exchange circular for upward [motion], but when it arrived at the top and became complete it would abandon that rectilinear [motion] appropriate to something incomplete just as it abandons its incompleteness, and exchange it for that which is appropriate to something complete, because it has become akin to that which is most complete.[199]

But it does not derive its circular motion from its place, but from the revolving body which is then adjacent to it; and it does not simply abandon its form in exchange for circular motion, given that rectilinear [motion] belonged to fire that was coming to be, while circular [motion belongs to it] when it has been perfected. For we do not say either that earth abandons its form whenever it rests at the bottom, but rather we assign rectilinear motion to it when it is incomplete, and rest to it when it has been perfected. However, someone who says that fire moves upwards *qua* fire, and earth downwards *qua* earth, without distinguishing between their incomplete and complete states and the motions and rests appropriate to each of them, would say that Alexander's remarks in this context were fine.

269b13-17 So someone drawing conclusions from all of these 55,1
things will be convinced [that there is some other body over and above those around here in our part of the world which is separate and distinct from them, having a nature as much more noble as it is far removed from these parts.][200]

Conviction comes in two forms, one arising irrationally without demonstration, as for instance when some cling even to the most absurd [beliefs], the other after demonstration and apodeictic syllogistic which is secure, irrefutable, and closely allied to the truth of things. So since what has been said has been said demonstratively, he reasonably says 'drawing conclusions ... will be convinced'. This sort of conviction is abundant in the case of scientific knowledge, as a result of our animal sympathy.[201] And this is why he uses the phrase 'will be convinced' both philosophically and appropriately, because animal sympathy is stirred by the secure knowledge of the more divine. He can say 'will be convinced'[202] because he has reasoned from hypotheses, and it is clear that,[203] insofar as the hypotheses are evident, so too will be what follows from conviction in them.[204]

It is better, I believe, to say that while he urges us in all cases to supplement demonstrative necessities with the sympathy derived from conviction, [he does so] particularly in the case of arguments concerning things divine, since it not only provides confirmation of true knowledge when it supervenes upon demonstration, but also unification with what is knowable, which is the end of human blessedness. For while the upward-leading love which arouses the desire for divine beauty exists already in the soul, the true revelation of it follows for the worthy, and for them conviction orchestrates a firm grounding in it and a unification with it.[205] For it is self-evident that the more removed in space the heavens are from the realm of generation and destruction, the more they exceed it in the worth of their substance. And in fact these things are the furthest removed at the extreme of the universe, while the heaven is endowed with the highest bodily form.

Xenarchus objects in the case of these principles which have just been related, and in relation to others which have already been discussed, and moreover to the dictum that for one thing there is one contrary. For he says, it is easy for people to move fire forcibly along a line of any form whatever, be it simple or complex. 'And we say' he says, 'in the ethical treatises too that there are two opposites for each of the virtues, e.g. wickedness and ingenuousness to prudence, over-confidence and cowardice to courage, and similarly with the others.'

It should be said against the first claim that it is necessary that the unnatural motions too be proper to each; for these too exist by nature and not as a result of contrivance. Complex forms of lines are beside the point, since the lines of simple motions are simple. Moreover, what is unnatural must be such as to be natural for something else.

In regard to the second [it should be said] that since each of the virtues is a balance, the two [opposites] to each of them are opposed as a single imbalance to a balance. And in fact while one is excess, the other deficiency, common to both is imbalance. Indeed, as he proceeds he himself is aware of this, namely that ingenuousness is opposed to stupidity and over-confidence to cowardice, while [opposed to] prudence is neither ingenuousness nor stupidity but what is common to both of them, and what is common to over-confidence and cowardice [is opposed to] courage, and just as the deficient is opposed to the excessive, the inequality common to both [is opposed to] the equality.[206]

'But,' he says,

> if these things are true, it is not necessary for the heaven to be of a fifth body on the grounds that two things cannot be opposed to one, the circular [motion] of the fire to that downwards and upwards.[207] For the upward is opposed to the downward as excess to deficiency, while that which is common to both, namely the rectilinear, [is opposed to] circular [motion] as imbalance to balance.

But while what he says here is elegant, I do not think that it relates to the contrariety as stated by Aristotle. For he does not oppose [motion] upwards and downwards to that in a circle, but rather the circular and the downward to the upward. But in regard to the supposition which says that it is fire which is carried in a circle, given that he says that [the motion] of the fire here has the structure of something which naturally moves upwards, it is not absurd for Aristotle to say that circular motion is no less unnatural for it than downward. And this is how he previously opposed them. So, since two things are reasonably taken to be unnatural for each natural, he concludes that there are two opposites for a single thing.

[Here a short section (56,26-59,23), containing Philoponus fragments 33-6 (see Wildberg, 55-7), is omitted]

[CHAPTER 3]

269b18-20 From what has been said (some things having been assumed, others demonstrated from them) it is evident that not every body has either lightness or weight. 59,24

Since 'all teaching and reasoned learning occurs as a result of pre-existing knowledge', as he himself told us in the *Analytics*,[208] certain things must exist prior to the demonstrations, some as being self-evidently credible, others as being previously demonstrated or as things yet to be shown. This is why some of the propositions are laid down in advance, and others demonstrated. Laid down in advance are the fact that there are two simple lines, rectilinear and circular,[209] that 60,1 upward motion is that away from the middle, while downward is that towards the middle, and that in a circle is around the middle,[210] and that for one thing there is one contrary,[211] and that there is one natural [motion] for each of the simple [bodies].[212] Of the propositions, it has been demonstrated that there are two simple motions, rectilinear and circular,[213] and that the motions of simple [bodies] are simple, and that simple motions are of simple bodies.[214]

And this was also shown, I think, by distinguishing the motions and the bodies, and the proper connections [between them]. And it was demonstrated from both assumed and demonstrated propositions that besides the four sublunary simple bodies there is a further fifth, for which circular motion is natural,[215] and that this is more complete, and prior, and more noble in nature than the other bodies.[216]

Then he says that it follows from these assumed and demonstrated [propositions] that not every body possesses either weight or lightness. For if weight and lightness emerge as properties from the very definition of things which move in a straight line,[217] and it was shown that what moves in a circle is distinct from the things which move in a straight line,[218] and it is distinct in such a way that rectilinear motion is incapable of belonging to it either naturally or unnaturally,[219] it evidently follows that not every body possesses weight or lightness, and consequently the heavenly [body] is shown to differ from the sublunary [bodies] in possessing neither weight nor lightness.

This will contribute towards his showing that the heavenly body is ungenerated, indestructible, unincreasing, undiminishing and unalterable. For if it possessed weight or lightness, there would be some motion contrary to its motion; and if this [were the case], there would something contrary to it moving naturally with the contrary motion;

and if this [were the case], it would be both generated from and destroyed into its opposite.

But if it possesses neither weight nor lightness, and does not in any way move in a straight line (for which there would be a contrary), but only in a circle, it being shown that there is no motion contrary to circular motion,[220] it is clear that what moves in a circle will have no contrary to itself, and so will neither be generated out of anything, nor be destroyed into anything.

So he necessarily assumed beforehand that what possesses neither weight nor lightness is the same as that which moves neither upwards nor downwards, which is the very same thing as that which does not move with a motion which has a contrary, in order that, having shown that there is no contrary motion to the circular motion with which it moves, it will have as a consequence that there is nothing contrary to it, from which it follows of necessity that it is neither generated nor destroyed, from which all the rest [follows].

61,1 **269b20-9** But we must first posit what we mean by heavy and light, [now only so as to suffice for our present purposes, later with greater precision when we come to examine their essential nature. Let the heavy then be that which moves naturally towards the centre, and the light away from the centre, while the heaviest is that which sinks below everything else which moves downwards and the lightest that which floats above everything that moves upwards. Everything that moves either downwards or upwards must, then, have either lightness or weight or both, although not in relation to the same thing, since things are heavy or light in relation to one another; for instance, air in relation to water, and water in relation to earth.]

He himself makes it clear in this passage that the discussion of the light and the heavy is not of primary relevance for him to the present issue in the way it is in the fourth book (where he discusses them in their own right); rather he now needs it in order to show that the revolving body is ungenerated and indestructible on the grounds that it possesses neither weight nor lightness.

Having in a way enunciated the conclusion of the argument in advance in saying 'it is evident that not every body has either lightness or weight' (for the conclusion is that 'it is impossible that the body which moves in a circle should have either weight or lightness'),[221] he defines what the heavy and the light are, and what is the heaviest and what is the lightest. For since one of the bodies which move downwards, namely earth, proceeds as far as the centre, or (what comes to the same thing) as far as the lowest point, while the other [proceeds] as far as the earth, and since one of the upwardly mobile ones, namely fire, [proceeds] as far as the highest point (i.e. the lunar sphere) while the other [proceeds] as far as the fire, it is reasonable that while one is heavy the other is the heaviest, and that while one is light the other is the lightest.

So if the heavy is what moves downwards and the light [what moves] upwards, and these are the definitions of heavy and light, it is clear that they must also convert, and that what moves either up or down possesses either weight or lightness.[222] And since of the upper [place] there is [a part] which is not completely up, but has a little of the down in it, namely the place beneath the fire, and of the lower [place a part] which is not completely down, the things which go to these places reasonably possess both weight and lightness, but not in relation to the same thing; for it is not possible to be at once lighter and heavier than the same thing.

Rather, for these things, heavy and light are relative. Air is light in relation to water, but not in relation to fire, and water in relation to earth, but not in relation to air (for it is heavy in relation to the latter). For these reasons they are neither genuinely heavy, nor genuinely light, nor genuinely simple. For fire is genuinely light and simple, earth genuinely heavy and simple, the one rising above all the other upwardly mobile things, the other settling out below the downwardly mobile. Consequently, if the intermediates are not simple in every way, the account concerning the simple [bodies] will not genuinely apply to them, and some people have undermined the
demonstrations propounded concerning the simple [bodies] by argu- 62,1
ing unsoundly on the basis of them.[223]

> **269b29-270a3** So the body which moves in a circle [can have neither weight nor lightness, since it can move towards the centre or away from the centre neither naturally nor unnaturally. For natural movement in a straight line is not possible for it, since there is one [natural movement] for each of the bodies, and so it would itself be one of those which move in one of these ways. But if it moved unnaturally, then if the downward movement were unnatural, upward movement would be natural, and if the upward were unnatural, the downward would be natural; for we laid it down that, in the case of contrary [motions], where one of them is unnatural,] the other is natural.

Making use of the definitions supplied of the heavy and the light, or rather of the conversions of those definitions,[224] he shows that it is impossible for the body that moves in a circle to possess weight or lightness. For if it did possess them, it would do so either naturally or unnaturally, and it will be demonstrated that neither of these is possible.

He makes use of two of the axioms, namely that for each of the simple [bodies] there is one natural motion, and that for the one of the contrary [bodies] for which one [of the motions] is natural, the other [motion] is unnatural.[225] He shows this as follows, as Alexander and Themistius[226] say: that which moves in a circle does not move either upwards or downwards naturally; that which moves neither upwards nor downwards naturally is neither light nor heavy. The minor [premiss] is not negative; for the argument would be inconclusive if derived from two negative [premisses].[227] But it has an indefinite predicate,[228] as if one were to say 'that which moves in a circle is such as to be moved neither upward nor downward according to its own nature'.[229]

Perhaps, however, preserving the indefinite nature of the predicate, he rather argued as follows: the body which moves in a circle can move neither naturally nor unnaturally either away from or towards the centre, which is the same as saying that the body which moves in a circle is such as to be incapable of moving either naturally or unnaturally either away from or towards the centre; and something of such a kind is capable of possessing neither weight nor lightness; and the conclusion is clear.

But it is clear from the conversion of the definitions[230] that it will possess neither weight nor lightness in moving towards nor away from the centre. For if the heavy is that which is such as to move towards the centre, and the light [is such as to move] away from the centre, it is clear that what moves neither towards the centre nor away from the centre is neither heavy nor light. He establishes the minor premiss implicitly as follows: since what moves in a circle is simple and moves with a single simple motion, it possesses a single circular movement by nature; [but] something of such kind will not possess rectilinear movement naturally.

The argument can be better presented in the second hypothetical mode[231] as follows: if rectilinear movement belongs naturally to that which moves in a circle, it will be the same as one of things which moves in a straight line; but it is not, as has been frequently shown; therefore rectilinear movement will not belong naturally to that which moves in a circle. He reminds us that the conditional 'if it were natural for it, it would be the same as one of the things that moves thus', is true with the words 'there is one [natural movement] for each of the bodies'.[232]

That there is no unnatural [movement] for them either, he shows, I think, in the same manner as follows: if there was unnatural rectilinear motion in any way whatever for that which moves in a circle, its opposite will be natural. And again he provides the reason for this conditional too in saying 'for we laid it down that, in the case of contraries where one of them is unnatural, the other is natural'.

He has taken the argument this far, omitting the rest as being clear on the basis of what has already been said. But for the sake of completeness, one further conditional is required as follows: if one or the other of the opposite [motions], be it be upwards or downwards, is natural [for it], it will be identical with one of the things which moves thus, i.e. with one of the sublunary [bodies]. But it has been shown that this is impossible. Therefore no kind of rectilinear [movement] will be unnatural for it. So if it is neither natural nor unnatural, and it is clear that it cannot be preternatural for it (since it is worse),[233] in no way will it move either upwards or downwards. Consequently it will be neither light nor heavy, since what [moves] upwards is light, and [what moves] downwards is heavy.

Themistius,[234] however, does not think that the argument goes this way, but rather [holds] that if it moves downwards unnaturally, the contrary motion to this, i.e. upwards, will be natural for it. But circular [motion] is natural for the revolving body; therefore one thing will have two contraries. And if it were to move upwards unnaturally, then downward motion will once again be natural [for it], and the same absurdity, that one thing will have two contraries, will follow; and the argument works this way too.

> **270a3-12** Since both whole and part move naturally in the same direction [(for instance all of the earth and a tiny lump of it), it follows first of all that it has no lightness whatsoever, nor weight (since otherwise it would have been able to move either towards the centre or away from it in accordance with its own nature), and secondly that it is impossible that it move in respect of place either by being forced downwards or dragged[235] upwards; for it can neither move naturally with any other motion, nor unnaturally, nor can any part of it, since the same argument applies to the whole as to the part.]

Having shown that the revolving body possesses neither weight nor lightness, he goes on to show that this is a property not only of the whole but of its parts as well. Moreover, they move with the same motion as the whole, since they possess neither weight nor lightness.

He shows this first of all, in my view as follows. Assuming that whole and the part move naturally in the same direction, he reasons as follows: if the whole moves neither upwards nor downwards [sc. by nature], the part will have the same property; and if this is so, it will possess neither weight nor lightness. But the antecedent [is true]; so therefore is the consequent.

That the axiom assumed at the outset is true, namely that whole and part move naturally in the same direction, he shows by way of 64,1
[the phrase] 'for instance all of the earth and a tiny lump of it'.[236] For

if the whole is all of its parts, and all the parts have the same inclination, clearly so too will the whole. And in this way, in my view, he shows the same thing to hold jointly for the whole[237] and its parts, namely 'that it is impossible that it move in respect of place either by being forced downwards or dragged upwards'.

He shows this by means of the demonstration made in the first place in respect of the whole, briefly recalling it: 'for it can neither', he says, 'move naturally with any other motion'[238] than the circular (since there is one natural motion for each of the simple [bodies]), 'nor unnaturally'[239] with one of the rectilinear [motions]. For its opposite would be natural, and there would no longer be one natural [motion] for each [body], but two natural contraries to one unnatural.

Clearly, if it is going to hold good in the case of a part as well, this demonstration also requires what has already been agreed upon, namely that both whole and part move naturally in the same direction. It was necessary to add this argument about the parts, wholly and in its own right, to what has already been said, showing that the parts are identical in nature to the whole, because even the entire masses of the sublunary elements do not possess weight and lightness, as they appear to,[240] but only the parts of them which have been separated [from the main mass]. And for this reason he immediately made the prior assumption that whole and part move naturally in the same direction.[241]

And furthermore he also answers objections, one of which holds that the comparison of the heavens and sublunary elements has not been made on the basis of similar things, since parts [only] of the latter were assumed to be placed unnaturally outside their proper place, while the whole of the former was.[242] Moreover [he answers] those who think that the heaven is similar in nature to the sublunary bodies, in that while it too is eternal as a whole, it is generated and destructible insofar as its parts are concerned.[243] For if it is evidently true, in the case of the sublunary elements, that parts which are separated from their proper whole and put in unnatural places possess an inclination towards rectilinear [motion], while none of the heavenly bodies in the whole of elapsed time, according to the traditions handed down from one generation to another, have ever apparently changed either as a whole or in part, it is clear that the heaven is rightly said to have a nature other than that of the four elements, and this seems to have its confirmation through observation handed down from time immemorial.[244]

But how was [the fact that] the part moves with the same movement as the whole confirmed by [the fact that] 'all of the earth and a
65,1 tiny lump of it' move in the same direction? For all of the earth moves with no movement at all when it is ensconced around the centre. But he talks of all the earth thinking of it in regard to all of its parts, as

I have said, and not in regard to its wholeness. For this reason he says 'all' and not 'whole', because if one says that all the earth is generated and destructible because all of its parts are of such a kind and none of them is eternal, it is still not true to say this of the whole.[245] So the whole earth, insofar as it is a whole, even though it does not move position, nevertheless possesses as a whole a tendency and inclination towards the centre.

For this reason the whole of each of the parts forms a sphere around it, each striving to get close to the centre, insofar as it is not prevented by some other part. For the drive of both the whole and its parts is towards the middle, and looking towards that it seeks to preserve and sustain the dissoluble composition which it naturally possesses as a result of its parts. In the same way, fire, both the whole of it and its parts, in their desire for divine body as being something akin to them, seek it out from all directions. For this reason this too [sc. fire] is formed into a sphere under it, all the parts of it [sc. the fire] seeking to associate with it and enjoy its living motion.[246]

Each of the intermediate [bodies] has the desire for association according to its own inclination: water [seeks out] earth, insofar as it settles over it, being fluid in its own nature. For this reason it flows around the earth and forms a sphere around it, and is sustained on account of the fact that the earth is in the middle, since it too enjoys association with the centre.[247] The air goes towards the fire wishing both as a whole and as parts to alter its turbid thickness, and to become airy.[248]

But the heaven, since it is more divine and superior to all the bodies in the universe, is not desirous of anything else, and does not seek out anything else, but inclining towards itself and desiring itself and its own soul and intelligence, it moves not with a deficient and incomplete rectilinear motion which consorts with much in potentiality and which seeks out something outside itself, but rather with a complete and actualized circular [motion] which possesses its good within itself.[249]

And if what I say here means anything, Aristotle was right to say that the totality and the part naturally move in the same direction, and that, of those things which have desires [directed] outside themselves, both the wholes and their parts, being desiderative, have an inclination in a straight line; and they have an inclination in general because they are desirous of something external, and what is external is spatially located. And if, hypothetically, the heaven were to be raised higher than its current place, the fire would follow it too. For the four elements seem to me to desire neither place nor wholeness 66,1
so much as contact with the better, which the whole desires no less than its parts.[250]

[66,4-91,20, containing Philoponus fragments 37-49, 51-61 (Wildberg, 58-76) omitted]

91,21 **270a12-22** Similarly, it is reasonable to suppose too that it is ungenerated and indestructible [and non-increasing and unalterable on the grounds that everything that is generated comes to be from its contrary and from some substrate, while likewise it is destroyed by its contrary and into its contrary, given that there is some substrate, as was said in our first discussions. And the movements of contrary things are themselves contrary. So if there can be no contrary for it on the grounds that there cannot be any motion contrary to circular movement, it seems that nature properly withdrew that which was to be ungenerated and indestructible from the contraries, since generation and destruction take place among the contraries.]

Having shown that there is, besides those under the moon, another
body which revolves and is more complete than and prior to them,
and which has neither weight nor lightness, he goes on to show that
it is 'ungenerated and indestructible and non-increasing and unalter-
able', and consequently that it can change in no way other than by
changing position, and that in a circle. Just as in the earlier discus-
92,1 sions he derived his division of the sublunary things from the differ-
ences of their motions, so now he derives the ungenerated [nature] of
the heaven as opposed to what is said to be the generated [nature] of
the sublunary things, and the fact that it is non-increasing and
unalterable, from the form of circular motion.

He first shows 'that it is ungenerated and indestructible' by arguing in the second figure, as I see it, as follows: the revolving body has no contrary; but things which are generated and destroyed have contraries, from which they are generated and into which they are destroyed; the conclusion is that therefore the revolving body is neither generated nor destroyed.[251] Of these two premisses he now proves the minor, namely that the revolving body has no contrary, referring the demonstration of the major to the first book of the *Physics*:[252] for these are the 'first discussions' which deal with natural principles.

Once again using the same method, he proves that the revolving body has no contrary, in the following way. The revolving body has no motion contrary to its natural motion; that which has a contrary also has a motion which is contrary to its natural motion, and in which its contrary moves naturally, which he posited when he said that 'the movements of contrary things' i.e. natural things, 'are themselves contrary'; and the conclusion [is that] what moves in a circle has no contrary.

In this case again he assumes the major premiss to be self-evident, for the natures of contrary natural forms are contrary and consequently the motions are too; for nature is a source of motion.[253] The minor [premiss], which says that there is no contrary motion for the motion of the revolving body, i.e. for circular motion, he demonstrates later on,[254] having said much in between.

But since the whole argument depends on these two things: first that if something is going to be generated and destroyed there must at all events be both a substrate and a contrary out of which it is generated and into which it is destroyed, and second that there is no motion contrary to circular motion, of which he will proceed a little later to offer a demonstration in many ways, while the former he now assumes without demonstration as having been proved in the *Physics*,[255] we must now recall what was said there, having first distinguished the various senses of 'generated' to clarify which one it is in respect of which Aristotle constructs his argument and what sort of generated thing he denies the heaven to be, so that we may also understand how, while Plato said that the totality was generated and Aristotle [said that it was] ungenerated, they did not contradict one another.[256]

Something is said in the general sense to be generated when it receives its own existence from some cause. Moreover what is produced is produced by some producer, and what is generated is gener- 93,1
ated by some generator, and it is impossible, as Plato says,[257] for there to be uncaused generation. It is clear that in this sense the only thing which is ungenerated is the first cause of everything, which is One and simplest, given that everything participates in the One, and what does not so participate is nothing. The One does not participate in plurality, so everything generated is pluralized. For the plurality is immediately brought into existence by the One, given that the plurality must participate in the One, in order that it not be infinitely infinite.[258] But the One has no trace of plurality, given that it is pre-eminently one.

The first plurality that proceeds from the One, since it participates in it immediately, is both unified and remains in the One, and insofar as it proceeds in some way from the One it has the character of something which is in a way generated. For this reason divine men[259] have provided us with theogonies, hymning on the one hand a multitude of gods remaining in the One and, as one might say, processing out of it in virtue of its multiplication,[260] and on the other hand hymning its generation, insofar as it came in to existence out of the One, in the same way as we consider progression out of the unit to be a generation of numbers.[261]

But insofar as it remains in the One it is unified in respect of the highest unity, and with no distinction yet appearing in which what its primarily non-existent comes to be,[262] it is primarily existent and a principle, and alone of beings it is itself and is not [derived] from a principle. For a principle is ungenerated, as Socrates proves in the *Phaedrus*.[263] And in fact this is the first thing which is in any way self-subsistent, and it is pre-eminently existent. For what is unqualifiedly One is the cause of being, and the self-subsistent excels, making manifest a certain doubleness both of the cause of existence and that which comes to exist.

But the first plurality is controlled by the One, and is the cause of existence because it is one, yet it is caused to exist because it is many, and is not simply one for this reason, namely that above it there is the One which is the cause of everything that is.[264] And the most primary and most genuine One is whole and simultaneously existent, both in respect of being and in respect of the temporal extension of being. And for this reason the eternity there[265] supplies the 'always' to being.[266] But since this eternity remains in the One, the 'always' is this eternity in a restricted form. And it exists as a unified plurality as opposed to a pluralized One, and it manifests neither extension in respect of its substance nor continuance in respect of genuinely being.
94,1 For this reason it is really real, and what it is.

After this it[267] immediately causes to exist what is immediately caused to exist by it, which, having been moved out of what is,[268] became something else besides; and it was made substantial as a result of this motion. And in the same way as the first became self-subsistent, this one became self-moving. For insofar as it was moved out of what is,[269] it came to exist as a result of motion, while insofar as it is proximate to what is and is not distinct from it, it became a self-mover because what was prior to it was self-subsistent, being able in the same way both to move and be moved on account of its still being glutted with the One and under its control.[270] And from this proceeds something pluralized, which also in a way has a share of the One, but not however by remaining in the One nor by being controlled by it, and because it is partitioned[271] it is no longer either self-subsistent or a self-mover, because it does not have within itself the cause of existence deriving from the One in the way that the unified thing and the thing after it both do.

This latter immediately admitted of extension both of substance and of continuance in respect of being,[272] insofar as it departed from the One and became extended in every way, body and the things akin to body came to be,[273] and time came forth along with it out of the eternity of it [sc. the One], measuring the continuance of being and providing the temporal 'always';[274] and it was no longer here simultaneously whole, either in respect of its substance or in respect of the continuance of being, but rather, as one might say, in respect of life. For this reason it is not genuinely real, since it has a large share of non-being. For neither is this part of its substance[275] what it is, nor is its being the same, but rather it is different at different times with the flowing of time.[276] Consequently neither does it receive the whole of its coming to be from the cause simultaneously (for then it too would have been something that actually was),[277] but part by part, as it is capable of doing. The plurality in it came to stand completely outside the One and, by participating in it as a result of its external influence, came to be composite instead of unified, and for this reason owes its existence entirely to something other than itself.

The unified plurality possesses within itself the One, since the One is the cause of being for everything and is genuinely the cause of being; even though it recedes from the unique cause of being, still it becomes self-subsistent by possessing within itself what causes its being. But the composite plurality, on the other hand, has its unity of composition as a result of external influence, and this one form immediately comes to be,[278] as [something which] comes to be in matter, [that is] in[279] the indefiniteness and extension of such a plurality, so that the self-mover shares intermediately in both of them.[280] Thus it has a share in the One as form in matter by way of composition, and not by being caused to be all at once, either in respect of substance or in respect of continuance of being, and in no way being the cause of being for itself, since it is partitioned,[281] as a result of which it no longer has the One within itself.

For what is partitioned[282] comes to be part by part and not as a whole; and nor is it genuinely self-subsistent, just as neither is what moves part by part genuinely self-moving. For what is genuinely self-subsistent and self-moving must be partless and unextended, and wholly fitted to itself as a whole; but what is partitioned[283] and extended only has its being from the outside. So for this reason, and because it is composite, and because it is not wholly and simultaneously what it is, but rather has its being in becoming,[284] it is genuinely generated as opposed to what genuinely is, which has its being from itself and is wholly and simultaneously what it is.

And something which is generated in this way has change and motion immediately out of what is, because it does not remain in what genuinely is. And for this reason it does not remain in the same condition completely, for then it would remain in the One just like what is genuinely real. For it is always changing and moving away from its previous state. For this reason time also goes along with it, measuring it and setting in order this outward movement,[285] just as something else sets in order the partitioned[286] extension of its substance and its corporeal nature, whether it be place or something else which possesses the same power.[287] So this is, for the reasons mentioned, what is genuinely generated.

As for what is immediately generated from the being of this thing itself, insofar as it is unmoved and is always in the same condition in respect of substance, potentiality, and actuality, it too must remain for ever [in a state of] coming to be, as on the one hand what genuinely is gives way to becoming, and on the other the always of eternity [gives way to] the temporal always. For it received, partially and insofar as it was capable, the completeness and the simultaneously whole universality of what is, which caused it to be, imitating the infinite power of the former[288] in its own [progression] to infinity.

Of such a kind did the much-honoured heaven first appear to us in its corporeal nature, emerging into being after the intelligible ordering as the finest of images representing the best of models. For, after proceeding from unity and sameness into similarity with respect to what is, what was generated came to be an image, insofar as it already resembled, but was not actually connected to, what is. And the heaven moves in an unmoving way and changes in an unchanging way, exhibiting only such changes as are capable of co-existing with something persistent.[289] For this reason it possesses that type of local motion which is capable of being complete while the substance and substantial disposition remain the same. For this is the type of change which affects substance and disposition to the least extent.

Moreover, it was assigned the type of local motion in which something moves locally without moving out of its place but rather keeps moving in the same place, while things which move in a straight line do not remain in the same place even for the shortest time. Consequently circular motion is more rest than motion, given that the things which move because of themselves in a certain quite remarkable way remain at rest as a whole while their parts whirl around. And being eternal, on account of owing its existence immediately to the unmoved, it transcends the change from non-being to being, and that from being to non-being, of which it is customary to call the one generation, and the other destruction. For if it came to be at a time, not having existed before, then its cause must also have done something at a time, not having done it before, and then it would no longer be unmoved, and would not preserve itself in the same way and in respect of the same things; and if it were destroyed, it would have departed from its similarity to the unmoved cause, and the cause would no longer be an immediate cause, and nor would it be the thing which makes exist[290] the things which are immediately caused by it to exist.[291]

And growth and diminution, being themselves kinds of generation and destruction, are constituted in a manner totally distinct from that which is immediately generated by the action of the unmoved cause;[292] but alteration of a certain kind, which we will perhaps come to know as we go along, can in a sense be seen in it.[293] So this sort of generator, which is most primarily and completely productive of bodily existence, is itself existent,[294] but is not however utterly unchangeable. For even if it shares in many blessed goods from its creator, as Plato says in the *Statesman*,[295] it still partakes of body as well, i.e. it is extended and partitioned[296] and undergoes an outward movement from what is.

For this reason, it was quite impossible for it to remain in itself and have no portion of change. So changing both in respect of local motion and configuration, existing at different times in different states in respect of one or another participation in the goodness imbued in it by the causes, it produces the things it produces no longer motionlessly, as it was itself produced, but rather brings them into being in a mobile way.

And so here too substantial change makes its first appearance, and generation and destruction of substance have their beginning. But generation is not from the utterly non-existent, nor is destruction into the utterly non-existent, because the causes also bring into being the differences of the things produced here[297] by changing from one state into another.

Perhaps it could be more clearly stated thus. The intelligible plurality is also unified in respect of its differentiation, which is conceived as being in the intelligible, insofar as all of what is really real remains in the One. For this reason not only are the different forms created together simultaneously in that substance, but also their contraries, and they participate in one another and are unified in relation to one another, so that their participation is no longer introduced from the outside, and they have no room there[298] either for acting or being affected, and for this reason they genuinely transcend generation.[299]

And in the first of the things which genuinely came to be, when distinction and partition[300] and change had appeared but a genuine similarity with the unpartitioned was still maintained, the things which filled out that substance were distinguished from one another both in parts and forms, while they both acted upon one another and were affected by one another, although the substance nevertheless remained, and the things that act act and the things that are affected are affected, since their activity on one another is perfective.[301] For by participating in one another, the forms in the generated [world] become like the unity in what is really real.[302]

But the things which are immediately caused to exist[303] by what is do this in a completed way, while those which are in turn caused to be by these things, and which have receded from the temporal always towards some particular time which is a part of time, become involved with other things in the manner of coming to be,[304] because they are caused to exist in accordance with the changing temporal dispositions of the heavenly bodies, so that some things [occur] when the sun happens to be in some signs of the zodiac, and others when it is in others.[305]

So when the great separation, which has constructed the sublunary substances out of things so distinguished, has come to be in the final plurality, neither does everything participate in everything, nor is everything in everything, but whichever differences have coalesced in a single form are capable of co-existing with one another and of participating in one another without conflict, while their contraries, withstanding all of the separation, are collected into it, especially and most of all the more generic ones, such as heats, coldnesses, drynesses and wetnesses, and what goes along with them and is grasped by each of the senses, such as palenesses, darknesses, sharpnesses, heavinesses, sweetnesses, bitternesses, roughnesses, smoothnesses, and the opposite olfactory qualities.

These are collected not by themselves, but along with the bodies which underlie them and in which they have their existence. These latter are the primary elements, fire, air, water, and earth, out of which the others things, both animals and plants, are composed. But whenever some harmonious and fitting combination derived from the heavenly things occurs, one which has an aptness for this or that composite form, at that moment that form shines forth, and it both binds together the bundle of contraries and is held together by it.[306]

98,1 And whenever contraries such as fire and water persist in conflict in accordance with their contrary qualities, since they are by nature disinclined to mix, one of them must at some time prevail and grow out of its opposite's diminution, and the composite form, such as that of a cow or a horse, which is such as to supervene upon such a balance of the elements, is then destroyed, while another form of balance and another suitability is generated in the elements according to the preponderance or scarcity of the elements; and bees are generated from the cow, wasps from the horse, and different grubs from different animals and plants.[307]

And it is the case that when a great over-abundance of elements has occurred in the composite things, as a result of weakness or old age they finally become unsuitable as a receptacle[308] for composite form, and in dissolution they flow into their own masses where, having been renewed and rejuvenated, they then move once again towards composition. This is made particularly clear by water, which is particularly suitable for generation and nourishment when it is pure and taken from its own entire mass, as is seen in the case of springs.

And it is clear that generation and destruction here[309] is a change which both occurs by [the action of] a contrary and takes place from contrary state to contrary, in the case of the elements with water, as it might be, being changed by fire into the fiery constitution which is contrary to it, and thus fire is generated from its contrary, water, in respect of contrary qualities, by [the action of] fire, which is the contrary of water.[310] For what is destroyed must be the contrary of what destroys it, while what comes to be is the same as what produces it.[311]

For the making of the elements into each other consists in a change [by the action][312] of the producers out of things which are suitable to be affected, i.e. the substrates for each thing, and equally destruction occurs of a contrary by [the action of] of a contrary: for water is destroyed by fire into fire. Consequently the destruction of one thing is the generation of another, and the generation of one thing the destruction of another, while the qualities are annihilated into non-existence. For whenever fire is generated out of water, the cold and wet quality disappears as the bodily substance[313] receives the qualities of the fire in exchange. And this happens whenever there occurs the change from some substance of water to another substance of fire.

But whenever some more indistinct doing and undergoing occurs between the elements in respect of their qualities, so that they induce in each other one another's disposition, and the water is warmed although it remains water, and the fire is cooled and moistened although it remains fire, then it is called an alteration and the result an affection, because no substance [has come to be] by the action of any other, but has only become altered.

And it is clear that not any and every disposition can come to be by the action of any other, but only contrary from contrary. For what is cooled is not cooled by the dryness, but by the coldness, since what is affected is affected by the producer, and the producer [does so] by its own nature and in its very essence. For this is how naturally productive things produce. And it undergoes an affection of the same kind as the producer is, or rather as that in respect of which the producer was producing, while the producer induces naturally and of itself an affection of the same kind as whatever quality it possesses in respect of which it produces.[314] For the natural producer wishes to change what is affected into itself, and the contrary is changed into the contrary, for example the heat in what is being cooled into the coldness in what is doing the cooling.

But whenever, as I said, alteration is what occurs, these things come to be incompletely, and what was previously hot is cooled, but not in such a way as to be completely cooled and to change into the nature of the thing doing the cooling, as happens in the case of things destroyed and generated. At any rate, the contrary acts upon the contrary, and it destroys what is affected since it wishes to change it into itself. For example, if fire acts upon air, wishing to change it into itself and inflame it, since air is fundamentally hot as well,[315] the fire does not wish to change the air's heat, since this can exist in the fire too, but rather its wetness, since this cannot co-exist with fire, and it destroys it not with heat in itself but with dryness, with the heat incidentally aiding the dryness.

Consequently one might construct an argument as follows: naturally active sublunary bodies act in the desire to multiply themselves; things which act in order to multiply themselves change what they affect into themselves; things which change what they affect into themselves destroy whatever is incapable of co-existing with them in what is affected; what is incapable of so co-existing are contraries, and contraries are destroyed by their contraries, since things which are capable of co-existing in the same substrate do not destroy one another.

So when the contraries in what is affected have been destroyed by the contraries in the producer, the substrate takes on the qualities [or quantities][316] of the producer in place of their contraries, which it had previously possessed, and changes into the nature of the producer. And what was formerly water becomes fire by the agency of fire and by way of air, first with the heat, which is the more active, driving the coldness out of the water, and then the dryness [driving out] the wetness as well.[317]

And whichever magnitudes and shapes are incapable of co-existing change into their contraries,[318] and so the corporeal extension of the water (or perhaps something else even more material within it), receiving into itself qualities contrary to those which it possessed, changes from water into fire, while whatever it has in common with fire, namely whatever it is which is capable of co-existing with each of the qualities, remains, whether it is its[319] corporeal nature with some things[320] common at some time, or whether it is prime matter.[321] For when change occurs, something must persist around which the change occurs; and this is the thing which genuinely changes, in respect of the qualities it loses.[322]

So of the qualities themselves, some are destroyed while some come to be, and the substrate changes in respect of them, and not only in the case of generation but in the case of alteration as well. For it was said regarding this that whenever the change in respect of contrary qualities in the affected thing does not come to completion, but is only a tinting[323] of some of them by others, as in the case of heated water, then the affected thing does not come to be something else, but is only altered.

And [this is true] not only in these cases, as I have said, but also in the case of natural growth and diminution. For what increases naturally, for example what is nourished, changes the contrary dispositions of the nourishment towards itself, and by assimilating it thus to itself grows and is augmented. And even if the nutritive capacity has something of the soul about it, it is none the less brought to completion in accordance with natural changes.[324] Furthermore, things which move locally change one place for another while the mover persists, so that every sublunary transformation is a change in which what changes persists in some respect. For this reason things which are temporally generated come to be not from what does not exist but from what exists.[325] And just as some other time pre-exists the time in which these things are generated, and which is subsequent to it, so too something else pre-exists what comes to be, after which and out of which what comes to be is generated.

Reasonably, then, Aristotle too treated change as being the genus of each sublunary transformation in the *Physics*.[326] And it is also reasonable that this change be everlasting, not only because it is brought into being by the eternity of the change in the heavens with respect to local motion and with respect to the different configurations, but also because the destruction of one thing is invariably the generation of another. And it is also reasonable that the simple bodies here should persist eternally as entire masses, while allowing generation and destruction as far as their parts are concerned. For if change of the composite things occurs primarily in respect of these [elements], and when they [sc. the composites] are dissolved, they [sc. the elements] move naturally towards their proper places and their proper entire masses, while they [sc. the entire masses] persist, alternately emitting parts of themselves and then reabsorbing them again, then this [will occur] forever because of the everlasting nature of the change.

And since generation is a change, it is reasonable that what is generated and destroyed, what is increased and diminished, what is altered and what changes place, and in general everything which undergoes change, is changed from contrary condition to contrary by a cause which is contrary to it. For this reason, in the first book of the *Physics*,[327] when Aristotle is searching for the principles of natural things in generation and destruction, he says that they are the contraries and the substrate for the contraries.

And it is clear that the things which are generated and destroyed in respect of qualities, for example in respect of heat or dryness, change out of the contrary qualities which they possess, while things which change in respect of substance, for example fire *qua* fire, or man *qua* man, although they too change in respect of the change of qualities into one another, *qua* fire and *qua* man they are substances, and there is no form contrary to substance. From what, then, do they come to be, not as hot or cold, but as man? Clearly from what is not man, but which is such as to become man. Of such a kind is the semen and the menses, not *qua* semen or *qua* menses unqualifiedly, but *qua* what is not man, but which is such as to become man.[328] For man could not come to be if man already was, since what is does not come to be what it is; but neither could what neither was nor was such as to become man become man.[329]

So what common name, then, do we use for this, insofar as it is not yet something yet is such as to become that thing? We standardly call it a privation,[330] and describe as deprived that which, while it does not possess the form of which it is said to be deprived, is yet such as to possess it. Thus the newly-born puppy is deprived of eyes, because it is such as to possess them; but something which has been completely blinded is said to be deprived of its eyes in respect of not this but a different sort of privation. For it cannot go back again, while the generation-producing privation from which the things which are said to come to be change into the form, can go back towards the form.

So even when something comes to be cold from [having been] hot, it comes to be from the non-cold which is yet such as to become cold, and for this reason [it comes to be] from [having been] hot. For the dry is not such as to be changed by the cold into the cold, because it can co-exist with it.

So if, while it is not always the case for everything which comes to be that what comes to be does so from the contrary form which is present in the substrate for a while, in the way in which, for instance, the hot comes to be from the cold (for first of all it is certainly not the case in the case of substances, since there is no contrary to a substance),[331] still [coming to be] from something which is not of such a kind, but which is such as to come to be of such a kind,[332] does hold for everything [which comes to be, both substances] and those things which change from contrary forms, then it is reasonable for Aristotle to maintain that the form, privation, and substrate are the common principles of generation. And he calls both form and privation contraries, but not according to the strict sense of contrariety (for [in that sense] both contraries are forms), but rather by opposition, since these too are opposed to one another.[333]

I have treated of these things at length, then, wishing particularly to straighten out my own thoughts about them, but also, probably, those of anyone else who will deal with them carefully. But that for the sake of which this entire discussion arose, how what is generated is generated out of the contrary and the substrate, and how what is destroyed is destroyed both with some substrate [persisting], and by its contrary and into its contrary, this I think has become clear from what has been said, which Aristotle here assumes without demonstration on account of its having been proved, as he says, in the first discussions.[334]

And one must remember that even if what is primarily substance neither genuinely comes to be from a contrary nor is destroyed into a contrary, on account of there being no substance contrary to substance,[335] but first of all it too has its generation from its proper privation, and then through the generation of contraries from contraries, and conversely its destruction through the destruction of contraries into contraries. For whenever the qualities and quantities in the semen and the menses[336] change into those contraries which are such as to be those of a man, being contrary to what they were before, then the form of the man supervenes. And conversely, whenever some of the elements over-reach themselves while their contraries are worsted, the substrate is reduced to disharmony, and then it[337] is destroyed; but otherwise it is not.

But since that is enough of that, let us see next in what sense of 103,1
generation Aristotle denies that the heaven is generated, seeking to demonstrate that it was ungenerated, and in what sense Plato says that both the heaven and the entire cosmos were generated.

That Aristotle means by 'generation' only the temporal change from non-being to being, and which invariably admits of destruction, on the basis of which he will demonstrate the heaven to be not only ungenerated but also indestructible as well,[338] is clear; and all the more so when he clearly demonstrates that what is generated is invariably destroyed, and what is destroyed comes to be. For it is clear that he treats generation and destruction as things which occur at particular times and which apply to sublunary things, having for this reason demonstrated that there is another fifth substance besides the sublunary ones, namely that of the heavenly body, which is naturally prior to and more complete than them.

And just as he denies heaviness and lightness and rectilinear motion to it as being properties of the sublunary [elements], so too [he denies] it their generability and destructibility. And this is I think indisputable, both from his saying that generation and destruction are the type of change in which one thing comes to be and is destroyed *after* another, and from his proving, in his refutation of those who say that the cosmos is generated but indestructible, that what is generated is invariably also destroyed. And it is not at all remarkable that Aristotle, who always wishes to take for granted things which are self-evident to everybody, says that what is generated is that which partakes of each kind of generation and which is clearly seen to be both generated and to be destroyed at particular times.

And Plato certainly knew of this kind of generation, which applies to sublunary things and is the opposite of destruction, when he wrote the following in the tenth book of the *Laws*:[339]

> and what sort of affection is it which is such as to bring about the generation of all things? Clearly whenever a first principle, having grown, comes to the second change, and from this to the next, and having come to the third allows perception to the things which perceive. So everything is generated by changing

> and being altered in this way. Something is really real whenever it persists; but when it is changed into some other state it is completely destroyed.

But he also knew of another sort [of generation], according to which what comes into a corporeal extension, not being capable of producing itself, but which is said to be generated only [in the sense that] something else produces its existence as its cause, in contrast with what is really real, which is its own principal cause.[340] For it is necessary that what is generated and derives its existence from something else should be caused to be by something real and self-subsistent, or [else it would] proceed *ad infinitum*, always positing some generated thing as prior to every other generated thing.

And having defined this sort of generated thing after that which really is in the sense of the *Timaeus*,[341] he says that the cosmos is, in itself, generated. And the definition of both of them, which derives from our internal cognitive powers, is as follows:

> what is it which always is and has no coming to be, and what is it which comes to be but never is? The one is apprehended by thought along with reason, and is always thus and in the same condition; the other is conceived by opinion along with irrational perception, and is generated and destroyed, and never really is.[342]

In this sense of 'generation', even the cosmos, which was immediately caused by God who is really real, is generated, according to Plato; and he writes the following about the cosmos: 'was it then always, having no principle of generation, or did it come to be? It came to be; for it is visible and tangible and possessed of body'.[343] And he makes it clear that everything of such a kind is generated and generable. For the self-subsistent must be partless and wholly fitted to itself as a whole, while what is distinguished and partitioned[344] is incapable of wholly fitting to itself as a whole, and for this reason, since it is not self-subsistent, it derives its being wholly from something else, and is said for this reason to be generated.

But since some people, lazily interpreting the 'destroyed' in the definition of generability, think that Plato obviously countenanced the destruction of the cosmos and of the heaven too, we must say what 'destroyed' means here. For by adding 'and never really is' immediately after 'generated and destroyed', he clearly indicates for anyone who has not prejudged the issue that what exists eternally transcends what does so only at some time. For 'never' is predicated in the strict sense of eternal things. For it [sc. the cosmos] exists for ever; and on account of its being derived immediately from what really is and is unmoved, and again on account of its being neither self-subsistent nor really real, and not what it is simultaneously wholly and completely, it is subject to change of a certain type at certain times, receiving a different completeness for itself at different times, but always receiving it on account of its immediate productive cause, which is unmoved, and on account of its own suitability, since it gets its existence immediately from what is really real.

And that Plato thinks that it is subject to change, not [in the sense of] its being generated and destroyed at a particular time, but on account of its corporeal nature (because of which it does not possess all of its blessedness simultaneously, in the way that what is really real does), may be easily learned, I believe, from what he wrote in the *Statesman*. For there he says something like the following, as I recall: 'what we have called heaven and the cosmos, has had a share from its creator of many blessednesses; but it also partook of body, wherefore it was impossible for it to remain entirely untainted by change'.[345]

Moreover, if it were indeed destroyed [by being turned] into another cosmos, the description 'change' would be appropriate, while if it were simply annihilated, it would not be said to have changed, since change is progression from one thing to another. And how could he say 'entirely untainted' if it did not possess something unchangeable?

But that Plato thought that the cosmos was neither created at a particular time nor destroyed at a particular time is clear from what he wrote in the *Timaeus*. First of all, he says quite clearly that time came into being along with the heaven, when he says: 'so time came to be along with the heaven';[346] so there cannot have been time before the heaven. But if this is so, the heaven will not have begun to come to be at a certain time. For time would have preceded it; and there would at all events have been some past time preceding that present time in which the cosmos came to be.

Nor is it capable of being destroyed at a particular time, since there would, conversely, be some future time after that present in which it is destroyed. And while he added 'in order that, having been created together they would also be destroyed together, if any dissolution should ever occur for them',[347] I think he indicates by this very statement that it was indissoluble. For if it were necessary for the cosmos to be destroyed together with time if it were to be destroyed at all, and time is indissoluble, then given that what is dissolved at some point has time after it (for 'at some point' is a part of time), clearly the cosmos is indissoluble.

Indeed, he added this to what had already been said: 'and [it was made] according to the model of everlasting nature, so that it would be as like to it as possible; for the model exists for all eternity, while it [sc. the cosmos] has been and is and will be for the whole of time'.[348] So how could such a thing have come to be at a certain time, six thousand years ago as it might be, or be destroyed at a certain time, if it has been and is and will be for the whole of time?

Those people who are incapable of distinguishing the everlastingness of time from the always of eternity, saying that time comes to be and is destroyed in a part of time, are not ashamed, and call Plato as their witness when he says 'so that it might be most like the perfect and intelligible animal by imitating its eternal nature.'[349]

But how could it be most like the eternal if it was produced for a period of time, and a very small one at that, as these people certainly hold, if it is compared to the eternal? And what need is there to say more, when Plato clearly says that on account of their own corporeal and extended nature, both heavenly and sublunary things, both earth
106,1 (for in this case he speaks clearly)[350] and obviously the entire masses of the other elements partake of change of a sort and are not utterly immortal, while on account of the goodness of their immediate creator, which always assigns to them their proper goods, they are indissoluble and will never meet with the fate of death?[351]

And it is better, I think, to attend to Plato's own words, or rather those of the Creator of all these things, whose thoughts and deeds Plato revealed as a prophet, saying

> so when all of the gods, both those which revolve unseen and those which are apparent insofar as they wish to be, had been generated, the creator of this universe spoke to them as follows: 'gods of gods, my works, of whom I am both creator and father, you are indissoluble by my will. Everything which is bound together may be dissolved, but to wish to dissolve something finely put together and well constituted would be the work of an evil being. For this reason, since you have come to be, you are neither immortal nor completely indissoluble, but yet you will not be dissolved or meet with the fate of death, since I have in my will a greater and yet more powerful bond than those with which you were bound together when you were created. Now, then, attend to what I have to say to you by way of instruction. Three sorts of mortals are yet ungenerated, and with them ungenerated the heaven is incomplete, since it will not contain in itself all the kinds of animals, as it ought to if it is to be sufficiently complete. But if they were generated by me and came thus to partake in life they would equal the gods. So in order that they be mortal, and that this universe might be really universal, turn yourselves according to your natures to the creation of the animals in imitation of my power regarding your generation. And insofar as it is fitting for them to be called similar to the immortals and divine, that which is the leader in them of wishing always to follow justice and you, I shall sow the

> seed, and having begun hand over to you. As for the rest, fashion and beget the animals, weaving the mortal in with the immortal, giving them food, and make them grow, and receive them again in perishing'.[352]

What could be clearer than this by way of showing that Plato thought that some things immediately created by the Creator of the whole are indissoluble and immortal on account of his own goodness, even if, on account of their having their unity (which he calls a 'bond') introduced from the outside, insofar as it is up to them (that is insofar as concerns 107,1
their proper separation and extension out of what is) they were dissoluble? What could be plainer than 'you are not completely immortal,' (i.e. unchangeable in respect of any change, as I see it), 'but yet you will not be dissolved or meet with the fate of death'? And who could be so shameless or so witless as to think, after this pronouncement, that Plato considered that the heaven was destructible?

And it was no less clear that these things were not mortal, when he said that there were still three kinds of mortal things left over, and when he ordered the eternal beings through their natural transformation and motion to interweave everything mortal with the eternal which was [produced] by the Creator; for otherwise the mortals would not be generated, if what created them did not change.

For the same reason, he also says the following: 'so in order that they be mortal, and that this universe might be really universal, turn yourselves according to your natures to the creation of the animals'. So how could the heavenly bodies be mortal, being created by the motionless and eternal activity of the Creator? And 'fashion and beget the animals, giving them food, and make them grow, and receive them again in perishing' is properly said, I believe, to the gods who control the elements, and who have presided over all the elements, insofar as they too possess something of the eternal. For from these primary sublunary elements they generate and nourish and increase the individual animals, and resolve them once again into the entire masses of the elements when they die.

But while I am not myself unaware that to speak so much seems beyond the normal measure required for exegesis of what Aristotle said, I, proposing to resolve the objections of those who fight against the heaven's being ungenerated and indestructible, who enlist Plato as agreeing with them against Aristotle, unreasonably in my view, have recorded Plato's opinions on these matters.[353]

But let us return to Aristotle's text. 'Similarly, it is reasonable to suppose that it is ungenerated and indestructible'. It was said earlier that, having proved the revolving body to be both prior by nature to and more complete than the sublunary [bodies],[354] and that it transcends rectilinear local motion, it was posited that it would transcend all other changes, generation, destruction, growth, diminution, and the alteration which is co-ordinate with them, so that it would possess local motion alone, the sort which least affects substance, and of that [motion] in a circle which befits eternal things.[355]

108,1 It was also said that it was first argued that what was ungenerated was also indestructible, and the analysis of the arguments was set out.[356] And [it was said] that Aristotle demonstrated the other relevant premisses, of which the first states that the revolving body has no contrary, because 'the movements of contrary things are themselves contrary'.[357] For if things which possess contrary sources of motion are naturally contrary, it is clear that the motions of contraries are contrary. So if there is no natural motion contrary to the natural motion of the revolving body, i.e. circular [motion] (for the argument concerns natural [motions]), it is clear that there is no contrary to the revolving body.[358]

Alexander draws the conclusion in the first figure as follows: all natural bodies which have no contrary motion have no contrary; the body which moves naturally with circular motion has no contrary motion; nor therefore [will there be a contrary][359] for the thing which moves naturally with this motion. Accordingly, he [sc. Aristotle] assumes without demonstration two premisses for the whole argument, one stating that what is generated and destroyed is generated from its contrary and is destroyed into its contrary, with something as a substrate for it, and the other stating that there is no contrary to circular motion. But the latter, which he now assumes, he later demonstrates in many ways,[360] and for this reason he refrains from inserting its demonstration here.

He refers the demonstration of the other one to the discussion in the first book of the *Physics*,[361] which I have also fully expounded to the best of my ability.[362] Having laid these things down, he infers that since the revolving body possesses neither that from which it is generated nor that into which it is destroyed, it will be ungenerated and indestructible.

Alexander further notes in this context that if indeed the things which possess contrary motions are most naturally contraries, then earth will be more naturally contrary to fire than water is. However water, being cold and wet, is opposed in respect of both its qualities to fire, which is hot and dry, while earth, being cold and dry, is so in respect of one only, namely the cold.[363] And he also notes that, in rightly saying that what is going to be ungenerated naturally transcends the contraries, he [sc. Aristotle] indicated that the heavenly bodies must possess ungenerability naturally, and not, as some people do, making it [sc. the heaven] destructible in its own nature, and then begging certain questions by wishing to make it indestructible.

And he seems to be rejecting Plato's claim (speaking in the voice of the Creator) that 'you are not altogether immortal, but you will not be dissolved'.[364] Plato indicates that, insofar as the nature of the heavenly bodies is extended and corporeal and descended from what 109,1 is really real, and is for this reason incapable of embracing the whole of eternity simultaneously, they are 'not altogether immortal'; but that they remain undissolved on account of their deriving their existence immediately from the unmoved cause which makes their change unchangeable and which precludes their dissolution by [way of their having] extension by the more powerful bond of unity. And he appends the 'not altogether immortal', I believe, to show that they do not possess immortality both as a result of themselves and as a result of the cause, as the self-subsistents do, but from the cause alone, from which alone they are produced.

I also note that the heavenly body wishes to transcend contraries not [in the sense] of things unconditionally contrary in property but rather [in the sense] of things which change into one another and are not capable of co-existing with one another, such as the sublunary contraries. For it is self-evident that the heavenly body participates at the same time both in motion and rest as it spins in the same place, and of sameness and otherness, unity and plurality, but these things co-exist with one another and support each other, and do not destroy or change into one another, as sublunary things do.

> **270a22-5** Moreover, everything which grows does so by the addition of similar stuff [which is assimilated into its matter: but for this thing there is nothing out of which it has come to be.]

Even though he inferred that the heavenly body is ungenerated and indestructible by assuming as a supposition that there is no natural motion contrary to circular motion, but being about to prove[365] what had been supposed, he employs what was inferred from [the assumption] – namely that it is ungenerated and indestructible – as if it were something already demonstrated. And making use of this as an additional assumption, he shows that it is also unincreasing and undiminishing, assuming that growth is a type of generation, and that just as nothing can be generated which does not possess a contrary out of which it will be generated, nor also can it grow (or diminish: for diminution is a type of destruction).

So once again the argument goes as follows: what grows grows from its contrary, out of which it is also generated; but the revolving body possesses no contrary out of which it is generated. But that growth is a type of generation, and that what grows grows from its contrary, is clear: for what is added to what grows is added in such a way as to become similar to it, and nourishes and augments that to which it is added; and what comes to be similar to that to which it is added does so from being dissimilar and contrary to it. So it is not possible for something to become similar to what has no contrary, because everything which comes to be does so from its contrary. But the same thing is contrary to similar things, so that what is contrary to what is added will also be contrary to that similar thing to which it is added.

Aristotle indicated something yet more precise by saying 'but for this thing there is nothing out of which it has come to be'; for something is nourished and augmented by that from which it comes to be, either directly or indirectly. For example, the animal is generated out of semen and menses;[366] but semen and menses are generated out of that by which the animal is nourished and augmented. So it is nourished and augmented by that from which it is generated. So what has nothing from which it is generated will have nothing by which it is nourished and augmented; for there will no longer be anything added to it, given that it too is generated from the same thing from which that to which it is added it [is generated].

Alexander says: 'if there is something similar to the revolving body which augments it when added to it, it too will be revolving, since the motion of the parts is in the same direction as that of the whole. And if this is so, the whole would be generable too, yet it has been shown to be ungenerable'. And he [sc. Aristotle] says that what is added is 'assimilated into the matter' of that to which it is added, i.e. into flesh and bones and the other uniform parts,[367] since it is these which are nourished in the first place; and these have the status of matter in relation to the organic parts and the whole animal.

It will also be shown by the same argument that it does not diminish. For what diminishes does so by the departure of one of its parts. But what departs does so by becoming dissimilar and changing into its contrary so that it no longer co-exists with it. Consequently what diminishes must possess a contrary, from which it is also added to and comes to be. But the revolving body is neither added to, nor comes to be, nor possesses a contrary. In general, what is not of a nature to be augmented is destroyed if it diminishes: and the heavenly [body] has been shown to be indestructible.

So why does Aristotle not, as we do, reason about growth on the grounds of [considerations regarding] nourishment, but simply says straight off that what augments must be akin to that which it augments? Is it for the sake of all-round accuracy? For in fact he believes, so it seems, that even the simple bodies also grow naturally by the addition of similar things (as he will make clear shortly,[368] when he says that we see that the elements also have growth and diminution), while the organic parts are not nourished naturally, but rather by the nutritive soul.[369] But it is clear that even if things are thus, they are no impediment to the demonstration given, since from that from which something is generated it also grows, as that from which it grows becomes similar to it and is added to it.

270a25-35 But if it is both non-increasing and indestructible, 111,1
by the same reasoning one may suppose it to be unalterable too, [since alteration is change in respect of quality, while the qualitative dispositions and states do not come to be without changes in respect of affections (as for instance in the case of health and disease). But we see that all physical bodies which change in respect of affection are also subject to increase and diminution, like animals' bodies and their parts, and those of plants, and similarly those of the elements; so that, if the circular body is susceptible neither of increase nor diminution, it is reasonable that it be unalterable as well.]

Just as he showed it to be non-increasing on the grounds that it is ungenerated – 'for there is nothing', he says, 'for this thing out of which it has come to be'[370] – so too he shows it to be unalterable on the grounds of its being non-increasing and non-diminishing (which, I believe, he now calls 'indestructible'), arguing as follows: what alters changes in quality; what changes in quality changes in affection. For corporeal qualities are of three types, either purely as perceptible affections (as when someone is warmed on the surface),[371] or in disposition (when he has been disposed in regard to heat so as to be called hot), or in state (when the disposition becomes persistent). Affection is observed in all of these cases, and for this reason Aristotle says that they occur not without changes of affection. For even if state and disposition differ in form, they are brought to completion with affection, since they occur when something is affected. Consequently what alters changes in respect of affection.

We see every natural body that changes in affection possesses growth and diminution: animals' bodies, and plants, and the simple bodies, and in general everything that changes in affection. So if what alters bodily grows and diminishes, what neither grows nor diminishes does not alter, since it does not change in affection. It may be expressed categorically as follows: what alters in affection grows and diminishes; the revolving body neither grows nor diminishes; therefore the revolving body does not alter in affection.[372] And Aristotle seems to me to argue rather in this way, and he draws the conclusion that it is unalterable in the sense that it does not alter in affection.

'It should be pointed out,' Alexander says,

that this is not stated in such a way as to imply necessity, but only reasonableness. For it is not the case that if states occur with affection in things which are naturally affected, this will necessarily also be so in unaffectible things; nor, if we observe things which alter in our region to grow and diminish, is it reasonable in general that if something alters it grows. If it is the case that insofar as something alters, it grows and diminishes, the argument possesses necessity; but if not, it does not. But Aristotle himself says in the *Categories*[373] that it is not necessary for things which change in affection either to grow or to diminish.

'For,' Alexander continues,

> those things which possess a contrary in substantial form and
> 112,1 affection will as a result of their substantial contrariety be both generable and destructible, and equally be subject to increase and diminution, as well as being alterable as a result of their contrariety in affection. But nothing will prevent those things which have no substantial contrariety, but consist in qualities which possess contrariety, although they are ungenerable and non-increasing, from being altered and affected in this way.

'And it should also be pointed out', he says,

> that he does not show that they are unalterable on the grounds of their having no contrary in accidental property; however he would have argued in this way, if he had thought it true, in the same way as he showed that things were ungenerable because they had no contrary. And, [he says,] to those who say that Aristotle holds that the fifth body is without qualities, it can be shown from this that they do not know what they are talking about. For if he had held that it was without qualities it would have been very easy for him to show thereby that it was unalterable, since what has no properties in the first place cannot change in property.

'And I have pointed this out,' he says,

> with a view to showing that even if it happens that the body revolving with the sun, being warmed by the sun's revolution, propagates warmth generated by its [sc. the sun's] motion through the body below it, this does not impute anything absurd to the substance of the revolving body. For it is not the case that alterable things in general are destructible, but only those

> things which can change in substance: and these are such as to possess contraries to their substance and form. For, as he says, that body is unaffectible by all mortal troubles, but not totally unaffectible. For it is not the case that if some accident of it has some contrary then it too must have some contrary. The stars possess colour, and if all colour is either light, dark, or mixed, there will either be some contrary to that colour or their colour will be mixed, but the stars will not on these grounds be destructible, since their colour is not part of their substance.

Since Alexander says this pretty much in these words, I think one should first consider carefully whether Aristotle did argue so poorly and fallaciously in this treatise, even if this man [sc. Alexander] out of respect [sc. for Aristotle] says that he [sc. Alexander] has taken [Aristotle's argument] as an appeal to something reasonable. Then it ought to be said, I think, that Aristotle does not deny every sort of alteration to the heavenly bodies; not of course fully-accomplished interchange or intertransmutation, but that of affection, which is frequently a cause of growth and diminution even if it is incidental.

For things which are dried and undergo the affection of desiccation shrink, particularly [if they do so] in respect of disposition, and even more particularly [if they do so] in respect of state, while things which are moistened grow with the added moisture; and similarly things condensed shrink, while things rarefied grow. But even if growth and diminution are not thought of as causes, yet at all events do accompany the passive alterations, nevertheless they do not [accompany] every type of alteration.

For it is I think clear that even the heavenly bodies operate upon 113,1
each other and impart to one another of their several proper goods in accordance with their different configurations. For just as the moon at different times clearly receives the sun's light upon different parts of itself according to its different positions in relation to it [sc. the sun], so too everything operates on everything else, even if those alterations are imperceptible to us.

This is, I believe, clear on the basis of the effects regarding things here.[374] For sometimes those things are the causes of other things because of their different configurations and combinations;[375] yet growth or diminution does not manifest itself along with this type of alteration in the case of the moon, even though it is so evident, nor [does it do so] in the case of the other stars,[376] except when they are at apogee or perigee: for then they are of different apparent size to us on account of their differing distances from us.[377]

And these changes are not merely passive ones, but perfecting ones; for opposites can co-exist there,[378] whereas here,[379] since they are not such as to co-exist with one another because of their distance from one another, they cancel one another out, and for this reason operate passively. For iron which has been heated by fire and passively altered is no longer capable of cooling even though it is cold by nature, because it acts according to its affection. But although the moon is in some way altered by the sun's rays and reflects the sunlight to us, [it does so] with its own proper property. For the alteration does not change any part of its substance, but merely perfects its inherent capacities.[380]

And Melissus was right when he said 'if it becomes different' – i.e. in respect of its substance – 'even by a single hair in ten thousand years, in the whole of time it would be destroyed'.[381] Consequently if someone says that the heavenly bodies are affected by one another, let it not be said that this alteration occurs passively, but rather that it is perfective, in the same way as the soul might be said to be altered by inspiration. For passive affection occurs because of a change in something substantial, which is why passive alteration is different in kind from that in respect of potentiality.[382]

And for this reason I think Aristotle was right not to deny every kind of alteration to the heavenly bodies, but only the passive kind with which growth, diminution, generation, and destruction are invariably associated. For this reason he changed the alterations, which he was going to deny, into [ones having to do with] affection, saying 'while the qualitative dispositions and states do not come to be without changes in respect of affections'. But [alteration] in respect of affection possesses the affection intrinsically.

114,1 He proceeds to make it clear that he means it to be unalterable in the sense of unaffectible in saying 'the first among bodies is unalterable and unaffectible'.[383] Consequently we may agree with Alexander that in Aristotle's view alteration is to be allowed to the heavenly bodies, since there is quality there as well, but not that there is in his view passive alteration. Otherwise he would not have sought to demonstrate its unalterability on the grounds of its unaffectibility.

And anyone who understands this by demonstration too must see the necessity in it. For those of the natural bodies which undergo passive changes both grow and diminish and are generated and destroyed, but they do not grow or diminish as a result of their being altered, but rather both [sc. growth and diminution] are to be found in mortal things, and [both of them] have their proper formula.[384] And for this reason Aristotle says in the *Categories* that things which are changed passively 'need neither grow nor diminish'.[385] For they do not grow or diminish in accordance with the formula of affection, even if growth and diminution belong to those affected things which have a changeable nature.

And how can Alexander say that these things grow and diminish, and are generated and destroyed, possessing some substantial contrariety, given that he[386] supposes that there is no contrary to their substances apart from a privation thereof, which has nothing of the active about it but only suitability,[387] and what is generated [is generated] not from this [privation] as something productive, but rather as simply following it and as a result of its suitability for it [sc. its contrary]?

So if generation is not merely out of the contrary but is also caused by the contrary, and contrariety is observed in the qualities, it is clear that both generations and destructions and growths and diminutions occur in respect of affections of the qualities. For these things occur when the elements change, in respect of qualities, into one another, and they change both actively into one another and passively as a result of one another.

Consequently, the substantial change that follows the [change] in respect of qualities is in a certain sense incidental, because it is necessary that whatever changes principally and primarily does so by a contrary, while there is no contrary to substance, but only to the qualities which pervade its substance. And the change is substantial in this way in that it is [a change] of the substantial properties.

So Aristotle rightly and accurately said that these things are both altered passively and are substantially affected; for an intensified affection invariably produces a change of the elements which constitute the substance. And he rightly denied passive change to the heavenly bodies on the basis of what he had already demonstrated. For if things which are passively altered are also substantially affected when they are generated, destroyed, increased, and diminished, then clearly things which transcend these things will be above passive alteration as well.

Consequently the heating by the sun of the adjacent spheres and the propagation of that [heat] to things here, as described by Alexander, should be understood cautiously: that a passive heat occurs there [sc. in the heavens] one should never concede, for then substantial change would invariably be consequent upon it. But the transmission by the sun should be said to be fully-accomplishing, one which produces animals and co-exists with their natural states; but it does not change them, as a passive alteration would. Moreover here the air passively receives the animal-generating heat, and passively warms things in this vicinity. For things here receive not only the solar effluences, but also those of the other heavenly bodies.

And if the heavenly [body] is impassive in regard to all mortal travail, it is clear that it will also spurn every affection which belongs to mortal things. Consequently this passive heat, which being intensified can dissolve even substance, is not appropriate for it, and nor is the form which is in general generative in this way. Consequently if this alone is called an affection, every generative affection of such a kind is excluded from the heaven.

But if there is said to be some affection which is perfective and which is appropriate to the heaven, it would have some other formula.[388] And even if someone postulates contrary colours or other qualities in the heavenly bodies, they would not be destructible, because the contraries co-exist there harmoniously and without conflict, as has often been said.[389] For this reason they possess neither passive action nor affection towards one another, since they have no desire to change one another.

> **270b1-4** So why the first among bodies is eternal, and is susceptible neither of increase nor diminution, [but is ageless and unalterable and unaffectible (if one is to believe what has been laid down)] is evident from what has been said.

He here reminds us of what was demonstrated in the first place of the revolving body, namely that it is eternal (since it is neither generable nor destructible), and that it suffers neither increase nor diminution. Being of such a kind, it is 'ageless' and 'unalterable', moreover unalterable in such a way as to be 'unaffectible'. For it seems to me that adding 'unaffectible' at the end is not redundant, but rather applies to all these things which occur in respect of affection.

'If one is to believe what has been laid down' might refer to the first hypotheses,[390] from which the demonstrations are deduced, concerning which Plotinus[391] said 'Aristotle would have no trouble [sc. in demonstrating everything else] if someone accepted his hypotheses of the fifth body', taking it, so I think, from this passage.[392] But he [sc. Plotinus] might also mean by 'hypotheses' all the premisses from which the demonstrations are deduced. However, it is more appropriate to interpret it as being the hypothesis which claims that there is no motion contrary to motion in a circle, and that what is generated and destroyed is generated from opposites and destroyed into oppo-
116,1 sites. For assuming these hypotheses, one of which[393] he is about to demonstrate, and the other[394] of which was demonstrated in the *Physics*, he inferred everything from them.

> **270b4-9** And it seems both that the argument confirms the appearances [and the appearances the argument. For as all men have some conception of the gods, and all of them, both Greeks and barbarians,[395] assign the upper region to the divine (at least those who think the gods exist), it is clear that immortal is associated with immortal –] for it could not be otherwise.

Both of these things, namely demonstrative argument, and mankind's common preconception[396] or the clear evidence of perception, contribute for us to the confirmation of the truth. When they are in harmony, and particularly in matters to do with nature when they have their proof through perception, the confirmation becomes indisputable; if they are in conflict some difficulty remains. Reasonably, then, after the demonstrations he adduces the confirmation derived from the appearances, which is sufficient to induce the appropriate belief in some, indeed in most people. He adduces three pieces of evidence from the appearances: one from human suppositions regarding the heavenly bodies, the second from perception and memory concerning them, and the third from the fact that they call it by the name of 'aither'.

Alexander divides the first of these into two: that all men believe the gods to exist, and that they suppose the divine [to be located] in the upper region. 'The argument', he says,

> showed both to be the case, and that there exists something divine. For the same argument which proved that there is some body which is ungenerated, indestructible, unincreasing and unaffectible, prior to and more perfect than all of the others, also established and proved that the gods exist. But [the argument] which showed that this thing is that which moves in a circle around the centre of the totality, also established that this is in the upper region.

So says Alexander. Perhaps, however, he [sc. Aristotle] calls to witness the supposition of all men of the gods' existence, because all men – 'at least those who think the gods exist', because of the Hippons and Diagorases[397] and any others there may be similarly unfortunate in places unknown to us; still, all those who do think this – 'assign the upper region to the divine'. But Aristotle did not establish that the gods exist on the basis [of the existence] of such bodies (except insofar they are the chariots of the gods), since he showed in the eighth book of the *Physics*[398] and in the *Metaphysics*[399] that the eternal gods are intelligible.[400]

Alexander understands 'immortal is associated with immortal' of the place and of the heavenly body, on the grounds that this is what is the divine,[401] and he understands 'for it could not be otherwise' to
mean that is it impossible for the upper region to be divine if there is 117,1
no god there. And this is true. But he [sc. Aristotle] says that it is the immortality of the heavenly body, and not of its place, which depends upon the immortality of god; and 'it could not be otherwise', i.e. for the immortal not to depend on the immortal. And the phrase 'all

people, not only Greeks but barbarians as well'[402] shows that this kind of supposition in their souls is something natural.[403]

270b10-11 So given that there is something divine (as there is)[, then what we have just said about the primary substance among bodies] has been well said.

Here Alexander propounds the argument in the following form: if 'there is something divine', i.e. if there are gods, then what we have said about the revolving body 'has been well said'. But there are gods both eternal and [located] in the upper region, and everything else we have said. So 'what we have just said about the primary substance has been well said'. But perhaps he [sc. Aristotle] does not say 'if there are gods', but 'if there is some divine' body, namely that which revolves, and that what has been said about it has been well said.

Alexander rightly notes that 'given that (*eiper*)' is equivalent to a factual connective, on account of its[404] being evident.[405] For if there are gods dwelling in the universe, which is taken as proven and evident, there will be some divine body which depends upon them; 'so if indeed there is some divine' body, what has been said concerning the revolving body, namely that it is, being thus, divine, has been well said, as the common preconception of mankind has also made clear.

270b11-16 The same result obtains on the basis of perception too, adequately [at any rate for human confirmation. For in all of past time according to the record handed down from one [generation] to another, neither the whole of the outermost heaven nor any proper part of it has ever apparently changed.]

He adds a second confirmation to what has already been demonstrated concerning the fact that the revolving body is ungenerated, indestructible, and unaffectible. This derives from our perception, and what has been handed down to us from earlier times, from which memories of their being thus have been handed down. For I myself have heard that Egyptians have got, recorded in writing, celestial observations going back for not less than 630,000 years, and the Babylonians for 1,440,000 years. In all this time in which reports have been handed down, it has never been reported that anything in the heavens was otherwise than it is now, either in respect of the number of the stars, or of their sizes, or of their colours, or of any periodic motions.

118,1 In so many years if it did not decline in any way but always remained at its peak, how is it possible for it, being at its peak, to be destroyed? For these people[406] say that these are already the final days of the world. But in my view in remaining in this unaltered state for even an hour it shows itself to transcend generation and destruction. For we see everything which comes to be beginning at the outset of a certain period of time and progressing from an incomplete condition to its completion and peak, and, in the same way, in moving from peak into decline it is destroyed. But something which has remained in the same condition for all of time known to man is clearly immune to generation and destruction and neither comes to be nor is destroyed. By 'the outermost heaven' he means the revolving body, distinguishing it from the whole cosmos, which he also calls 'heaven'.[407] And note how he employs as confirmations of the demonstrations what someone else would have used as the clearest demonstrations.[408]

> **270b16-25** It even seems that its name has been handed down from the ancients [to the present time, and that they conceived of it in the same way that we too speak of it; for one must think that the same opinions occur to us not once or twice only, but countless times. So because the primary body was distinct from earth and air and fire and water, they dubbed the highest place 'aither', deriving its name from its 'always-running' [*aei thein*] throughout eternity. (Anaxagoras misuses the word infelicitously;] for he uses the term 'aither' instead of 'fire'.)

He adduces as the third confirmation of its eternality its name, which has been handed down from the ancients to the present time. And he reveals to us two intentions of those who gave [the name] in regard to it. For they called it 'aither' as being the highest thing, and one exalted above all of the sublunary elements, each of which they call by a particular name, having especially honoured the heaven with the name of 'aither', which emphasizes its height and exaltedness, and the fact that it is much the lightest and purest by comparison with the things under it. And the name shows that it is 'always-running', indicating its eternal self-motion, as well as emphasizing its eternal existence.

And wishing to show that it is not only people in the tradition from those who established the name until now who have held this opinion, he says that the same opinions frequently occur to men, even if there are sometimes gaps between them. And it is clear that we must suppose that same true opinions come [to us] many times. For the nature of things is enduring, and leads those people who have briefly strayed back to itself once again,[409] while I do not see how the same false opinions, being both themselves indeterminate[410] and occurring 119,1 to souls which are moved indeterminately, could invariably recur.

He censures Anaxagoras for having incorrectly derived the name 'aither' from '*aithein*', i.e. to burn, and for this reason having applied it to fire. For if this were the natural conception of the name, then we would call fire 'aither'. So what need is there to use two names to signify one thing, and so to obscure the other of things signified by it [sc. '*aither*']?

[119,7-144,4, containing Philoponus fragments 63-75, 77-8, 80 (Wildberg, 77-91), omitted]

144,5 **270b26-31** And it is evident from what has been said why it is impossible for there to be a greater number of simple bodies than those mentioned. [For the motion of a simple body must itself be simple, while we say that only these are simple, namely the circular and the rectilinear, of which the latter has two parts, that away from the centre and that towards it.]

He has shown that the heaven is ungenerated and indestructible, and on that basis of that it is non-increasing, undiminishing, and unaltering as well. He employed in the proof two premisses, one stating that what is generated from its contrary (for the demonstration of which he referred us to the first books of the *Physics*),[411] the other that there is no contrary to the revolving body. He proved this from the fact that if there were some contrary to the revolving body there would have to be a motion contrary to circular motion; and he grounded this conditional on the claim that 'the movements of contrary things are themselves contrary',[412] it follows by contraposition that if there is no movement contrary to that in a circle there will be no contrary to the revolving body.

So, wishing to demonstrate this premiss,[413] he reminds [us] once again of [the facts about] the simple bodies and the simple motions. He needed to consider these because, given that circular motion is simple, if it were to have a contrary it would be one of the simple [motions]. And he reminded [us] of the simple bodies because if there were to be something contrary to the revolving body, which is simple, it would have to be one of the simple [bodies].

These things serve to establish one another: for if simple bodies are [just] those which move with simple motions, then if these five [bodies] are the only simple ones, then these three motions are the only simple motions; and there will only be these five simple bodies, since there are only these three [simple] motions, namely in a circle, upwards, and downwards.[414] So once again he adduces these premises so that we look for the contrary of the revolving body and circular motion not among the indefinite things but among the simple and definite ones.[415]

The reason why the simple motions are three but the simple bodies five is that, in the case of the bodies which move in a straight line, there is one which is unqualifiedly heavy and one which is unqualifiedly light, which are contraries to one another, but there are also two intermediates which have a share in each of them,[416] although more of one than the other.

These move with the same motion as those in which they have the greater share; for they move in respect of that which predominates. But they do not move in the same way as them;[417] for earth [moves] towards the centre and fire towards the heaven, while the intermediates [only move] towards the extreme elements, because air is not fully light and water not fully heavy: and so it is possible for the motions to be divided into five.

And if it has been shown that there is no contrary to circular motion, it is reasonable that circular motion remain undivided; for there is nothing which is less circularly moved, as [there is something which] less light and less heavy; for the lesser occurs because of the mixture of the opposite.[418]

[CHAPTER 4]

> **270b32-271a5** That there is no other movement contrary to circular movement one may confirm from a variety of sources. [First of all, we state that the rectilinear is most opposed to the circular, since concave and convex seem to be opposite not only to one another but also to the straight, when they are taken together and as a unity. Consequently, if anything were contrary to it, rectilinear motion necessarily would be particularly contrary to circular motion. But the rectilinear motions are opposed to one other in regard to place, since up and down is both a difference and a contrariety of place.]

He shows by many arguments that there is no other movement contrary to circular movement, using division, as I see it, to drive the argument forward. For since the simple motions are the circular and the two rectilinear [motions], if there is a contrary to circular motion, it either must be one of the rectilinear [motions] or else one of those along the periphery; and either those along some segment of a single circle will be contraries, or those along a greater or lesser semicircle, or those along a single semicircle, or those along two semicircles of a single circle, or those along a single circle. But if none of these is a contrary, there will be no contrary [motion] at all.

Of these [arguments] the first is the following. If there is some motion contrary to circular motion, it would most likely be along a straight line. But rectilinear motion is not contrary to circular; therefore there will be no other motion contrary to circular motion. He proves the conditional effectively as follows. If the straight line seems most opposed to the circular (as that which is undeflected to that which is deflected at every point), then motion in a straight line will seem most opposed to circular motion. But the antecedent [is true]; so therefore is the consequent.

He then, in the middle [of the proofs], rebuts an objection brought to bear against the additional premiss,[419] one which holds that in the [case of the] circular the concave is most opposed to the convex. Thus he says that the concave and the convex are the same in substrate, differing only relationally;[420] and even if they are opposed to one another in respect of relation, when taken together and unified into one circle they are then opposed to the straight line. But a difference of motions is not generated in respect of relations. Consequently what was said at the outset was true, namely that the circle is opposed to the straight line, and the earlier conditional, which stated if there was some contrary to circular motion, that in a straight line would be particularly contrary, is also true.

But he shows also that the additional premiss of the original argument is true, namely the one which says that rectilinear motion is not contrary to circular [motion],[421] from [the fact that], of the rectilinear [motions], that upwards is the contrary of that downwards. For upper and lower are the contrarieties of place, and the movements get their contrarieties most of all from places, since contrary movements are those which occur from and to contrary places. Therefore if the rectilinear [motions] are contrary to each other, and for one thing there is one contrary (which can now be taken for granted, having been stated many times),[422] and the rectilinear [motions] are two and no more (and for this reason he set out earlier the differences of the simple motions), then [motion] in a straight line will not be contrary to that in a circle.

If, as Alexander says, this argument is from the more [*to mallon*] and the less [*to hêtton*],[423] then since, as I see it, 'less' is opposed to 'more', but it is not opposed to 'most particularly' ['*malista*'], one must wonder whether 'most particularly' is used here instead of 'more', or whether the demonstration from [what is] 'particularly' [the case] and what is opposed to it in no way belongs to the genus of [proof from] the more and the less.[424]

> **271a5-10** Furthermore, if someone supposes that the same reasoning [applies in the case of the circular as it does in the case of the rectilinear (i.e that movement from A to B is contrary to that from B to A), in fact he is speaking of rectilinear motion, since this is finite, while there will be an infinite number of arcs[425] through the same points.]

Having said that contrary motions are those from contrary places, it is easy to suppose that movements from and to opposite [places] along a greater or a lesser arc of a semicircle will also be contraries: for example, that the movement from A to B is the contrary of that from B to A.[426]

However, he says that even though this assumption seems [to involve motion] along the arc, what is in fact assumed [is motion] along straight lines, namely those which are drawn from one contrary place to another.[427] And he added the reason for this wonderfully, by saying 'since this is finite, while there will be an infinite number of arcs[428] through the same points', saying 'is finite' instead of 'is single'; for it is impossible to link one point to another with more than one straight line, since the straight line is the shortest of those which have the same extremities, and the shortest [line] is unique.

He makes it clear that he means that the straight line is finite in number rather than size by saying that the arcs are infinite: for these are infinite in number and not in size,[429] since it possible to inscribe 147,1 an infinite number of arcs.[430]

For if (i) the motions from A and B are contraries, and (ii) contrary motions are from contrary places, and (iii) those from contrary places are those from [places] furthest apart, and (iv) those from [places] furthest apart are from [places] separated by a determinate distance (since the greatest distance is determinate); and if (v) those [motions] from [places separated by] determinate distances are [from places] which have a straight line between them (since what determines and measures distances is a straight line, since this alone is determinate, because it alone is the shortest one of those which have the same extremities); and (vi) if those motions which occur between distant points which have a straight line between them occur as though along straight lines – then (vii) if the motions from A to B are considered to be contraries, they are so considered [as if they took place] along straight lines.[431]

The circular lines drawn between the same points are indeterminate[432] and infinite.[433] So if indeed contrary [motions] are those from contrary places, the circular path along the shortest arc[434] from A will be no more the contrary to that from B along the same line than it is to that from B along the longest, since B is contrary to A equally along the longest [line]. The same argument applies also to the infinite [number of arcs].[435] For it is not possible to take either the greatest or the determinate [distance] in the case of the circular lines, since for every inscribed arc it is possible to take one either larger or smaller.[436]

Furthermore, if the movement from A is contrary to that from B, movement in a straight line will be contrary to that in a circle, if that from A takes place along the straight line between A and B, while that from B [takes place] along the circle.

> **271a10-13** The same thing holds too for the single semicircle, [say from C to D and from D to C: it is the same as motion along the diameter, since we always posit each thing's distance along a straight line.]

In refuting [the suggestion that] motions along greater or lesser arcs of a semicircle are contraries on the grounds that the curving lines are infinite and indeterminate, he gave us to suppose that what was said followed from their plurality rather than from the nature of the circular and the straight: so now in the case of a single semicircle, which obviously has a single circumference, he proves the same thing once again.

In the case of the semicircle drawn from C to D,[437] the motions from C and D along the circumference, if they are to be taken as contraries,
148,1 will equally [be contrary] to that along the diameter. For if contrary [motions] are once again those from places which are furthest separated from one another, and the greatest separation is determinate, and we judge the determinate separation as being the shortest of those which have the same extremities, and this is a straight line, then it is clear that the motions will take place as though along straight lines and according to the same hypothesis, and the demonstration will hold no less if it takes place in a single semicircle.

And the case is the same here as it was there: if [motion] from A is contrary to that from B, and the one occurs along a straight line and the other along the circumference, the rectilinear will be contrary to the circular. And that the contrariety of things moving along the circumference is to be ascertained as though they were moving along a straight line is clear from [the fact that] they are ascertained according to the greatest distance, and the greatest distance is determined by a straight line.[438] For it is possible to draw different curves between the same points, some bigger and some smaller, and to draw a longer segment of a circle between points closer together, and a shorter between [points] further apart.

'If someone', says Alexander,

> after defining the contraries of up and down and joining them with [the straight line] C to D were to draw a semicircle around it, and were then to think that up and down were not determined rectilinearly: [what then?] First of all [he says], none of the things which move naturally up or down move in a semicircle but along a straight line; for they do so along the shortest [line] (for even donkeys, according to Diogenes, go towards food and drink in a straight line).[439] And secondly, motion along such a semicircle, having as its extremities up and down, will not be simple, since it is not simply circular, but also upwards and

downwards. For not even if you drew a whole circle [he says] around the straight line from earth to the heaven would what moves along it move with a simple motion, but there would also be upward and downward motion at the same time as that along the circumference. For the only simple circular [motion] is that around the middle.

271a13-19 The same thing would hold even if, having constructed a circle, [one were to suppose that the movement along one semicircle were the contrary of that along the other: that is, in the whole circle, the movement from E to F in semicircle G is contrary to that from F to E in semicircle H. And even if they were contraries, it would not be the case that movements around the whole circle would for this reason be contrary to one another.][440]

He has shown that, even in the case of a single semicircle, motions 149,1
taking place along it from the extremities of a diameter are not contraries, because the greatest distance, which produces the form of contrariety, is not determined by the circumference but by the straight line. Now he shows by way of two semicircles G and H joined together to form a single circle,[441] that even if I move something from E to F around semicircle G, and around H from F to E, not even thus will the motions be contraries, and for the same reason. For the circumferences do not define the greatest distance in respect of which contraries are characterized: rather it is defined along the diameter EF. And for this reason again, if the motions are treated as contraries, they are so treated in virtue of motion along the rectilinear distance and not that around the circumference.

Having shown in the case of the greater and lesser arcs in the semicircle,[442] and in the case of the single semicircle,[443] and in the case of the two joined together,[444] that movements along them are not contraries even if they seem to take place from opposed [positions], he concludes that 'even if they were contraries, it would not be the case that movements around the whole circle would for this reason be contrary to one another', arguing indirectly.[445] For it is not the case that someone who has shown that [motions] in the semicircles are contraries has thereby shown that those in the circle are too, which was what required demonstration. For while in the case of the arcs and the semicircles the motions appear to be contraries on account of the opposition of the extremities of the arcs from which and to which they move, in the case of motions taking place around a whole circle, there are not two opposing starting-points for motion for two things moving in opposite directions, since each of them [moves] from and to the same [place].

He will make clearer the difference between motion along a semicircle and motion along a circle in what he proves next, namely that motions occurring along a complete circle are not contraries. Consequently the demonstrations he adduces in the case of the arcs and semicircles are surplus to requirements, although not without point, since he shows by way of them that the nature of the arc is in general such as to preclude contrariety of motion.

150,1 **271a19-23** Nor is it even the case that the circular movement from A to B is the contrary of that from A to C, [since the motion is from the same to the same, while contrary movement was defined as that from one contrary to the other.]

Now he proves what is at issue – namely that motions which take place in opposite directions around the whole circle are not contraries – immediately. And he proves it on the basis of the definition of contrary motions (for contrary motions are those which take place from places to their contraries), and the definition of circular motion.

For whenever there is a circle ABC,[446] and something starting from A moves along the B part of the circle as far as A, while something else, also starting from A, but going along the C part of the circle, also arrives back at A, both of the motions take place from A and to A, i.e. from and to the same place, since what moves in a circle describes the whole circle. But contrary motions are from contrary places to contrary places, not from and to the same place: consequently circular motions are not contraries; the argument is in the second figure.[447]

'It was possible', Alexander says,

> to employ this argument in the aforementioned cases as well; for none of them take place from contrary to contrary. But it is clearer in the case of the circle, in which motion not only does not take place from contrary to contrary, but not even from one place to another, but rather from and to the same place. For this reason he adduced it in this case as well.

271a23-33 Yet again, if circular [motion] is contrary to circular [motion], one or other of them will be pointless; [**for they are towards the same thing, because the circular mover must arrive equally at all the contrary places no matter where it starts (the contrarieties of place are up and down, front and back, and right and left), and contrarieties of movement depend on contrarieties of place.**[448] For if they were equal, there would be no motion for them, while if one motion prevailed, the other would not exist. Consequently, if one of them exists, the other body would

> be pointless and would not move with the motion proper to it; for we would call a shoe with which one could not be shod pointless.] But God and nature do nothing pointlessly.

Having shown that motions which take place in opposite directions along the same [circle] are not contraries, he now proves the same thing by *reductio ad impossibile*, arguing as follows; if motion along one circle was the contrary of that in the opposite direction on the same circle, one of them would be pointless. But what is pointless is impossible. Therefore circular motion is not contrary to circular [motion].

He proves the conditional as follows. Things which move in opposite directions along the same circle both arrive at all the points in the circle no matter where they start from, and even if these movements were contraries, as is supposed, and the contrarieties of movement exist in virtue of the contrarieties of place, both of them equally will arrive at all of the contrary places in the circle.

The contrarieties of place are up and down, front and back, and right and left, and if there is indeed contrariety of place in the circle,[449] they will all exist simultaneously, since no one of them is any more [of a contrariety] than any other. So as both of them move in opposite directions through all of the circle they confront one another and conflict with one another, as everywhere coming from contrary places and possessing contrary natures (for they would not move in a contrary fashion if they did not possess contrary principles of motion).

And if they were of equal strength (this is what 'equal' means here), there would be no motion for them; for things of equal strength moving from contrary [positions] will bring each other to a halt, so that both of them will remain motionless, pointlessly. But if one of the motions prevails, that which is prevailed over by the prevailer will be moved with the prevailing motion, and thus a single circular motion will occur, with that which is prevailed over failing to complete its circle.

Thus the latter would be pointless, being unable to carry to completion its proper activity; for we call something pointless when it does not fulfil its function, as in the case of the shoe. Consequently if they are of equal strength both of them will remain motionless pointlessly. But if one of them prevails, that which is prevailed over will be pointless, and thus the conditional of the argument is demonstrated.

For it follows from their moving in opposite directions along the same circle that they run into one another, and [it follows] from their having, by hypothesis, contrary natures and coming from contrary places that in running into one another they conflict. I believe that Aristotle posited contrary places and called them as such for this reason, namely to indicate that if there are indeed contrary circular motions the places throughout the circle will be also contraries; for [it will be the case] no more here rather than there.[450] And things which move and arrive similarly at all of the contrary places possess a constantly renewed contrariety towards each other, and for this reason conflict.[451]

And it follows from their conflicting that either they bring each other to a halt or that the one which prevails drags around with it the one it prevails over, from which [it follows that] either one or both of them is pointless. But the additional premiss states that it is impossible for any of the natural things to be pointless.[452] He proves this by assuming another premiss in addition which says that none of the things of which God or nature are causes is pointless, because they do nothing pointlessly.

152,1 I derive the conclusion effectively as follows: God and nature are the causes of those things which are by nature; nothing of which God and nature are the causes is pointless; therefore none of the things which are by nature is pointless.[453] I have thought it necessary to unpack Aristotle's demonstration in this manner, and for the reasons mentioned.[454]

However, Alexander says:

> in saying that it 'must arrive equally at all the contrary places', he is not saying that there are some contrary places in the circle, but is rather seeking to clarify [the fact that] something moving in a circle must pass through every part of the circle. But what moves in a circle necessarily passes through every part of the circle, and there is no need in addition to this for contrariety of places.

But I think that he [sc. Aristotle] proceeded in a better way, when he noted that if there were contrary motions in a circle there must be contrary places too. For contrary local motions take place in virtue of contrarieties of place.

'But,' he [sc. Alexander] says,

> he draws the conclusion that there are contrary places in the circle, from the the fact that the contrary motions would take place in the circle, and that there are both an up and a down along the circumference, and the other oppositions, as something absurd.[455]

But it does not seem so much to infer this as being simply absurd, even if it is absurd, as to [to infer it] as something which follows from the hypothesis,[456] while it contributes the fact that they set out from contrary places to the tendency of the things which move in opposite directions to conflict. As evidence for this I adduce [the fact that] this absurdity is a consequence of there being contrary places, while he makes use in addition of [the fact that] what moves, no matter where it starts from, 'must arrive equally at all the contrary places', from which the constant renewal in respect of the contrariety of power follows.[457]

'But,' says Alexander,

> two arguments can be propounded on the basis of this statement;[458] one, that one or other of them will be pointless, he speaks of later, in giving the reason for it after the other argument, in the words which he adds: 'if they were equal, there would be no motion for them'. For these things tend to show that one or other of them would be pointless.

But 'there would be no motion for them' means that both will be pointless,[459] and Aristotle infers that 'the other body would be pointless' on the basis of the other hypothesis, according to which one prevails and the other is prevailed over; but common to both is that 'God and nature do nothing pointlessly'.

'But,' says Alexander,

> what lies between these statements[460] should be another argument. Indeed, some copies transmit not the reading 'because the circular mover must', but rather '*moreover*, the circular mover must', as though he were adding something new to what has been said already.[461] And what was added would be that, if contrary motions are to occur along the same circle, they must 153,1
> pass through all of the contrarieties in respect of place in the circle, and he added [a specification of] what sorts of things these contrarieties in respect of place are. Consequently there must be contrarieties in respect of place along the circumference. For contrary motion along a circle must

he says,

> either take place towards contraries (as in the case of straight lines), or if not that, then rather through contrary places (which the circle will possess if it possesses contrariety), since it cannot take place towards contrary places, at any rate if [it is] towards the same one.[462]

Having said this, he says,

> he no longer continues with the point that it is absurd to say that on the single, continuous circular circumference there are contrary places (one up and one down, or any of the other oppositions,[463] or all of them), but taking up the argument again he proves, as[464] he previously said, that one or other of them would be pointless.

So Alexander. But perhaps whoever wrote 'moreover it must' was not sensitive to the coherence of the argument as a single entity,[465] nor to the fact that it is not in accordance with Aristotelian usage to employ such transpositions.[466] And how could he [sc. Alexander] say that 'circular motion cannot take place towards contrary places, at any rate if [it is] towards the same one'? For in general if the circle is assumed to have contrary places, then its motion would, at all events, be both through them and also, I believe, towards them.

However Alexander set out the demonstration concisely, as he says, in the manner of his master Aristotle, that there is no motion contrary to circular motion and no contrary to the revolving body, in the following way.[467] 'For if', he says,

> there is a motion contrary to circular motion, it will either be rectilinear or circular; but neither of these [is the case], as will be shown; consequently there is none. Well, motion in a straight line is not contrary to circular [motion]: for what kind of rectilinear motion will be its contrary, and why one rather than the other?[468] Moreover those along straight lines are contrary to one another, and to each thing there is one contrary. And if we are unable to show that either of those along straight lines is contrary to that in a circle, then in general those along straight lines will not be contrary to that in a circle. But then circular [motion] is not contrary to it either. For contrary [motions] are those which take place from and to contraries; for contrarieties of movement are so in virtue of contrarieties of place, but things which move cyclically along a circle move from the same thing and to the same thing even if they are moving in opposite directions, and one and the same thing is not contrary to itself. Consequently things [which move] in a circle will not be contrary to one another. Things moving thus in opposite directions are subcontraries of a sort, but their motions are not contraries, since they do not admit of the definition of contrariety.[469] And if neither motion in a straight line nor that along a circle are contrary to circular motion, then neither will there be any contrary to that which moves with such a motion by nature. That things moving along a semicircle are not said to move in the same way as those along a circle is clear from [the fact that]

> things moving in a circle move from and to the same [place] continuously, while motions across a diameter[470] are not continuous, since the mover must turn back, and what turns back must first come to a halt.[471]

Let these things suffice, then, in regard to the clarification of what Aristotle says. But in addition, for those who think that Aristotle says that God is not a productive but only a final cause,[472] we must bring up what he says here in such a clear fashion, namely 'God and nature do nothing pointlessly'. However there are those who take 'God' to mean the heaven, in a forced manner, because its motion is the cause of the nature of things down here. And they would speak truly, were they to add 'immediately';[473] for God, bringing the heavenly bodies to be through his own agency, creates through their motions the things which come to be and are destroyed in the sublunary realm. For the unmoved cause makes all of those things it makes through its own agency eternal and equal to the gods, as Plato says.[474] But some say that Aristotle loosely equates God with nature in this passage by means of this phrase.[475]

But since Aristotle has proved by what he says here that, since motion takes place as though around one circle, there is no motion contrary to circular motion even if things move in opposite directions around the same circle (for either both will be pointless and both forcibly at a standstill, or one of them will be, when it is carried around along with the stronger), it is right to inquire how the motion of the planets is not contrary to that of the fixed sphere.

For not only do they move in opposite directions, but they appear to move from and to opposite places, if indeed the fixed [sphere moves] from east to west, while the planets [move] from west to east. For the fact that they do not move along the same sphere does not seem to prevent their being contraries, since it is neither necessary for everything [which moves] from the middle or to the middle to move along the same straight line, nor for them invariably to meet one another.[476]

And in general apparent contrary motions around a single circle possess an apparent contrariety to those moving in the other direction, but not in that they take place from contrary places, which is the particular property of contrary motions. But the fixed [stars] and the planets seem to move from contrary places. So it should be said that contrary motions, which are the current subject of inquiry, must be both from and to contrary places: for this is the definition of 155,1
contrary motions.

But it is appropriate for things which move in respect of their own [motions] to be as far as possible as strong as one another, at least if the contrariety is not quickly to disappear when one of them prevails. But things which move in respect of their own [motions] and are contraries by nature must clash with one another, given that we say that the motions of things contrary by nature are contrary; and they must transmute into one another, since they have a common substrate. For things which are thus generated from one another are contraries: and this has been, I believe, adequately proven.[477]

Let us see, then, if the motion of the planets and of the fixed [stars] have something of these differentiations. First of all, east and west, from which as opposites they appear to move, have their existence relative to us and not to the totality, since what is east to some people is west to others. Each of them, then, may be said to move in the same way both from the east and from the west. For just as that hemisphere of the fixed [sphere] which is above the earth appears to move from east to west, the one under the earth [seems to move] in the opposite direction from west to east, otherwise stars which have set would not rise again.

And that of the planets seems to move above the earth from west to east, while [it moves] under the earth in the opposite direction, and both move by circling round from and to the same places; and if you imagine some point independent of each of them, each part that starts from it finishes up at it again, and in the same way both of them would naturally start off from it and go towards it.

But how can they be said in general to move from contraries to contraries, when each of them is always in all the places, even if at different times with different parts, and they move equally naturally from all of them and to all of them?

Moreover, in the case of the sublunary elements which move in a straight line, if they made continuous returns in their movement, and equally by nature both went up and came down, and particularly if they did so in different places so that they did not run into one another, some of them moving on the right and others on the left, no one, I think, would say that either their motions, or indeed the things themselves which moved equally towards all places, were contraries. For each thing that moves in a contrary fashion moves from one contrary place to another, having an affinity with one and an aversion to the other.

The motion of both of them will not be of equal strength, at least if the fixed [motion] drags the planet around with it; but the one which prevails will not however force the one which it prevails over, nor will it destroy its natural motion, as occurs in the case of contrary motions. That it is not forced is clear from the [fact that] although the planet is imbued with the natural motion of the fixed [sphere], it none the
156,1 less preserves its own motion, revolving in its own eternal measures.[478] Furthermore, if indeed it was forced in this way by a contrary more powerful motion, it would long ago have finally ceased its own motion; and if it has not, it cannot have preserved its own identity

through whole of time while being subject to such force. Consequently things that move in this way are not contraries.

And even if these motions were contraries insofar as they are moving in opposite directions, they will not be contraries in the same way as if they were of things which were contrary and such as to change into one another, at least if things which move in respect of their own [motions], when removed from their proper places, are not such as to clash with one another, either as wholes or in part. For even if they touch one another, [they do] not [do so] by coming from contrary places and in virtue of contrary natures, but as things which have always gone together and which are compatible with and agreeable to one another.

In general, things which change into one another and have a common substrate and are not capable of co-existing, both conflict with one another over their substrate and change into one another. But these things do not have a common substrate, but each has its own, and they are such as to co-exist with one another in friendly contact. But then neither even do the entire masses of the sublunary [elements] change into one another, but only parts separated off from them. So if no part were separated off from them, they would not be such as to change into one another, while if they changed as wholes, if the totality persisted, one world would be generated from another, while if it were destroyed, it would no longer change but be destroyed along with it.

What then? Might someone say that the opposite movement of the spheres had no power, and that it made no difference whether it was this way or that? But it has the greatest power, which holds the whole world together and provides the cause for sublunary generation and destruction,[479] not however in such manner that one thing is changed by the other,[480] which the argument was looking for, but so that a concordant ordering of secondary things comes into being in relation to the prior things.

[156,25-201,10 containing Philoponus fragments 81-107 (see Wildberg, 92-121), and fragment 50 (Wildberg, 67), omitted]

Notes

1. Alexander of Aphrodisias, fl. AD 200, head of the Aristotelian School in Athens and inaugurator of the great commentary tradition. His commentary on *de Caelo* does not survive, but much of it can be reconstructed from Simplicius' remarks.

2. 'Subject' translates *skopos*, which is difficult adequately to render in this context. Its usual meaning is 'aim', 'goal', or 'target'; but here it means something more like 'theme', 'ambit'. The desire to discover a single, unifying *skopos* behind any work became a Neoplatonic commonplace, traceable back to Iamblichus.

3. *kosmos*: I have usually rendered this as 'world', although on occasion 'cosmos' or 'universe' have seemed more appropriate. For Alexander's view, see further ad *Cael*. 1.5, 271b1.

4. This sentence is confusing, and may be corrupt: for there to be three distinct senses of '*ouranos*', 'the whole of the divine revolving body' must refer not merely to the outermost sphere of the fixed stars, but to the whole ensemble of heavenly spheres, a sense which '*ouranos*' certainly can bear in Aristotle; but in that case the subordinate clause 'which ... he also calls the furthest heaven' seems misplaced; the simplest solution would be to move the clause back to qualify 'sphere of the fixed stars'; the MSS tradition is in any case poor for the opening lines of the treatise.

5. *Timaeus* 28B.

6. *arkhai*: principles here in a causal sense.

7. By 'body' (*sôma*) here and elsewhere Simplicius, following Aristotle, means something like 'elemental mass'.

8. i.e. the ether, the incorruptible element of the heavenly bodies: Aristotle argues for the necessity of postulating such a body at *Cael*. 1.2-4.

9. *Cael*. 3.1, 298b6-8.

10. Iamblichus (*c*. 245 – *c*. 325) was a pupil of Porphyry, himself the pupil, editor, and biographer of Plotinus. Iamblichus composed commentaries on Aristotle, none of which survive (the Greek fragments, most of which derive from Simplicius, are collected in D.G. Larsen, *Jamblique de Chalcis, Exégète et Philosophe* (Aarhus, 1972), vol. 2; see also J.M. Dillon, *Iamblichi Chalcidensis in Platonis Dialogos Commentariorum Fragmenta* (Leiden, 1973); he was committed to a strikingly powerful version of Platonico-Aristotelian syncretism, holding that Aristotle did not deny the Theory of Forms. His *On the Mysteries*, an analysis of theurgic ritual, and the strikingly different *On the General Mathematical Science*, a sophisticated account of role of mathematics in science, which do survive, confirm Simplicius' high opinion of him (his name is often qualified in Simplicius' works with the epithet 'divine': cf. e.g. *in Phys*. 639,24).

11. Syrianus (d. 437) was the teacher of the great Neoplatonist systematizer Proclus; although a syncretist himself, he rejected Iamblichus' claim about Aristotle's accepting the Theory of Forms (above, n. 10) in his surviving commentary on the *Metaphysics*.

12. i.e., it is neither a mixture of the four elemental stuffs nor wholly composed of a single one of them.

13. *aitia poiêtika*: this is not an Aristotelian category, but a later (Stoic-influenced) categorization of efficient causes: cf. e.g. Alexander, *On the Soul* 24,11-15 Bruns; *On Fate* 3, 166,22-9; 23, 173,10-17 Bruns.

14. See n. 2 above.

15. Almost certainly Nicholas of Damascus (64 BC – *c.* AD 20), tutor to the children of Antony and Cleopatra, friend of King Herod, and in old age associate and hagiographer of the emperor Augustus. He was the author of a vast and polymathic *oeuvre*, including comedies, tragedies, and a *Universal History* in 144 books, of which fragments survive; Simplicius mentions him (as Nicholas the Peripatic) at *In Cael.* 398,36ff. as the author of a treatise *On the Philosophy of Aristotle*; and elsewhere (*in Phys.* 23,14ff.; 25,1ff.; 151,20) in connection with a volume *On the Gods*. This is the only surviving reference to *On the Universe*. Fragments of *On the Philosophy of Aristotle*, mostly preserved in Syriac, are edited by H. Drossaart Lulofs, *Nicolaus Damascenus: On the Philosophy of Aristotle* (Leiden, 1965).

16. 4,16-21 below.

17. Simplicius is here referring to *Cael.* 3.1, 298b1-4, which echoes (although not word for word) 1.1, 268a1-4.

18. *Cael.* 3.1, 298b6-8.

19. *Meteor.* 1.1, 338a20-5.

20. i.e. in the *Physics*.

21. i.e. *de Caelo*.

22. i.e. it does not form the basis of further compounds as the four sublunary elements do.

23. *Cael.* 1.2, 268b11; 'the Universe': literally, *to pan*, 'the All': *to pan* is standardly contrasted with *to holon*, 'the Whole', where the latter, but not the former, connotes structure.

24. Reading *to auto* with D.

25. *Cael.* 1.1, 268a1-3.

26. *Cael.* 1.1.

27. Reading *en toutois hoti*, with bc.

28. *Cael.* 1.2.

29. *Cael.* 1.3.

30. *Cael.* 1.4.

31. *Cael.* 1.5-7.

32. *Cael.* 1.8-9.

33. i.e. Plato: see *Cael.* 1.10, 279b17-80a11.

34. This view was held by no ancient theorist (*Cael.* 1.10, 279b12), but is refuted by Aristotle for the sake of completeness: *Cael.* 1.12, esp. 283a4-24.

35. *Cael.* 1.12.

36. *kinêsis*: I generally translate this as 'motion', although its Aristotelian ambit is frequently broader than that, and includes all sorts of change (cf. the definition at *Phys.* 3.1, 201a10-12: '*kinêsis* is the actualization of the potential *qua* potential'; and cf. ibid. 200b25-34, where four types of *kinêsis* – substantial, qualitative, quantitative, and positional – are distinguished); this restriction is harmless enough in most contexts in *de Caelo*, where motion (in our sense) is generally what is at issue; although it is awkward, for example, at 7,10-15 below.

37. The meaning of this sentence is obscure; perhaps the sense should be: 'and it is clear that in these books bodies and the study of them are more important'.

38. *Cael.* 1.2, 268a1.

39. 'and act', *te kai poiousi*, seems out of place here, and may well be an unintelligent intrusion into the text.

40. *Cael.* 1.1, 268a4.

41. *Cael.* 1.1, 268a1.

42. *Phys.* 1.2-3; since Parmenides and Melissus deny the reality of change, and since nature for Aristotle is a principle of change (*Phys.* 2.1, 192b8-15; cf. *in Cael.* 1.2, 12,3-5 below), to adopt the Eleatic position is *ipso facto* to deny that there can be a study of nature, or physics, at all: *Phys.* 1.2, 184b25-185a20.

43. For the atomists the minimal bodies were without (divisible) magnitude, and Aristotle is about to define magnitude in terms of divisibility.

44. i.e. magnitudes in less than three dimensions, and hence not bodies as such.

45. Aristotle does in fact say this explicitly in our treatise – but it clearly implicit in what he says in the next lemma; at *Phys.* 6.1-2 he explicitly talks of the continuousness of time and motion as well as body.

46. What is at issue here is the direction of (formal) explanation. Alexander holds that the totality has beginning, middle, and end because it is complete; but why should it not be the case that it is complete because it has beginning, middle, and end, since to be complete just is to have an end?

47. 'Everything' and 'total' render *panta* and *pan* – the natural contrast between the plural and the singular in Greek is hard to reproduce in English.

48. Simplicius' point is pithier in the Greek: he contrasts Pythagorean *endeixis* with Aristotelian *apodeixis*. *Apodeixis*, as described in *Posterior Analytics*, is supposed to be the ineluctable derivation of necessary consequences from necessarily true axioms; by contrast, *endeixis* here denotes an altogether woollier, more defeasible procedure of informal argument (at least in this sense: in Stoicism and medical contexts it may refer to the perfectly respectable process of inferring to a hidden internal condition on the basis of evident signs and symptoms). The argument is uncharacteristic not only because Aristotle rarely has much favorable to say for the Pythagoreans, but rather because this sort of appeal to plausibility has no place in a properly-organized science (see *Top.* 1.1).

49. Ptolemy of Alexandria (*c.* AD 100-175), famous astronomer and geographer, author of the hugely influential *Syntaxis* (or *Almagest*, as it was known in the Arabic world), as well as an *Optics* which survives largely in a Latin translation. See also n. 113 below.

50. Thus Ptolemy's method is, in Simplicius' view, superior.

51. *Phys.* 6.1, 231a21-b18.

52. The argument appears to be this: take any magnitude composed of discontinuous magnitudes, and divide it down to its atomic constituents: what is left will no now longer be divisible, no matter how small the component parts; hence if anything is to be indefinitely divisible, it must not contain atomic parts, and consequently will be continuous.

53. i.e., the fact that it has not yet been demonstrated that whatever is continuous is divisible (a more controversial contention, at least in regard to actually extended objects) is not germane to the issue: all that is required is the converse claim.

54. The connection of thought is confused by the distinction of senses of 'divisible in every way'; a continuous magnitude is 'divisible in every way' (i.e. everywhere) in that there is nowhere that it cannot be divided; a three-dimensional body is 'divisible in every way' (i.e. in all possible manners) in that there are no more than three dimensions. First appearances notwithstanding, Simplicius is not here suggesting that another argument based on the impossibility of 'progression to another type' is here invoked in order to bolster the claim that a continuous magnitude is 'divisible in every way'.

55. i.e. of completeness.

56. i.e. the realm of the fifth element.

57. Here conceived to as a body, the totality of the cosmos.

58. Aristotle's remark that 'hence in a way each of these bodies is many' is very puzzling; Guthrie (1936) remarks ad loc. that 'it is not easy to say in what sense limitation by contact makes each body many', but thinks that Aristotle may be thinking of Plato's *Parmenides* 138A doctrine that anything with boundaries cannot be wholly one in the strongest sense 'of being without parts and indivisible (like a point)'. But that is surely not to the point here, since the totality (which is supposed to be complete in the requisite way) avowedly has parts. It would make more sense in the context for Aristotle to have said that 'each of the bodies is one of many'; Simplicius evidently knew of no such reading, yet seeks to interpret the text in such a way as to extract something like that moral from it: in the case of each element considered on its own there is a 'progression to something else', in the sense that there is something more beyond it, in something like the same way as there is a second dimenison beyond the first and a third beyond the second. But this is not achieved without strain.

59. Read *haplou* for *haplôs* here.

60. *Cael*. 2.1, 284a2ff.

61. This is indeed the standard interpretation of these lines, which are usually translated 'formally distinct parts' (W.K.C. Guthrie, *Aristotle: On the Heavens* [Loeb Classical Library: London/Harvard 1936], 11) – Hankinson and Matthen prefer the stronger 'the parts it has in virtue of its form', i.e. the (spherical) form of whole dictates that it possess certain formally distinct parts; which actually coheres better with what Simplicius has just said in the previous paragraph. See also M. Matthen and R.J. Hankinson, 'Aristotle on the form of the Universe', *Synthese* 96.3 (1993), 417-35.

62. Simplicius here differentiates, in un-Aristotelian fashion, between *meros* and *morion*; 'piece' is a translation of art: the idea seems to be that *x* and *y* are parts (properly speaking) of *z* just in case *x* and *y* are individually uniform but differ from one another in form; distinct pieces, on the other hand, may share a form.

63. In calling these propositions *hupotheseis*, Simplicius does not mean that they are mere assumptions, nor does he imply that they have the same logical or evidential status: some rest upon others (and further assumptions), [5] is pretty clearly supposed to be an *a priori* truth and perhaps also a truth of analysis, while [6] is explicitly said by Aristotle to be obvious to perception. Rather they are the propositions which Simplicius sees as doing the most important work in the course of the argument. They are indeed all to be found at various points in the course of *Cael*. 1.2; and Aristotle himself talks of 'the assumptions regarding motion', and 'these assumptions' at 1.8, 276b8, 277a9, some (although not all) of which are clearly Simplicius' six.

64. [2] and [3] (my numbering, of course) are distinct: [2] states that simple motions belong only to simple bodies (if a simple motion, then a simple body), while [3] holds that simple bodies have only simple motions (if a simple body, then a simple motion); their conjunction expresses the claim that all and only the (natural) motions of simple bodies are simple. Aristotle enunciates these principles at 269a3-4.

65. 'At most' is not justified by the Greek – but that is clearly the sense required for the principle (since it is crucial to Aristotle's argument that some things – pre-eminently circular motion – have no contrary); Guthrie translates Aristotle's enunciation of the principle as 'a thing can have only one contrary' (*Aristotle VI: On the Heavens* [Cambridge Mass./London, 1936], 13), which gives the right sense. I have not added this supplement in what follows, however.

66. Plotinus, 2.1.2, 12-14 (cf. *in Cael.* 1.3, 115,30-1 below); what Aristotle would have had no trouble with is accounting for the eternal existence of the heavenly bodies; Plotinus goes on to say, after this aside, that this is a problem for those who do not accept the Aristotelian postulate of the ether, but rather (as orthodox Platonists do) construct the heavenly bodies from elements which elsewhere are capable of resolution and destruction; *pace* Simplicius, in this passage Plotinus seems simply to be referring to the postulation of the ether itself with his talk of hypothesis here, rather than the six propositions discerned by Simplicius. Plotinus (AD 205-70) was the founder of Neoplatonism, the doctrine which sought to systematize the Platonic picture of the world; although Plotinus borrowed judiciously from Aristotle, he would not go to anything like the syncretist lengths of his successors, and was quite happy to allow that Aristotle and Plato frequently disagreed. In Plotinus' hugely influential metaphysics, the universe is organized in a hierarchy with formless matter (identified with non-being and evil) at the bottom, and the pure, ineffable actuality of the One at the top, which creates all the other levels of reality by means of a spontaneous outpouring of its own actuality. His writings were arranged into six groups of nine ('Enneads') by his pupil and biographer Porphyry.

67. i.e., its persistence as a single, eternally-existing object, by contrast with the persistence, for example, of the human species.

68. i.e. the five regular solids which Plato assigns in the *Timaeus* (53C-56C) to earth (the cube), water (icosahedron), air (octahedron), fire (pyramid), and the cosmos as a whole (dodecahedron).

69. Fr. 265 Isnardi Parente (fr. 53 Heinze). Simplicius repeats this quotation verbatim twice elsewhere (*in Cael.* 1.3, 87,23-6; *in Phys.* 1165,33-8). The ascription of a fifth element to Plato is startling. It is usually supposed to be Xenocrates' creative re-interpretation of his master's doctrine (see Isnardi Parente, *Senocrate – Ermodoro: Frammenti* [Naples, 1982], 433-5, for a sage assessment), and it is of course *ben trovato* for someone like Simplicius wishing to buttress the notion of the essential unanimity of Plato and Aristotle. But as Simplicius goes on to imply, the 'fifth element' here amounts to no more than the particular geometrical construction associated with the heavens; and elsewhere Xenocrates 'says that the stars and the sun are composed of fire and the primary density, the moon from the secondary density and its proper air' (Plutarch, *On the Face in the Moon* 943f. = fr. 161 IP).

70. I cannot find in Plato precisely the claim that 'heaven comes to be from fire'; but at *Tim.* 40A, he writes 'the gods [i.e. the stars] he made mostly out of fire', while at 31B he says that the universe had to be visible, and nothing can be visible unless composed of fire.

71. cf. *Tim.* 58C-D; see 16,18-21 below.

72. cf. *Tim.* 31B-32C.

73. Some such supplement here and at 13,2 below seems required by the dialectic of the argument: see next note.

74. At *Cael.* 2.2, 285a27ff.

75. The thought of this passage is difficult to unravel: in particular, the two sentences beginning with the logical connective 'for' seem not, as it turns out, to explain their predecessors. I have supposed that some sentences of the form I supply within the pointed brackets have fallen out of the text, to restore the dialectic of the argument. An alternative, avoiding the supplementation, would be to translate *auton apophaskein eikos* in 13,2 as 'it is probable that he will *assert* that'; the sentence would then read: 'and even if he *says* it is simple, he would likely have to allow that it is a composite of them: for we shall learn, etc.'. The overall result is much the same; but while *apophasis* (generally 'denial') often appears in logical Greek in place of *apophansis* ('assertion') in a positive sense, I can find no parallel for a similar positive use of *apophaskein*; however, Simplicius may originally have written *apophainein* here, which would give the requisite positive sense.

76. *Phys*. 8.7, 260a27-61b26.

77. The argument would run better if *sunthetou* ('composite') were read in place of 'simple' here.

78. For this Stoic-influenced later Peripatetic designation of efficient causes, much employed by Alexander, see *in Cael*. 1.1, 2,21-2, and n. 13.

79. *hôn ouk aneu*: cf. Plato. *Phd*. 98B-99B, esp. 99B.

80. 'Matter' here in the technical Aristotelian sense. If *A* is the matter for *B*, ten *B* requires *A*, but *A* does not entail *B*'s existence.

81. Again a technical Aristotelian usage: the magnitude 'underlies' the movement precisely in the sense that without magnitude there could be no movement: it is the 'matter' for the motion; cf. *Metaph*. 8.1, 1042a32-5.

82. Simplicius may mean that the motion is the formal cause of the magnitude, or more probably that in this particular case it is its efficient cause: the existence of the motion brings about the actualization in this case of the abstract magnitude.

83. Xenarchus of Seleucia, who taught in Alexandria, Athens and Rome at the end of the first century BC, was the teacher of the geographer Strabo, and an associate of the emperor Augustus and his court philosopher, Arius Didymus. Almost all the surviving fragments of *Against the Fifth Substance* are preserved by Simplicius in this chapter; an exception is found at Julian, *Speeches* 8 (5) 3. He rejected the Aristotelian notion of the ether, apparently supposing the heavenly bodies to be made of fire, possibly under the influence of Strato; but unlike the latter, he retained (although with amendment) the concept of natural places and motions for the elements. His philosophy of mind, although fundamentally Aristotelian, was materialist, and he appears to have accepted the Stoic notion of an extra-mundane void (Simplicius, *in Cael*. 1.9, 286,2). See H.B. Gottschalk, 'Aristotelian philosophy in the Roman world', *Aufstieg und Niedergang der römischen Welt* II, 36 2, 119-20; P. Moraux, *Der Aristotelismus bei den Griechen*, vol. 2, 197-212 (Berlin, 1984).

84. See 13,15-17 above.

85. This does not indeed figure among the six assumptions laid down by Simplicius at 12,6-11 above, where only simple motions and simple bodies, not simple magnitudes, are put into one-one correspondence; this leaves open the possibility, canvassed here by Alexander, that while there will be a simple magnitude for every simple motion (and hence for every simple body), there need not conversely be a simple motion for every simple magnitude; this amounts to saying that the magnitudes are matter for the motions.

86. Material causes make their 'effects' possible, but they do not necessitate them: thus a supply of bronze is a necessary, but not a sufficient, condition of the generation of bronze sculpture: cf. *Phys*. 2.3, 194b24ff.; 2.9, 200a6-b9.

87. i.e. it corresponds to the characterization given at 13,25-6 above.

88. i.e. the sun's motion along the ecliptic; although this is not a uniform motion in Simplicius' sense.

89. The point appears to be that any motion of a body can be viewed as some combination of the simple motions (although of course it *need* not be so in reality, as the special case of animal motion shows). Consider the celestial sphere and any point within it – now consider any possible motion of that point. Either it maintains a constant radial distance from the centre, in which case its motion is circular; or it does not, in which case the radial distance either increases (and it moves upward), or decreases (and it moves downward).

90. i.e., simple motions occur either along a straight line or along a circle.

91. As plainly it cannot: if it were to do so, the three motions should be along each of the three perpendicularly-oriented dimensions.

92. Of [1]-[6] above: 12,7-11.

93. i.e. in virtue of their being animals and plants; any animal has a natural tendency to fall, but it has it in virtue of its being predominantly earthy, not because it is an animal: see Simplicius' own example of the man falling from the roof: 40,17-20.

94. i.e. elements, as distinct from complex biological structures.

95. cf. *Tim*. 58C.

96. cf. 14,21-4 above.

97. i.e., presumably, in a complex motion two separate trajectories will combine to produce a new vector which is in some sense their sum, but does not consist of their each actually being realised, either successively or simultaneously. Simplicius however interprets him differently as talking about motions with successive distinct directional components: see below.

98. i.e. Alexander thinks these motions are 'in a way' mixed because they are not, properly speaking mixed at all; Simplicius rather takes 'in a way' not to compromise the genuineness of the mixture, but simply to signal that it is a mixture of a particular type, namely one involving motions.

99. i.e. in a universe constructed as ours is, there can be no freely-existing pure elements: they will always be found in admixture with others.

100. i.e. of elemental earth and fire (cf. 12,31-3 above): this is of course not a view acceptable to Aristotle, but derives rather from Plato's association of the visible and the tangible with fire and earth respectively (*Tim*. 28B, 31B; nn. 70-2 above); Simplicius would like to reconcile Plato and Aristotle in good, Neoplatonist syncretist fashion – here the strain is evident.

101. Here Aristotle expresses [2] and [3] of Simplicius' six hypotheses: cf. 12,8-9 above.

102. The logical form of this argument merits a brief comment. First, it is introduced by the categorical connective *epei* ('since'), which amounts to an assertion of the antecedent of a conditional – this is reflected in Simplicius' remark that the antecedent has already been established (but conflicts with his reluctance below to accept Alexander's intepretation of '*eiper*' as factual: 18,9-15). Secondly the antecedent in question is a complex of two propositions ('circular motion is simple' and 'of a simple body, etc.'). Thus, effectively, a two-premiss argument is presented as a conditional in which the conjunction of the first two premisses (the second of which is itself conjunctive in form) forms the antecedent, with the conclusion as consequent (this mirrors Aristotle's own preferred presentation of arguments in *Prior Analytics*). Finally, the second conjunct of the second premiss ('simple motion is of a simple body') is redundant in the argument (a fact implicitly noted by Simplicius in his 'categorical' presentation of the argument: 18,16-19 below).

103. i.e. in either of the two other distinct, natural motions (up or down for the revolving body, and so on).

104. Here Aristotle introduces [5] of Simplicius' six hypotheses (12,10 above; 19,20 below); on the addition of '<at most>', see n. 65 above.

105. 'Other' (*allê*) is the reading of all the MSS of Aristotle at this point; however Simplicius (see 20,3 below) apparently read 'simple' (*haplê*) here, perhaps rightly.

106. Aristotle's argument in this chapter is vitiated by a lack of rigour in regard to the meaning of *enantion*, which may mean either (a) 'contradictory opposite' or (b) 'contrary opposite'. Simplicius' inference here only requires that unnatural motion is the contrary of natural motion in sense (a); however, later Aristotle apparently behaves as though he has established that is contrary in sense (b). However, Aristotle can still be acquitted of a serious fallacy of equivocation: see Hankinson and Matthen ad loc. for details.

107. The argument is that if circular motion were to have a contrary at all it would have to be of the whole ensemble of rectilinear motions: but that would violate the hypothesis [5]; however, see the objections of Xenarchus, and Simplicius' replies: 55,25-56,12 below.

108. Here Simplicius attempts to finesse the problem noted above (n. 107): any two simple motions, if they are opposites at all, must be contrary opposites. Thus he takes 'unnatural' to indicate contrariety, while the mere contradictory opposite of natural motion will be 'non-natural' (for this reason it might be better to translate Simplicius' uses of *para phusin* here as 'counter-natural' rather than 'unnatural': but I have opted for consistency of translation); Aristotle does not make use of such a distinction; but his text can be read consistently in accordance with it.

109. By 'intermediates' Simplicius here means composite motions containing both upward and downward components (see 20,6-10 below) – cases where, according to Aristotle, the object moves in the direction of that element which predominates (*Cael.* 1.2, 269a7-9).

110. i.e. if a body does indeed move unnaturally (i.e. counter-naturally) in a circle there must be some simple motion which is natural for it – but there are only two other simple motions available, and they are already taken by other bodies, namely the four sublunary elements, which are in any case contraries of each other.

111. i.e. *Cael.* 4.1-6; but see also 1.3, 269b23-6.

112. Or perhaps: 'although not in the same proportion'.

113. *Optics: On the Elements* is lost, as is the first book of *Optics*, much of the rest of which survives in a Latin version of an earlier Arabic translation survives; but in what survives there is no mention of the movement of the elements, which would in any case be more appropriate to a proem: see A. Lejeune, *L'Optique de Claude Ptolémée* 1989[2] (Leiden, repr. from 1956), 13*-15*.

114. *Enneads* 2.2.1,19-30.

115. *Cacl.* 4.3, 310a33-4.

116. This reference is usually taken to be to Aristotle's *On Generation and Corruption* (the translation would then read 'and in *On Generation*, as Alexander also does on these matters'); but if so it is very obscure. Simplicius may mean to refer to *Gen. Corr.* 2.8, 335a19-23 – but Aristotle is making a rather different point in that passage. The reference is picked up at 22,18-21 below, where Heiberg refers to *Gen. Corr.* 2.10 – but again, that does not seem precisely to the point, either here or there. I tentatively suggest that *On Generation* here refers to a work of Alexander's of that name (the latter passage can be made to square with this interpretation), although I can find no other reference to an *On Generation* of Alexander. It is conceivable that the text here should read *peri kinêseôs*, 'On Motion': and the reference would be to *Phys*. 3.1 (see below, n. 130); for this designation of (parts of) the *Physics*, see *Cael*. 1.5, 272a30-1.

117. At 22,18-21 below.

118. This account of the structure of the cosmos is not to be found in *Cael*., but it follows closely that of *Meteor*. 1.3 and 1.7, 344a9ff.

119. *Meteor*. 1.7, 344a9ff.

120. 21,33-23,10 below.

121. Lit. non-wandering, i.e. not like a planet.

122. i.e. the proper motion of the planets is from west to east along the ecliptic, each carried on its own sphere; but that sphere is itself carried by the westward-moving diurnal sphere of the fixed stars (plus a good deal of other apparatus), giving an appearance of east-west motion, albeit somewhat retarded by comparison with that of the outermost sphere. But this is not an unnatural motion, since it has no tendency to destroy or damage the proper motion of the planet's sphere by fighting against it or restraining it – it simply affects its apparent motion (for Aristotle's Eudoxan, or perhaps better Callipan, celestial mechanics, see *Metaph*. 12.8, esp. 1073b1-1074a16).

123. Reading *erôtêsei*, with BEb, against Heiberg's *erôtêsoi* <*an*>.

124. *Cael*. 1.3, 270a3-5; cf. 1.8, 276a31-b22; 4.3, 310b3-5.

125. Involving the example of the helix: 13,22ff. above.

126. i.e., when they are in their natural places: see 20,10-18 above.

127. One might supply 'in its place' after 'coming to be' in this sentence – but it is better to take Xenarchus as making a perfectly general point, in which case the verbs 'to be' should be read as being generalized incomplete predicates: 'being *F*', 'coming to be *F*', and so on: when you are coming to be something you are not yet really that thing.

128. i.e. around the centre of the cosmos; Aristotle confusingly uses *to meson* sometimes to mean the centre of the universe, sometimes (as Xenarchus does here) to mean the place of the body surrounding it (i.e. that occupied by earth), sometimes to mean the intermediate position between fire and earth (occupied by water and air), and sometimes to mean that between the heavens and the lower body (i.e. that occupied by fire, air and water).

129. cf. n. 115 above. Heiberg, taking *On Generation* to be a text of Aristotle, refers to *Gen. Corr.* 2.10 here, where Aristotle stresses that the intermittent rectilinear motions must themselves be caused ultimately by a continuous circular motion, which none the less has cyclical qualities, namely the motion of the sun along the ecliptic: but this is not germane to the issue.

130. To understand this apparently paradoxical phrase, cf. Aristotle's definition of motion at *Phys*. 3.1, 201a10: 'the actuality of the potential *qua* potential is motion'; in other words, motion (or change in general) represents the thing's potentiality *as it is becoming actualized*.

131. i.e. the thing is no longer merely being actualized, but is now fully actual: cf. *Cael*. 4.3, 310a21-b1, b9-11, 311a2-6: things achieve their full form in their natural places.

132. The argument is as follows: whenever earth is in contact with earth at the centre of the cosmos, it is in its proper place. But then consider the behaviour of mountains, which have been raised upwards by geological activity: their earth is still in direct contact with the earth at the centre (and hence is, by definition, in its proper place); but it retains its tendency to move downwards (in erosion, as scree). So even in its proper place (where it is fully actual), it has the inclination to fall; hence the inclination to fall cannot be proper to its non-actualized state. It is unclear, however, whether the earth at the summits of mountains does count, for Aristotle, as being in its proper place, if the proper place for earth (however it is precisely to be defined) is properly spherical (as it seems to be for Aristotle: see *Cael.* 1.7, 274a19; *Phys.* 3.5, 205b10-13); see Hankinson and Matthen, ad *Cael.* 1.6, 273a7 ff.

133. *Tim.* 62c-63e.

134. cf. 22,22-3 above.

135. i.e. there need not be an infinite number of *types* of composite motion; the only sense in which composite motions may be said to be infinite is numerically, since in an infinite time (as in Aristotle's universe: *Cael.* 1.12) there will as a matter of fact be an infinite number of them, just as there will be an infinite number of bodies, although not of types of body.

136. cf. nn. 83-5 above.

137. cf. *Cael.* 1.2, 269a5, above.

138. Reading *prosupethemetha* with Heiberg for the MSS *proüpethemetha*.

139. *Cael.* 1.2, 269a7-9.

140. i.e. even though air is not as light as fire, it does not thereby possess a different *type* of lightness. In general for Aristotle differences of degree ('the more and the less') do not amount to differences of form; but there are exceptions: *PA* 1.4, 644a16-b15.

141. Reading *einai hêtton* with E in place of *hêtton einai*.

142. Simplicius' argument is difficult to follow here. As I translate it, the opinion ascribed to Aristotle is that there is a sense in which the intermediate elements are not genuinely simple, but presumably not one strong enough to entail that they are properly compounds of opposites. However the text might mean: 'he will not be saying that these things are genuinely simple, as Aristotle holds', which attributes to him the opposite view. In favour of the version I favour is the Greek word-order and the *kai* ('even') in the second clause. The point is made clearer by supplying only: perhaps read *ou monon* before *erei*, and *kai* before *kineisthai*. In favour of the second reading is the fact that, in *Cael.* at least, Aristotle does appear to uphold the simplicity of all the elements; but Simplicius may be thinking of the quality theory of *Gen. Corr.* 2.1-5, esp. 2.3, 330b30-331a5, where Aristotle refers to all four elements as 'simple', yet also claims that 'earth and fire are ... purest, while water and air on the other hand are intermediates and more combined'.

143. i.e. that which moves up, and that which moves down: see *Cael.* 1.8, 277b13-17; 3.1, 298b6-8. It is of course a theoretical problem for him as to why there should indeed be four sublunary elements, rather than two: see *Cael.* 3.1, 298b6ff. But Simplicius (or perhaps Alexander) is here urging that, if air and water are properly to be elements, they had better have only one intrinsic tendency, and not be compounds of opposites, as the suggestion a few lines earlier has it.

144. i.e. the equator.

145. Presumably Xenarchus. Simplicius' solution to the problem here is not a particularly happy one – effectively it requires that we conceive of the celestial sphere as being composed of infinitely many circular slices. It would probably be better to take issue with the premiss that every part of a simple body ought to move with the same speed – but Xenarchus makes a telling point in favour of its plausibility by pointing out that simple bodies are uniform, and so if they have their tendency to move (at a given velocity) in virtue of their form, and their form does not differ from one part to another, then every part should move at the same speed. Equally, of course, the different spheres on the Eudoxan model of the universe move at different speeds; yet they are made of the same stuff. It seems, then, that Aristotle must reject the claim (which he never in fact endorses) that bodies have their tendency to move *with a particular velocity* (as opposed to their tending to move in a certain direction: *Cael.* 2.7, 289a14-16) in virtue of their form. Their different particular velocities (and *a fortiori* the different particular velocities of their parts) will then have to be explained by appeal to some further principle (cf. *Cael.* 2.8).

146. i.e. a circumpolar circle: Simplicius' expression is less than rigorous here – of course there are infinitely many such circles (and their maximum magnitude depends upon the observer's position); hence there is no single 'slowest' one, as he goes on to say. But the lack of rigour is harmless in this context.

147. cf. 12,6-11 above.

148. 269a5, above.

149. Uncharacteristically, Simplicius quotes only the opening clause of the lemma and not the final words; but he discusses all of the passage here translated in the next section of commentary.

150. i.e., he employs hypotheses [1] and [2] (above, 12,8-10); see n. 63 above.

151. Retaining *oude kata phusin*, against Heiberg.

152. i.e. at *Phys.* 8.9.

153. See below, 39,21-32.

154. It might be objected that a circle could be added to by expansion (consider a meridian on a gradually-inflating spherical balloon); but then the degree of curvature would change: you cannot add to a circle simply by patching in new arcs.

155. i.e. the circumference: the Greek word *arkhê*, here translated 'beginning', is ambiguous between the meanings 'beginning', 'starting-point', 'source', 'origin', and 'principle'.

156. i.e. both in respect of having beginning, middle, and end, and in that it cannot be added to.

157. 269a22-3; 'beyond' here means 'greater than'.

158. i.e., since straightness is a property (or form), something ought to be able to possess it completely: a line may be perfectly (as opposed to approximately or partially) straight.

159. i.e., presumably, it is not the straightness of the line that can be increased, but its length; and *qua* straight, a line is (conceptually) extendable, although in the case of a cosmic diameter it will not be so in actuality.

160. i.e., the magnitude as such is complete only in the longest possible physically-realisable straight line, a diameter of the cosmic sphere, and hence it is not complete as a function of its straightness, but only as a result of particular (formally contingent) limitations that happen to be placed upon it.

161. The Demiurge is, of course, not an Aristotelian notion, but rather derives from the *Timaeus*; here Simplicius' Platonism (and his syncretism) come to the fore.

162. i.e., even though the cosmic straight line is the longest physically possible (and hence is complete in the sense that none larger can be constructed, and so in a sense there is nothing beyond it), none the less this is only true on virtue of the actual limitations placed upon the size of the cosmos by the Demiurge (or, for Aristotle, by the nature of things as they happen to be), and not because of any intrinsic limitations having to do solely with the form of straightness. Thus, the straight is inferior to the circular not because straight lines are deficient *qua* straight, but rather because the form of straightness is inferior to that of the circular.

163. Hypothesis [2] once again: 12,8-9 above.

164. i.e. the circular and the rectilinear.

165. i.e. the circular.

166. *Phys.* 8.9, 265a13-b16.

167. I find it difficult to make sense of this clause (*alla kata phusin*), which seems to attach naturally neither to what precedes it nor to what comes after. Perhaps it should be secluded.

168. This rather obscure phrase looks to the doctrine of the *Timaeus*, in which the physical universe as a whole is an animal, but a mere physical representation of the intelligible idea of such an animal in the mind of the Demiurge: *Tim.* 28c-29b, 30a-31b.

169. Simplicius here characteristically infuses the authentically Aristotelian notion of the priority of the whole to its parts with the Neoplatonic idea of the One generating diversity from itself.

170. Again utilizing hypothesis [2]: 12,8-9 above.

171. The distinction between the two formulations is subtle, not to say evanescent. Simplicius' is, I suppose, somewhat more emphatic; it may also signal his greater willingness (as a Platonist) to embrace the notion that the heavenly body is in fact composite, a position Aristotle floats only (as Simplicius rightly sees) for the sake of generality of argument ('*even if* the heavenly body is composite, *still* there must be something within it which is such as to move naturally in a circle, and which is more powerful than the other constituents: so there is a fifth simple body').

172. cf. 25,11-21 above.

173. cf. 24,21-34, and n. 145; but here the different speeds are not those of the celestial equator and other latitudes, but rather of the exterior of the shell, the interior of the shell, and the parts between the two.

174. i.e. when they are in their natural places: cf. 21,33-23,10 (and cf. *Cael.* 4.3, 310a20ff.; n. 131). The example given here is that of the fire-sphere; cf. *Meteor.* 1.4, 341b5-22.

175. cf. 23,31-24,10.

176. It is not clear what Simplicius refers to here; in *in Cael.* 1.1, he frequently refers to the celestial body as divine, but he is not quoting Aristotle when he does so; at 1.2, 11,18-25 he refers to *Cael.* 2.1, 284a2ff., on the reasonableness of supposing that there is something divine and immortal – but that is of course proleptic; and at 38,11-14 he speaks of Aristotle proceeding 'to show that the revolving <body> is prior to and more divine than the rectilinearly-moving bodies'; but again there is no mention of divinity in Aristotle's text. What is required is some premiss to the effect that simplicity and priority are divine attributes – but this has not been previously established.

177. *Meteor.* 1.3, 340b32-341a12; 1.4, 341b5-22.

178. cf. 23,31-24,10; 42,10-14.

179. Thus conflicting with the basic principle (hypothesis [5]) that for a single thing there is a single contrary: *Cael.* 1.2, 269a11; 12,10, 19,21 above, etc. I translate *enantion* here neutrally as 'opposite' rather than 'contrary' in order not to prejudice the eventual run of the argument.

180. The argument is a reductio: suppose circular motion to be unnatural for fire; but we already know that upward motion is natural for it, so downward motion will be unnatural for it; but this conflicts with hypothesis [5]; therefore our original supposition must be false.

181. Reading *lithinês* with D for *plinthinês* (cf. 51,9).

182. Presumably rotating it about its axis rather than swinging the whole thing in a circle (on the end of a piece of string, for instance).

183. i.e. the hypothesis that circular motion is unnatural for it is self-refuting, since it entails that some other motion (downward, say) is natural for it, but this in turn entails that upward motion is unnatural for it, and so circular motion cannot be unnatural for it, otherwise the same thing will have two contraries. But in that case, circular motion must be natural for it (since that is the only alternative).

184. Simplicius apparently assumes that the bulk of the argumentative work in Alexander's thought-experiment is being done by the fact that the wooden object is spherical; the idea then would be that it is somehow natural for spherical things to revolve, which Simplicius counters by observing that other shapes can revolve on their axes. But this seems to misconstrue the point of Alexander's objection.

185. It is hard to see why a revolving sphere should be said to be moving up and down, unless we are to suppose that its axis is horizontal (or at any rate off the vertical); then its motion will be equivalent to that of the wheel: above, 15,2-4.

186. This Platonic, *Timaeus*-type solution could not of course have been accepted as a resolution of the difficulty by Aristotle; again Simplicius' Neoplatonist syncretist predilections come to the fore.

187. In other words, that it is preternatural: 21,25-7 above; 51,24 below.

188. i.e. the circle of the moon, against which the fire-sphere abuts, one of the seven 'planetary' or wandering spheres (which include that of the sun), by contrast with that of the fixed stars.

189. Reading *parapheromenon* with E^2; or possibly, reading *auto* [with E^2b] *peripheron*, 'which carries it around'.

190. i.e. the risings and settings of the stars due to motion along the ecliptic.

191. 269b7-10; cf. 53,4-18.

192. cf. 21,20-7.

193. Simplicius' phrasing here is slightly different from that found in the texts of Aristotle, and in his own lemma (50,5-6 above).

194. i.e. the strongly contrary, as opposed to the simply contradictory.

195. *Phys*. 8.8.

196. Again, Simplicius does not quote the end of the lemma, although he discusses it: cf. 38,7, n. 149 above.

197. In the mood of Cesare (roughly speaking): no revolving body is moved in a circle unnaturally; all fire is moved in a circle unnaturally; so no fire is a revolving body; categorical syllogistic is not well adapted to handling such arguments, where the subjects are properly-speaking particulars and the conclusion is a (negative) identity-sentence, and the strain is palpable.

198. i.e. the upward force of what it is which nourishes the fire finally gives out and the fire at the limit begins turning; it is not clear whose theory Alexander refers to here, although it may well be Strato of Lampsacus, who rejected both the theory of natural places and that of the ether (cf. frr. 50-5 Wehrli).

199. i.e. the eternally-revolving spheres: here Simplicius canvasses the view of Xenarchus (as well as Ptolemy and Plotinus): above, 20,10-32; 21,33-23,10.

200. See n. 195 above.

201. i.e., because of our 'animal sympathy' with the truth, when we are confronted with it in the form of ironclad deductive ('scientific') knowledge, we cannot fail to be convinced of its truth; this notion of sympathy or kinship derives ultimately from *Meno* 81D; see also *in Cael*. 1.3, 65,7-16 below.

202. Delete *kai* here: but see n. 200.

203. Or, retaining the first *kai*, and reading *dioti* with Bc for *dêlon, hoti*: 'because he has reasoned from hypotheses, and because insofar as …'; or, reading *dêlonoti*: 'and <because> clearly, insofar as …'.

204. Here it is clear that the 'hypotheses' are more than mere suppositions: they are premisses which command assent, and as such so do their implications.

205. This is an expression of the standard Neoplatonist goal of mystical union with the highest reality of the universe, the One.

206. sc. of courage, since it is a mean between extremes; 'inequality' and 'equality' here refer to the states of imbalance and balance mentioned above: 56,5-7.

207. Reading *êtoi*, with D. The text which Heiberg prints here, which translates as 'the circular [motion] of the fire and that downwards to that upwards' cannot be right, since it opposes the ensemble of circular and downward motion to upward motion: but on the hypothesis being entertained by Xenarchus, circular motion will be natural for fire, as will upward motion (moreover, this opposition is precisely that which is attributed to Aristotle a few lines later, where it is explicitly said to be different from Xenarchus' opposition: 56,18-20). Transposing the 'upwards' and the 'downwards' is also possible, yielding the sense: 'both the circular [motion] of the fire and that upwards to that downwards' (i.e. opposing the two supposed natural motions of fire to its unnatural motion); but that would make Simplicius's reply an *ignoratio elenchi* (although it is possible that Simplicius misconstrued Xenarchus' text here).

208. *An. Post.* 1.1, 71a1-2: the opening sentence of *Posterior Analytics*.

209. *Cael.* 1.2., 268b19-20; *In Cael.* 1.2, 13,14-14,29 above.

210. An elaboration of hypothesis [1]: 16,3-5 above; *Cael.* 1.2, 268b17-21.

211. Hypothesis [5]: 12,10; *Cael.* 1.2, 269a10, 13.

212. Hypothesis [4]: 12,10, above; *Cael.* 1.2, 269a8-9.

213. The first hypothesis: 12,7-8 above; *Cael.* 1.2, 268b17-19.

214. Hypotheses [2] and [3]: 12,8-9 above; *Cael.* 1.2, 269a3-4.

215. *Cael.* 1.2, 269a2-18.

216. *Cael.* 1.2, 269a18-b2, 269b13-17.

217. *Cael.* 1.3, 269b29-270a3, below; cf. 61,16-18 below.

218. In Chapter 2.

219. This will be argued for at *Cael.* 1.3, 269b29-270a3, below.

220. This is the burden of Chapter 4.

221. *Cael.* 1.3, 269b29, below.

222. Because definitions are equivalences: if A $=_{\text{df.}}$ B, then any A is B and *vice versa*; this is the meaning of 'conversion' in this context: the Greek word *antistrophê* usually translates as 'contraposition' in logical contexts (as at 144,15 below), i.e. the inference from 'all A's are B's' to 'all non-B's are non-A's' (or from 'if *p* then *q*' to 'if not-*q* then not-*p*'): but here that obviously gives the wrong sense.

223. It is not clear to whom Simplicius refers here, nor what is precisely the nature of the unsound arguments he castigates: but it is easy to see how someone (Xenarchus?) might have argued that there was an inconsistency in the Aristotelian scheme of things: having proposed that there is one and only one simple motion for each simple body (hypotheses [2] and [3]) he finds himself with three simple motions (up, down, and around), but five simple bodies (earth, water, air, fire, ether); for Philoponus, see *Against Aristotle on the Eternity of the World* fragments 1-5 (Wildberg, 1987, 41-5); below, n. 414. Simplicius' solution is that air and water are not, properly speaking, simple bodies, since they possess only relative, and not absolute, heaviness and lightness.

224. 61,15-18, n. 222 above.

225. See *Cael.* 1.2, 269a2-12; *in Cael.* 1.2, 12,7-11. The axioms he has in mind are 'hypothesis' [4], plus a substitution-instance of a compound proposition derived from 'hypothesis' [5] and the Aristotelian claim (269a-10) that 'unnatural motion is contrary to natural motion'.

226. *CAG* V.4, 12,6-10. Themistius (*fl.* late 340s to 385) considered that the form of the commentary was already played out (*in An. Post.* 1,2-12), and turned instead to creative paraphrase, a style he claims to have invented. His paraphrase of *de Caelo* survives in a Hebrew version of an Arabic translation, but it is of fairly limited value. It is disputed whether Themistius was a Neoplatonist, or rather a more or less orthodox Aristotelian (see H.J. Blumenthal, 'Themistius, the last Peripatetic commentator on Aristotle?' in Bowersock *et al.* (eds) *Arktouros*, Hellenic Studies presented to Bernard M.W. Knox [Berlin and New York, 1979], 168-82); at all events, his version of Aristotle is much freer of Platonizing accretions than that of later writers such as Simplicius.

227. No mood of the syllogism with two negative premisses is valid.

228. Simplicius' point here is that we cannot construe the premisses as being of the form 'it is not the case that A is B' and 'it is not the case that B is C', since nothing follows from two such premisses (n. 227); hence to say that 'A is not B' is to predicate something, the lack of B, positively of A. Such a 'positive' predication is indefinite, in that there are indefinitely many ways of not being something or other (compare 'Socrates is not white' – non-whiteness is not a particular colour); Simplicius is not here speaking of indefinite propositions, i.e. those in which the quantity is not specified (e.g. 'pleasure is not good': *An. Pr.* 1.1., 24a19-20; cf. *Top.* 3.6, 120a5ff.).

229. To put the matter syllogistically, we cannot treat the premisses as being of the following form: (a) no circular-mover moves up or down by nature (minor premiss); (b) nothing which does not move up or down by nature is light or heavy (major premiss) – for nothing follows from two universal negatives (*An. Pr.* 1.4, 26a9-11). Simplicius construes the minor as (ai) all circular-movers are such that they move neither up nor down by nature; which, with (b), entails (c) no circular mover is light or heavy, in the first-figure mood Celarent: AeB, BaC $\vdash$ AeC ('A' and 'B' are term-variables; 'e' translates as 'belongs to no', 'a' as 'belongs to all'; thus 'AeB' represents 'A belongs to no B', 'AaB' represents 'A belongs to all B', or idiomatically, 'no B's are A's' and 'no A's are B's').

230. See n. 222 above.

231. i.e. the second Stoic indemonstrable: if A then B; but not-A; therefore not-B: Sextus, *PH* 2 157.

232. Hypothesis [4]: 12,10 above; *Cael.* 1.2, 269a8-9.

233. i.e. the revolving body could not possess rectilinear motion preternaturally, since rectilinear motion is inferior to its proper nature, while something moves preternaturally only if it moves in a manner which is intrinsically superior to its own natural motion, under the influence of a superior body. Simplicius' invocation (and rejection) of the preternatural option shows that he is sensitive to the danger of Aristotle's being taken to equivocate in his talk of what is unnatural (see *in Cael.* 1.2, 50,7-52,18 (cf. 19,11-21,32). He might also have noted that, even if it were to move upwards or downwards preternaturally, that could have had no implications for its being either heavy or light (for it is only if movement downwards is *contrary* to its nature that it would be implied that it were light, and similarly for heaviness). For the concept of preternatural motion, see 21,20-5, 51,22-6.

234. *In Cael.* 5.4, 12,11-19; Simplicius offers a similar exposition of the succeeding lemma: 64,6-12.

235. The word 'dragged' (*anelkomenon*) does not appear in the MSS of Aristotle, but Simplicius apparently read it: 64,5-6 below.

236. Reading *hoion pasa gê kai mikra*, with Dc, and *bôlos* for *bôlon*; *pace* Simplicius, it is hard to see how these considerations count as a proof of the axiom; such a proof, if one is required, would follow more readily from the consideration that, since an element is homogeneous, the whole and its parts do not differ on nature; however, see further below, 64,14-17, and nn. 240-1.

237. Here the reference must be to the whole mass of the ether, in view of the subsequent quotation from the lemma (270a8-9) which refers to the ether, and not, as one might otherwise suppose, to whole elements and their parts in general, or even (as would be linguistically possible) to the whole Universe and its parts (since of course in the latter case the parts are not identical in nature to one another and to the whole, but are rather differentiated).

238. *Cael*. 1.3, 270a9-10.

239. *Cael*. 1.3, 270a10-11.

240. Or perhaps: 'as they suppose', referring to some unnamed opponents: see next note.

241. The sequence of Simplicius' thought here is confusing, and it is unclear precisely how he takes the argument to run. That any part of a uniform mass of stuff must possess the same intrinsic properties as the mass of the whole is a consideration that crops up in a variety of places and is put to a variety of uses (e.g. at *Cael*. 1.8, 276a31-b22; 4.3, 310b3-5); it is also on occasion turned against Aristotle by his opponents: see Xenarchus' objection about the non-uniformity of movement of the parts of the heavenly spheres (*in Cael*. 1.2, 24,21-25,10). Simplicius seems, however, to be arguing that the principle of the uniformity of nature of part and whole in homogeneous substances may not be enough on its own to secure the requisite conclusion, that if the whole cannot behave in a certain manner neither can its parts, since the whole mass of earth in its proper place has no weight, although parts of it removed from that place do. But Aristotle seems not to have subscribed to the view that elements in their place are weightless; and if weight is defined as the tendency to move down if unimpeded, any particle of earth apart from the central point itself (which is not of course a particle) will have weight. Aristotle does allow that the elements only possess their fully actualized form when they are at rest in their natural places (*Cael*. 4.3, 310a33-4; see *in Cael*. 1.2, 20,11-22,29), but this is compatible with their parts still having weight (cf. Alexander's thought-experiment involving excavating under earth in its natural place: 22,19-29; and n. 132); and this is precisely what Simplicius seems to allow a few lines below: 64,32-65,16. Furthermore, Aristotle explicitly says that all the elements have weight in their natural places, except fire, and they all have lightness, except earth: *Cael*. 4.4, 311b4-9; 4.5, 312b2-19 (although he also says that air in its natural place is really light: 4.3, 311a1-3). MS c seeks to resolve the problem by reading a different text, which would make the claim that the masses are weightless (and lightnessless) in their proper places part of the assumptions made by unnamed opponents, which Simplicius rejects; but the textual changes are not convincing, and look to have been made by someone sensitive to the difficulties occasioned by the best-attested readings here. Thus it seems best to retain the text as printed by Heiberg.

242. i.e., if whole and part behave in the same way in regard to natural motion, then if the whole cannot move from its place, neither can any part of it.

243. It is not clear who Simplicius has in mind here: the position attacked seems to be that although the heavens are distinct from the sublunary world, still as a whole they are conserved, although their parts may change, rather than the claim that the heavens, being not elementally distinct from the rest of the world, are equally subject to change and decay, although conserved as part of the whole (this latter position is common, in very different ways, to both the Stoics and the Epicureans, and was probably held by Anaximander and Heraclitus as well).

244. See 270b11-16. This absolute prohibition on the unnatural motion (and hence positioning) of even a part of the ether also allows Simplicius, on Aristotle's behalf, to sidestep the question of what would happen to a piece of ether detached from the whole: would it continue to spin in place in the sublunary realm, or would it first seek to rejoin the main body of ether in the heavens? In the latter case, it would have to have a natural tendency upwards (when in an unnatural place), as well as in a circle (when in its natural place), in opposition to what Aristotle has so far established (cf. Xenarchus' objection and Alexander's reply, *in Cael* 1.2., 21,33-23,10).

245. We might make Simplicius' point here by distinguishing between the collective and the distributive senses of 'all'; all the earth is destructible in the latter sense, but not in the former; but it is doubtful whether he rightly understands Aristotle's point here; elsewhere Aristotle is perfectly happy to consider, thought-experimentally, what would happen if all of an element were removed from its natural place (*Cael.* 4.3, 310b3-5).

246. i.e. the circular motion of the celestial spheres, in which the fire-sphere participates 'preternaturally': see *in Cael.* 1.2, 21,20-5, 51,22-6; above, n. 39. Although the basic notion (of the circular motion induced in the fire by the lunar sphere) may be Aristotelian, Simplicius' language and mode of explanation here is distinctively Neoplatonist.

247. cf. *Cael.* 4.3, 310a32-311a12: the intermediate elements (water, air) move towards their likes (earth, fire), which give them form: 310b7-15.

248. The Greeks were accustomed to distinguish between two types of air, *aêr*, the thick, cloudy stuff in the vicinity of the earth, and *aithêr*, the bright, pure, gleaming substance of the upper sky: see e.g. Empedocles, fr. 31 B 38 DK, and 31 A 49 DK; but the distinction is already commonplace in Homer and Hesiod; cf. 54,16-17 above; and *Tim.* 58D.

249. Simplicius here stresses a crucial Aristotelian distinction, between process (*kinêsis*), which is intrinsically end-directed, and hence (while it is going on at any rate) incomplete, and activity or actuality (*energeia*) which is complete at every moment of its continuance. Rectilinear motion, since it is motion *towards* something, is a *kinêsis*, and hence is defined in terms of a deficiency, and hence irreducibly involves the notion of potentiality (at *Phys.* 3.1, he defines *kinêsis* as 'the actualization of what is in potentiality, insofar as it is such'; cf. *Cael.* 4.3, 310a20-b1); the same is not true for circular motion, which has no beginning and no end. On the distinction, see further *Phys.* 3.1-3.

250. i.e., the fundamental explanation of the elemental tendencies of the elements has to do with a desire for communion with higher beings, from which their tendencies to aggregate as wholes in specific places (which might have been thought to have been primary) follow. Thus Simplicius seeks to give a Neoplatonist twist to Aristotelian theory. But while it is true that Aristotle does characterize the structure of the universe as a whole in terms of its lower parts striving to emulate its higher ones, to the limit of their capacities for so doing (cf. *Cael.* 2.12, esp. 292a22-b25), it is difficult to see how the tendency of earth (and derivatively water) towards the centre can be accounted for in this way, unless those tendencies themselves are made, in un-Aristotelian fashion, to be derivative of the upward inclinations of the lighter elements (see further *Cael.* 1.8, 277a27-b9). However, at *Cael.* 4.3, 310b14-15, Aristotle does say, somewhat anomalously in the context, that the higher body always stands to the lower as form to matter.

251. A syllogism in the mood Camestres (AaB, AeC $\vdash$ BeC): contraries belong to what is generated or destroyed; contraries do not belong to the revolving body; therefore being generated or destroyed does not belong to the revolving body.

252. i.e. *Phys.* 1.7.

253. cf. *Phys.* 2.1, 192b8-15.

254. *Cael.* 1.4.

255. *Phys.* 1.7.

256. At this point, with a proleptic endorsement of his own syncretist position, Simplicius begins a long digression which occupies him until 107,24, first outlining a version of the Neoplatonist account of the emergence of the various levels of reality from their archetypical first principle, the One; proceeding therefrom to a general discussion of the metaphysics of generation, destruction, and change, which is more securely Aristotelian in tone and inspiration (although with some distinctive Neoplatonic elements, notably the suggestion at 100,9 that pure physical extension alone may be the proper candidate for the prime matter underlying change at the deepest level), and concluding with a few pages on the whether Aristotle's and Plato's account of the nature of the cosmos can be squared, an issue to which he returns in Chapter 8.

257. *Tim.* 28A; this is a Greek commonplace, one Aristotle accepts, his theory of spontaneous animal generation notwithstanding (cf. *Gen. An.* 2.6, 743a34-5: external heat is the efficient cause of the spontaneous generation of animals).

258. Or perhaps rather 'indefinitely indefinite': the idea is either that plurality is, in a sense, a particular (and hence single) thing (or possibly the thought is that a plurality is a plurality of units: but see 93,22-5 below).

259. Simplicius here refers to his Neoplatonist predecessors; the fundamental notions here are derived from Plotinus, although Simplicius regularly refers to Iamblichus, one of his teachers, as 'divine': *in Cael.* 1.1, 1,24, above; *in Phys.* 639,23.

260. In the Neoplatonic hierarchy of being, each level creates that beneath by an outpouring of its own being (procession); the created reality retains within itself the form of the higher level – or, as the Neoplatonists preferred to put it in order to emphasize the proper ontological structure of things, the created reality in part remains or rests within that which created it; finally (although Simplicius does not deal with this here), each level of created reality seeks to return to that which created it (reversion).

261. The Greeks standardly considered two to be the first number, generated from the non-numerical unit; Plato generated all numbers from the Unit (or the One) and what he called the 'indefinite dyad', a general principle of multiplicity: *Phil.* 15B-17A; Aristotle criticizes the theory at *Metaph.* 13.7, 14.1.

262. All of the various hypostases, or generations of reality beneath the One, are inferior to it in being, and hence participate in non-being, the more so the further down the hierarchy one goes, until one arrives at absolute non-being, matter and evil: cf. n. 66 above.

263. *Phdr.* 245d.

264. See 93,7, n. 258 above.

265. i.e. in the transcendent world: see n. 298 below; but cf. n. 378 below.

266. i.e. at the lower levels of reality; the One does not exist 'always', since that implies an everlasting period of time, which in turn would endow it with temporal parts ('temporal extension of being': above); but whatever does exist for ever (in time) does so in virtue of participating (to a limited extent) in the timeless eternity of the One.

267. i.e. the unified plurality, or One-Many as Plotinus calls it (*Enneads* 5.4.1-2). In these pages Simplicius offers a version of the standard Plotinian generation of reality from the One, by way of the First Hypostasis (Mind) and the Second Hypostasis (Soul); see further *Enneads* 5.2.1, a version whose clarity is not aided by its extreme abstraction (a clearer account is given by Proclus, *Elements of Theology*, 1-57, esp. 1-7, 18-20); it does this 'after' what comes earlier in a metaphysical and not in a temporal sense.

268. What is = *to on*, i.e. what really exists, the transcendental, formal world, of which the physical world is a copy; these Neoplatonic categories are owed ultimately to Plato's discussion of reality in *Rep.* 6, esp. 508A; but the cosmogony is that of *Timaeus*, esp. 28B-42E.

269. Reading *apo tou ontos* (cf. 94,2); the MSS simply have *tou ontos*, or *hupo tou ontos* (c).

270. i.e., it is because it still partially remains in the One that it partakes of the autonomy of the One to the extent its motion is self-subsistent.

271. Or 'because it is separated off <from it>'; a similar reading is possible at 95,1-2.5.15; 96,20; 97,6; 104,14; as I translate, it is the internal plurality of the created world which is at issue; on the alternative version, which fits this context well, but suits others less well, it is the fact that the created world is distinct from the transcendental world which does the explanatory work.

272. Perhaps reading *kai tên kata to einai paratasin*: 'admitted both of extension of substance and of continuance in respect of being', i.e. both physical and temporal extension.

273. The 'things akin to body' are presumably those things mentioned by Aristotle at *Cael.* 1.1, 268a1-6, and presumably at least include spatial extension and magnitude.

274. cf. 93,27-8, and n. 266, above; the everlastingness of the created world mirrors and represents, but is not the same as, the timeless eternity of the transcendent world, in the same way as physical substance represents its non-physical being.

275. This may refer to the non-being component of the physical world (i.e. that 'part' in virtue of which we say that it is not so-and-so); or it may refer to the physical world as a whole, considered as a part of the whole system of being. Simplicius' language is highly arcane and obscure here.

276. The thought here is reminiscent of Heraclitus (frr. 22 B 12, 49a, 91 Diels-Kranz: cf. *Theaetetus*, 179E-83B). A more direct source of Simplicius' contentions here is probably *Tim.* 59b-61b, on the instability of the elements in the material world, which are never really what they seem to be, but are always in a process of becoming.

277. As opposed to something which is merely coming to be, and which is hence incomplete (and has non-being in it, in the sense that something which is coming to be *F* is not yet *F*).

278. Or 'it immediately comes to be the single form', or 'the form One'.

279. Or 'as a result of'.

280. i.e. the self-mover lies midway between the pure formal unity of the One, and the indeterminate material plurality.

281. See above, 94,10, n. 271.

282. See n. 271 above.

283. See n. 271 above.

284. For this phrase, cf. *Tim.* 27D-29D, 51E-52B; *Phil.* 53C-54D; *Theaet.* 152D-E.

285. Or possibly 'extension'.

286. See n. 271.

287. i.e. time and place are responsible for the fact this particular stage of the development has parts and extension, both temporal and spatial.

288. i.e. of the wholeness and completeness of what is.

289. i.e. the sort of change exhibited by the heavens, the regular alteration of position associated with rotation, is something which is itself stable and unchanging, an *energeia* rather than a *kinêsis* (see above, n. 249); moreover, it does not involve the transformation of something into something else, as in the case of the sublunary elements.

290. Reading *oude to einai*, of MS c, for *oude tôi einai*, which Heiberg prints, and which would translate: 'nor would it create by its being the things which, etc.'

291. i.e., if the visible heaven came to be at a time, then it would be the result of some action in time, and hence it could not have been directly generated by something unchanging – but in that case it could not be, as Plato says it is, properly an image of the eternal: *Tim.* 29A-B, 30C-31A, 38B-C.

292. i.e. circular motion.

293. Aristotle will explicitly say (1.3, 270a26-35) that it is unalterable, and he defines alteration as 'motion [or change] in respect of quality', as opposed to motion in respect of place (270a28); but Simplicius, following Alexander, refuses to think that Aristotle denies alteration in every sense of the heavens, and gives as an example of such an alteration the moon's receiving light from the sun: see below, 111,24-114,6.

294. i.e. it has genuine, eternal existence and is not relegated to the sphere of mere becoming.

295. *Pol.* 269d.

296. See n. 271 above.

297. Either in the sublunary world, which is the proper locus of generation and destruction (cf. n. 379 below), or perhaps more generally in the perceptible, physical world, as opposed to the intelligible world (which is indicated by 'there' at 97,4: see n. 298).

298. i.e. in the intelligible world; see nn. 265, 298 above; but cf. n. 378 below.

299. i.e., in the intelligible world, the forms all exhibit timeless mutual relations between one another, but they do not interact as such.

300. See n. 271 above.

301. i.e., in the physical world, there is genuine interaction between the things which represent the forms of the intelligible world, and hence there is temporal change, which involves the closest to complete perfection to which these things may aspire (see n. 302 below); all this again in Neoplatonic orthodoxy, but Simplicius could legitimately claim at least a partial antecedent for it in Aristotle's claim that everything in the world strives to emulate the perfect activity of god insofar as it is capable of so doing: *Metaph.* 12.7, esp. 1072a26-b31; *Cael.* 2.12.

302. i.e., the closest they can get to the genuine unity of timeless inter-relation that holds in the transcendental world is constant physical combination and re-combination.

303. i.e. the transcendent Forms.

304. Reading *proskeitai en allois genesiourgôs* from the margin of D.

305. What is at issue here is not any developed suggestion of connections between astrological conjunctions and terrestrial events (although such connections may be hinted at at 97,28-32 below), although Neoplatonism was, by and large, perfectly accommodating to such connections (cf. Plotinus, *Enneads* 2.3). Rather Simplicius simply means that at different times of the year, different natural events occur, because of the different positions of the sun relative to the earth, a point made by Aristotle himself at *Meteor.* 1.9, 346b35-347a8.

306. Presumably the idea here is that certain composite forms occur which, even though they involve the elements, are themselves properly unified, and reflect transcendent forms (e.g., that of Man); 'derived from the heavenly things' might mean 'under the influence of the heavenly bodies' (the usual meaning of *ourania* in Simplicius: cf. 23,8; 64,27; 97,15); but 'heavenly things' here probably refers to the transcendent Forms which Plato sometimes locates 'beyond the heaven' (*Phdr.* 246E-49C, esp. 247C-E), and to which Simplicius at any rate supposes Aristotle to be obliquely referring at *Cael.* 1.9, 279a18-35.

307. For this widespread ancient notion that some creatures were generated asexually from the decaying matter of others, see e.g. *Gen. An.* 1.1, 715b4-7; 3.11, 762a8-18; Sextus Empiricus, *PH* 1.41.

308. The use of this Platonic term (*hupodokhê*) is significant: it is the word Plato uses in the *Timaeus* to refer to the basic substrate of the universe before it is endowed with qualities: 48E-9A, 50B-51B; Simplicius assimilates it to Aristotelian prime matter, which he is consequently more prone to regard as mere extension: see nn. 256 above, 321 below; however, compare 98,28: n. 313.

309. i.e. in the sublunary world; cf. n. 297 above.

310. Fire is composed of the hot and the dry, which is why it is contrary to water (which is composed of the cold and the wet): *Gen. Corr.* 2.3-4, esp. 331a16-b26.

311. Here Simplicius gestures towards the fundamental Aristotelian account of the nature of generation: the producer possess a form similar in type to what it produces ('man begets man': *Phys.* 2.1, 193b8, 2.3, 194b31), in virtue of which it induces in material which does not yet possess that form (and hence is in a contrary state) the form in question; cf. *Phys.* 1.7, *Met.* 7.7-9.

312. Perhaps reading *hupo* here before *tôn poiountôn*; at any rate this must be the sense of the genitive.

313. This phrase shows that Simplicius at any rate believes that Aristotle is committed to qualityless prime matter: see 100,9 below, n. 321.

314. i.e. the producer causes the thing affected to take on whatever quality is primarily involved in the production: the producer's *F*-ness induces *F*-ness in the thing affected.

315. According to standard four-quality theory, air is a mixture of the hot and the moist, fire of the hot and the dry: see *Gen. Corr.* 2.1-4; and see n. 363 below.

316. This phrase, *ê posotêtas*, should probably be deleted; although it may anticipate 'magnitudes and shapes' of 100,8.

317. For the idea that heat and cold are active qualities, while wetness and dryness are passive, see *Meteor.* 4.1.

318. It is not immediately obvious what Simplicius has in mind here. The point may simply be that when stuffs change state they do not maintain their volume (boiling a gallon of water produces more than a gallon of steam); but he is perhaps referring obliquely to the Platonic theory of the *Timaeus*, according to which the fundamental structures of the elements are the regular solids, the cube, the pyramid (tetrahedron), the octahedron, and the icosahedron (corresponding respectively to earth, fire, air and water), and the triangles which form their sides (*Tim.* 53C-57C); transmutation of the elements takes place when the faces of the solids are re-areanged (thus a twenty-sided unit of water can re-combine into two of air and one of fire: 56D). A consequence of this is that, in spite of what Simplicius will later claim (105,34), earth (being made of square faces, which resolve into pairs of equilateral right-angle triangles) cannot change into any of the other elements (as Plato acknowledges: 54B-C), the faces of whose bodies are equilateral triangles, conceived by Plato as pairs of scalene right-angle triangles: 54A-B; see further n. 350 below.

319. The antecedent of this pronoun is not clear, but it should probably be taken to be 'bodily extension'.

320. Presumably this picks up 'qualities' of the previous line.

321. The Greek is tortuous here, but the sense is clear enough: something must stay constant through any change of fundamental quality (since unless something remains, it is not a change at all: *Phys.* 1.6-7): the alternatives, for the continuant substrate of the change, are (i) the quality which doesn't alter in this particular transformation (i.e. the hot in the case of the transformation from air to fire), and whatever physical extension is appropriate to it, or (ii) some still more fundamental 'prime matter' which is the substrate for all of the qualities, although in fact exhibits none of them. Simplicius is studiedly neutral here; Aristotle's position is controversial: cf. *Gen. Corr.* 2.1, 329a30-b5, which apparently (although this is disputed) favours (ii); on this issue, see King, 1956; Williams, 1982; Charlton, 1970.

322. i.e. change has the fundamental form of *x* coming to be *F* from having been *G* (for some *x*, *F*, and *G*), where *F* and *G* are contraries, and where *x* is what persists through the change (and hence is what *is* changed): again see *Phys.* 1.7; and see 100,28-32 below: this analysis of change was motivated in large part in order to obviate the challenge of Parmenides and the Eleatics, that since coming to be was the coming to be of something from what is not, and since what is not is nothing, and hence can have no causal or explanatory power (and cannot even properly be referred to), generation is impossible: Parmenides, fr. 28 B 8 Diels-Kranz.

323. *parakhrôsis*: a technical term for a slight change of degree; see n. 371 below.

324. Aristotle referred the capacities for growth, metabolism and reproduction common to both animals and plants to a part of the soul, the nutritive soul (cf. *de An.* 2.2, 413a21-414a4; *Gen. An.* 2.1, 735a15-19); the Stoics preferred to consider such capacities merely as natural (*phusikai*) rather than psychic (*psukhikai)*; Galen dismisses the difference as being purely a matter of terminology (*On the Natural Faculties* II 1-2 Kühn). The point here is that even if the overall processes of growth and metabolism are under the control of the soul (the self-regulating living organism), none the less the processes which it involves are physical processes of qualitative change.

325. See n. 322 above.

326. *Phys.* 5.1.

327. *Phys.* 1.7.

328. Aristotle held that in animal generation the male contributed form, in the form of the semen, the female the material in the form of the menstrual fluid: *Gen. An.* 1.2, 716a3-15; 1.20, 727b34-729a32; and generally 1.18-23.

329. In the case of substantial change, something coming to be a particular type of thing, like a man, it does not do out of its opposite (for there are no opposites to substantial forms: cf. 102,9, 22-3 below; and see n. 387); but it does not thereby come to be out of nothing – it comes to be out of material constituents which were such as, prior to the generation of the individual, such as to be an individual of that type potentially but not yet actually: *Phys.* 1.7, 190b1-10; 1.8, 191b13-17.

330. cf. *Phys.* 1.8, 191b14-17; 1.9, 192a3-6.

331. See n. 329 above.

332. Reading *ek mê toioutou, pephukotos de <ginesthai toioutou>, pasin*, etc., paralleling 102,3-4 above. The sentence is extremely tortuous, and something appears to have gone wrong with it; one might also supply *kai tais ousiais* before *kai tois ex enantiôn*, although that might simply be understood from the context, as indicated by my supplement '[both substances]'.

333. Here ends the first substantial portion of Simplicius' long digression.

334. See above, 92,10: the reference is to *Phys.* 1.7.

335. See 102,9 above; n. 329.

336. See n. 328 above.

337. i.e. the form of man.

338. See *Cael.* 1.10-12.

339. *Laws* 10, 894A.

340. In other words, the sort of generation Simplicius has in mind here, and which he goes on, in standard Neoplatonist fashion, to ascribe to the Plato of the *Timaeus* (cf. *in Cael.* 1.8), is not generation in time on the Aristotelian model, but rather the continual metaphysical dependency of the subsequent hypostases on the prior beings, in the manner he sketched a few pages earlier; this allows him to make the syncretist move of saying that Aristotle and Plato do not in fact contradict one another.

341. *Tim.* 27D-28C.

342. *Tim.* 27D-28A; cf. *in Cael.* 1.8.

343. *Tim.* 28B; cf. *in Cael.* 1.10, 297,1-301,28.

344. See n. 271 below.

345. *Pol.* 269D-E.

346. *Tim.* 38B.

347. *Tim.* 38B.

348. *Tim.* 38B-C.

349. *Tim.* 39D-E.

350. This is in fact a problem for Simplicius. Plato does indeed talk of the transmutation of all the elements, including earth, at *Tim.* 49B-C: but he is cautious about it ('first we see – or think we see – what we have just been calling water condense and turn into stones and earth .... So in this manner they transmit their generation to one another cyclically, or so it appears'), and explicitly withdraws the claim in the case of earth (54B-C: see n. 318 above). This is of course a difficulty for Simplicius' syncretist project, sice the transmutability of earth is never in doubt for Aristotle (cf. e.g. *Cael.* 4.5; *Gen. Corr.* 2,3-5), who in any case heavily criticizes Plato's account (e.g. at *Cael.* 3.7-8).

351. Heiberg punctuates with a full stop here, but grammatically this long sentence is a rhetorical question, paralleling the previous one.

352. *Tim.* 41A-D.

353. Here ends the long digression that has occupied Simplicius since 92,32.

354. *Cael.* 1.2, 269a18-b2, 269b13-17; see *in Cael.* 1.2, 40,1-41,32 above; cf. *in Cael.* 1.3, 60,11-12; 91,23-4; 103,11-12.

355. cf. 95,24-96,25.

356. *Cael.* 1.3, 270a12-22; 91,23-92,31 above.

357. *Cael.* 1.3, 270a17-18; 92,11-93,31.

358. *Cael.* 1.3, 270a18-20; cf. 92,11-27, above.

359. Either the text is elliptical here, or something has fallen out; the sense, however, is not in doubt.

360. *Cael.* 1.4.

361. *Phys.* 1.7.

362. This appears to be a reference to Simplicius' own commentary on the *Physics*, which is usually thought to post-date *in Cael*; either the conventional dating is wrong, or this is a later insertion; or, just possibly, all of this passage, from 108,10-23, is a quotation from Alexander.

363. cf. *Gen. Corr.* 2.4, 331a16ff.; and n. 312 above.

364. *Tim.* 40b; the passage is more fully quoted and discussed in relation to *Cael.* 1.12, 283a24-9 below.

365. At *Cael.* 1.4.

366. See n. 328 above.

367. At *Part. An.* 2.1, 646a13-24, Aristotle distinguishes types of levels of composition: (1) formation of stuffs from the elements and qualities; (2) formation of the 'uniform substances' (*homoiomerê*) in living bodies (e.g. blood, bone and flesh), also from the elements; and (3) formation of the non-uniform parts (e.g. the face, the hand) from the uniform parts. The distinction between (2) and (3) is fundamental to his biology; members of set (2) are dissective (any part of bone is bone), while those of (3) are not (a nose is not a face).

368. 1.3, 270a30.

369. i.e. nourishment, under the influence of the nutritive soul (for which see *de An.* 2.2-4), is not the only form of augmentation or growth – so merely showing that the heavenly body is not subject to nourishment would not be enough to show that it cannot grow in any way.

370. 270a25 above; Simplicius 'quotation' here differs slightly from Aristotle's words as reported in our MSS; but the sense is unaffected, and there is no need to suggest emendation to either text.

371. This is an example of 'tinting' (see n. 323 above), a superficial and evanescent change which contrasts with the more permanent (but still alterable) condition of a disposition (*diathesis*) and the completely unalterable condition of a state (*hexis*); see *Nic. Eth.* 6.5, 1148b18-34; *Pol.* 2.1-2, 1220a18-b20; *Metaph.* 5.19-20, 1022b1-14, although in the latter passage Aristotle differentiates the two concepts along rather different lines. The distinction between disposition and state was to have a long history in ancient medicine.

372. A syllogism in the mood Camestres.

373. *Cat.* 14, 15a19-25.

374. The word translated 'effect' (*apotelesma*) is standardly (although not exclusively) used in later Greek in the astrological sense of the effect on human destiny of the arrangement of the heavenly bodies – and that is almost certainly its sense here, although Simplicius might have been thinking, in good Aristotelian fashion, of the explanation of seasonal change on the basis of the sun's tropical movement (see *Meteor.* 1.9, 346b36-47a5; *Gen. Corr.* 2.10); see 1.4, 156,20-4 below.

375. This word, *sunkrisis*, also has an astrological sense, of 'combination of influences'.

376. In this case planets.

377. Although they have not really either grown or diminished.

378. i.e. in the heavens; but see nn. 265, 298 above.

379. i.e. in the sublunary realm: see n. 298 above.

380. i.e. the heavenly bodies like the moon can take on properties (by alteration), such as the ability to illuminate, from something else without thereby compromising any of their own actual inherent causal properties; but when iron is warmed, although it is naturally cold, it is no longer cold, in the sense of actually possessing the power to cool, other than potentially.

381. Fr. 30 B 7 Diels-Kranz (part): a longer extract is preserved by Simplicius *in Phys.* 111,19-112,15.

382. Simplicius' point is that the type of affection which the heavenly bodies may be said to undergo is not such as to affect their fundamental constitution, and hence has no tendency to diminish and destroy them – this is why he insists that even some property such as the moon's shining by reflected light belongs in a sense intrinsically to the nature of the moon.

383. 270b2 below.

384. i.e. growth and diminution are specifically different from, and not merely types of, alteration.

385. *Cat.* 14, 15a23.

386. It is not clear whether this pronoun refers to Aristotle (as is perhaps more likely on grounds of sense), or Alexander (which is slightly favoured by the grammar).

387. i.e. what substantial individuals like human beings are generated out of are not their contraries (since there is no contrary to 'man'), but simply out of something (matter) which was not (yet) a man, but was none the less such as to be suitable matter out of which a man could come to be; see 101,17-28, and nn. 328-9 above.

388. i.e., it would be different in definition from the passive affection.

389. cf. 113,13 above.

390. See *in Cael.* 1.2, 12,7-12 above.

391. Plotinus, 2.1.2, 12; cf. *in Cael.* 1.2, 12,11-15 above.

392. i.e., apparently, the hypothesis of the ether; but Plotinus rejected it (*Enneads* 2.1.2, 11-14); see n. 66 above.

393. That circular motion has no contrary: *Cael.* 1.4.

394. Generation and destruction take place from and into opposites: *Phys.* 1.5, 188a30-b26; cf. 1.7-8.

395. The MSS of Aristotle have 'both barbarians and Greeks' here; but Simplicius quotes the sentence later in this form (139,28-9); and cf. 117,4-5 below, and n. 402; however, re-quoting the sentence later (370,6) he writes 'both barbarians and Greeks'.

396. 'Preconception' (*prolêpsis*) is originally a technical term of Epicurean philosophy, describing the basic, untutored intuitions that all humans bring to bear upon their experience of the world.

397. Notorious ancient atheists.

398. *Phys.* 8.6.

399. *Metaph.* 12.6.

400. And hence not physical objects, like the heavenly bodies. Simplicius denies that Aristotle here seeks to prove the existence of the gods, or even the existence of a universal human belief in them, as Alexander supposed. Rather, the almost universal belief in the gods is simply a confirmation from what is apparent that the argument so far is on the right track.

401. Reading *theiou* (as in the equivalent clause at 117,18-19), as against *theou*, printed by Heiberg.

402. This is problematic: the grammar suggests that Simplicius is quoting a phrase directly from Aristotle here; however, he gives the phrase in question in the accusative case, whereas in the text of Aristotle as we have it it is nominative. Simplicius probably read a different text of Aristotle from the one we have here – see n. 395 above – but even so it is very difficult to see how his text could have contained accusatives at this point. An alternative translation might be: 'the fact that it is everybody, not only Greeks but also barbarians, shows that this kind of supposition in their souls is something natural'.

403. It is something natural because it is (almost) universal, and hence exhibits an intrinsic trait of human nature rather than one which merely culturally conditioned.

404. i.e. the following clause.

405. i.e. it asserts the existence of the gods, rather than making it the antecedent of a genuine conditional, since (in Simplicius' view at any rate) would deny the truth of the clause; see *in Cael.* 1.2, 18,9-19 above.

406. This is probably a reference to the Christians, as prone in Simplicius' day to think that the end was nigh as they are now: the *houtoi* would then simply be a contemptuous appellation (compare *houtos*, 'this one', for Philoponus: 119,7); it is just possible, however, that it refers to the Babylonian and Egyptian astronomers mentioned in the previous paragraph, as was suggested to me by a reader (however, I can find no indications that they tended suppose that the end was at hand).

407. cf. *in Cael.* 1.1, 1,1-6,8 above, on the different meanings of *ouranos*.

408. In other words, he does not treat the 'confirmations' as though they were themselves, independently, genuinely demonstrative; this is probably a dig at Alexander: see 118,15-29 above.

409. The idea that human beings are naturally equipped to arrive at the truth echoes earlier remarks about 'animal sympathy' and the source of proper conviction: *in Cael.* 1.2, 55,3-13; cf. n. 201.

410. Indeterminate in the sense that while there is only one way of being right, there are indefinitely many ways of being wrong.

411. Especially *Phys.* 1.7.

412. 270a17 above.

413. i.e. 'that the movements of contrary things are themselves contrary'.

414. This sentence brings out starkly the problem confronting Aristotle and his faithful disciples like Simplicius in maintaining that simple bodies and simple motions are in one-one correspondence at the same time as holding that there are five bodies but only three motions. Aristotle will on occasion speak as if there are only three elements (*Cael.* 1.8, 277b13-17; 3.1, 298b6-8; cf. Simplicius, *in Cael.* Prooemium, 1,18-24; 1.8, 272,11-12; 3.1, 555,7-12); but in his treatment of the properties of the sublunary world in *Cael.* 3-4, he is clearly committed (as he is elsewhere) to there being four properly distinct sublunary elements. This difficulty was seized upon by opponents of the Aristotelian scheme, notably Philoponus (*Against Aristotle on the Eternity of the World* fragments 1-5; Wildberg, 41-5); Simplicius tries to evade it in the next paragraph.

415. i.e. if there is to be a proper contrary of the circular, it must be a properly-defined, definite trajectory: it cannot simply be the non-circular.

416. i.e. the heavy and the light: see *Cael.* 4.4.

417. i.e. the pure elements.

418. And there is no opposite to circular motion, so there can be no such admixture. Of course, any Aristotelian must accept that different heavenly spheres move with different speeds, and it is not clear how they are to account for that: see the objections of Xenarchus, *in Cael.* 1.2, 24,21-25,10.

419. *proslêpsis*, the Stoic technical term for the categorical premiss in a hypothetical syllogism: ps.-Ammonius *in Anal. Pr.*, *CAG* IV, 68,4ff. = *SVF* 2.236; cf. Sextus Empiricus, *adv. Math.* 8.413 = *SVF* 2.239; Galen, *Inst. Log.* 7 = *SVF* 2.244.

420. i.e. whether a particular curve is considered to be concave or convex depends on one's point of view.

421. This premiss is not explicitly stated by Aristotle; but it is both implied by and required for the argument.

422. See *in Cael.* 1.2, 12,10; 19,17-29; 20,35-21,7; 55,26-7; 1.3, 60,3.

423. On arguments 'from the more and the less', *ek tou mallon kai hêtton*, see *Top.* 2.10-11, 114b38-115b10; 3.6, 19b18-30; 4.6, 127b18-128a11; 5.8, 137b14-138a29.

424. It is hard to see, however, why it should not be seen as a limiting case of it.

425. Most MSS of Aristotle have *periphereis* ('curving') here, with 'lines' being understood; Simplicius clearly read *periphereias* ('circumferences', or 'arcs'): 146,25-6. There is of course no difference in sense.

426. Fig. 1:

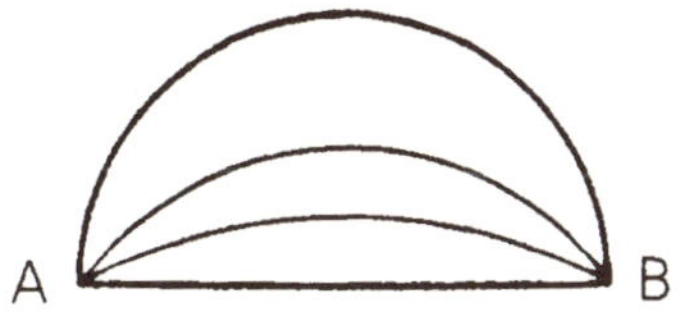

427. The expression is difficult, but the sense clear: the sense in which the motion from A to B along the circumference is contrary to that from B to A is given by the contrariety of directions along the straight line linking the two points on the circumference directly (see Fig. 1; *Cael.* 271a8-9, 12-13); this amounts to determining the nature of a motion solely in terms of its beginning and end-points, independently of the particular trajectory the moving object takes between them. It is of course a further question why anyone should think this, one which Simplicius tries to answer in the following paragraphs.

428. See n. 425 above.

429. Aristotle will go on to argue that there cannot be an infinite circle: *Cael.* 1.5.

430. sc. which join the two points: see Fig. 1 above; the straight line between the two points is numerically finite in the strongest sense – there is only one of them. Heiberg prints *periphereis* here; but see n. 425 above; it seems better to adopt the reading of MS D, *periphereias*, for the sake of consistency.

431. This very long complex conditional is difficult and unwieldy to reproduce in English; I have added the roman numbering for convenience. (i)-(vi) are conjuncts of a conjunctive antecedent, of which (vii) is the conclusion, which itself has the form of a conditional; in addition, premisses (iv) and (v) have appended sub-lemmas supporting them, the second of which is itself complex in form.

432. In length, i.e. there is no one particular length they have, whereas contraries are supposed to be separated by a determinate distance.

433. In number: see Fig. 1.

434. Strictly speaking, of course, there is no shortest circular arc that links two points, as Simplicius implicitly notes at 147,16-19: but this lack of rigour does not affect the argument here.

435. Perhaps 'to an infinite number of cases'.

436. This sentence is difficult to construe, and seems on the face of it false: for while it is true that there is no least circular line that can be drawn linking two points (see n. 434), it is false that there is no greatest: the longest circular trajectory between any two points is that which is such as to make them diametrically opposed on the circle thus drawn. Of course, if we are allowed to go from A to B not only along the arc which links them but also around the rest of the circle, there will be no longest circular distance between two points (as the curvature of the arc linking the two points tends to zero, so the length of the remainder of the circumference of the circle as a whole tends to infinity). It seems perverse to treat such trajectories as marking the distance between points in any sense, and this seems ruled out by Simplicius' claim that he is treating of circles drawn 'in a semi-circle'; but the argument apparently needs this assumption here, in order to generate the requisite conclusion that no two points considered as being separated by arcs can ever be maximally distant from one another (and hence candidates for being in contrary places: 147,2-3), since for any arc you draw connecting them, you can always draw a larger one; see n. 438 below.

437. Fig. 2:

438. This claim is puzzling at first sight, given the previous paragraph's acknowledgement that the straight line is the shortest distance between two points; but Simplicius' point is that contrariety is measured in terms of the greatest possible opposition, and so in spatial cases by the largest possible spatial separation – but in view of the fact that there is, as we have seen, no largest circular line linking any two points, the greatest separation must be determined by a straight line. Moreover, consider two points on a particular circumference: they will be furthest apart if they are diametrically opposed – and the diameter is, of course, the longest chord inscribable in the circle.

439. It is unclear which Diogenes this is supposed to be. Heiberg suggests Diogenes the Cynic, and he is probably the most likely candidate. This looks like a reference to a *bon mot* of a typically cynical kind; donkeys were proverbially stupid – but presumably even they are not so foolish as to take a circuitous route towards nourishment (or something else of value, as presumably some hapless victim of Diogenes' wit is being accused of doing).

440. See n. 448 below.

441. Fig. 3:

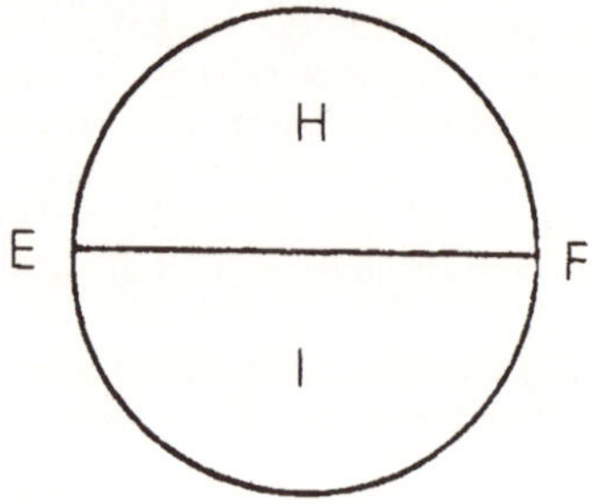

442. 146,18-147,21: Fig. 1.

443. 147,23-148,26: Fig. 2.

444. 148,28-149,10: Fig. 3.

445. Or perhaps 'by way of a counter-objection' (see LSJ s.v.); the sense seems to require something like 'concessively'. I read *antiparastasin*, with BE²bc, against *antiperistasin*, with ADE, as printed by Heiberg, here; the later would mean 'by mutual replacement', a term in Greek physics owed originally to Empedocles to describe the way in which motion in a plenum is possible, and hence to undercut the atomist arguments for the void – but that is not to the point here.

446. Fig. 4:

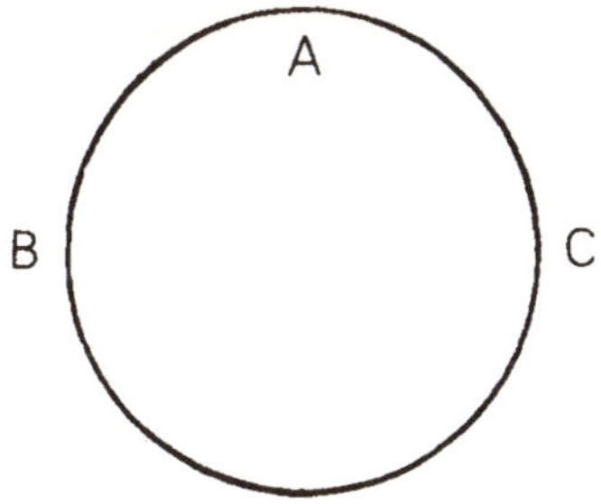

447. i.e.: all circular motions are from and to the same place; no contrary motions are from and to the same place; so no circular motions are contrary motions; an argument in the mood Cesare.

448. The lines between the asterisks seem out of place here, and their interpretation caused trouble to both Alexander and Simplicius (see below); Moraux suggests transposing them to the end of the lemma which ends at 271a19 above (see n. 440), which makes good sense; but such a dislocation must have happened relatively early in the tradition. Other alternatives are possible: see n. 461 below.

449. Aristotle in fact does argue, not entirely comfortably, for there being distinctions of up and down, front and back, and right and left in the cosmos: *Cael.* 2.2.

450. cf. 151,9 above.

451. Thus Simplicius supposes that the invocation of the contrariety of places within the circle is supposed to underwrite the claim that such counter-motions will inevitably conflict, and constantly so – but this hardly seems needed; see n. 448 above.

452. Nature does nothing in vain: a cornerstone of Aristotle's natural philosophy, and a slogan repeated constantly throughout his works – here, however, is the only occasion on which he refers to God, as well as nature, as doing nothing in vain, a fact which suggests that *de Caelo* (or at any rate this part of it) is one of his earlier surviving works; see further below, 154,6-17.

453. A reformulation in the categorical syllogistic mood Camestres of the argument of 150,25-151,2 above.

454. At 151-23-30; see n. 451.

455. i.e., according to Alexander, the argument is a *reductio*: the supposition that there are contrary circular motions entails that there must be contrarieties of place in the circle, which is absurd; so the supposition is false. See nn. 448, 451, 454 above.

456. i.e., that there are two contrary motions in opposite directions around the same circle.

457. i.e. on Simplicius' view the argument is not a simple reductio, as Alexander has it (n. 455); rather the proposition that there are contrarieties of place in the circle is used to reinforce the point that the opposing motions will constantly be at war with one another.

458. 'If circular [motion] is contrary to circular [motion]'.

459. Since neither of the two motive forces, by hypothesis, achieves anything.

460. i.e. 'one or other of them will be pointless' and 'the other body will be pointless'.

461. On this reading, a new, self-contained argument begins at 271a23, with *epi to auto gar* ('for [they are] towards the same thing'). The difficulty with this suggestion is that the new argument seems irrelevant in the context (see n. 448 above; although, as Alexander says, it depends upon the proposition that 'circular [motion] is contrary to circular [motion]': n. 458); and that it is grammatically awkward (see n. 467 below). A better option (but evidently not Alexander's: see 153,7) would be to take *epi to auto gar* with the previous sentence, supporting the claim that one of the two circular motions would be pointless.

462. This clause shows that Alexander, on the option being canvassed, treats *epi to auto gar* as part of this argument: see n. 461 above.

463. i.e. front and back, right and left: 271a26,7.

464. Reading *hôs* in place of the *pôs* of the MSS.

465. It is doubtful if it has any such coherence, however: see nn. 448, 451 above.

466. *huperbata*, i.e. the figure of speech still known as hyperbaton, or inversion; in this case, placing 'for <they are> towards the same thing' before the 'moreover' clause which introduces the new argument: see nn. 462, 465 above.

467. Or possibly: 'However Alexander set out the demonstration that there is no motion contrary to circular motion and no contrary to the revolving body, <which had been expressed> concisely, as he says, in the manner of his master Aristotle, in the following way'.

468. i.e., why should motion upwards, rather than motion downwards, be the contrary of circular motion?

469. A is contrary to B in the strict sense just in case A and B cannot both hold of the same thing, although their negations can; and these negations are themselves subcontraries. Alexander cannot mean to invoke precisely this technical distinction here – but the opposite motions are 'subcontraries of a sort' in that they both hold of the same thing, or set of things, namely the points they move from and to.

470. i.e. around a semi-circle, to a point diametrically opposed to the starting point: see Fig. 2.

471. Alexander's reasoning is obscure here: he seems to treat motion in a semi-circle as though it is in fact motion along the diameter (and not simply measured by it): then, viewed from the perspective of the diameter, the mover must stop its progress away from the starting point along the diameter before beginning to reverse that process along the other semi-circle. Or perhaps Alexander is considering motion back and forth along the same semi-circle (i.e. from C to D in Fig. 2 and then back again); at all events, his argument is unclear.

472. A major bone of contention among the commentators: Alexander, the orthodox Aristotelian denies that Aristotle made God an efficient cause; Simplicius, the Platonist, demurs. The key texts are *Phys.* 8.10, 266a12-b27, which may appear to make the Prime Mover an efficient cause, and *Metaph.* 12.7-8, which does not (although some have read 12.7, 1073a5-11 in this way). See Introduction p. 7; and *in Cael.* 1.8, 269,31-271,27.

473. i.e. if they were to claim that God is not *immediately* a productive cause of sublunary events; cf. *in Cael.* 1.3, 104,8-28; 106,25-107,25.

474. *Tim.* 41C.

475. i.e. 'God and nature do nothing pointlessly'.

476. i.e. a piece of fire ascending from one point on the earth's surface and a lump of earth descending towards a different point will none the less be moving with contrary motions, even though their directions of travel are not diametrically opposed.

477. cf. *in Cael.* 1.3, 60,20-9; 98,15-30.

478. i.e. there is no clash of force between the two motions in which one actually impedes the other, and hence two motions 'opposed' in this way can have no tendency to impede, and ultimately destroy one another, which has been a definitional characteristic of contraries properly so called.

479. See *Meteor.* 1.9, 346b36-47a5; *Gen. Corr.* 2.10; see 1.3, n. 374.

480. i.e. not in such a way that one circular motion tends to destroy the other.

Bibliography

Arnim, H. von (1903-5) *Stoicorum Veterum Fragmenta* [*SVF*], 3 vols (Leipzig); (1924), vol. 4, indexes, by M. Adler (Leipzig)

Blumenthal, H.J. (1979) 'Themistius, the last Peripatetic commentator on Aristotle?' in Bowersock, G.W., Burkert, W., and Putnam, M.C.J. (eds.) *Arktouros*, Hellenic Studies presented to Bernard M.W. Knox (Berlin and New York), 168-82

Cameron, A. (1969) 'The last days of the Academy at Athens', *Proceedings of the Cambridge Philological Society* 195, n.s. 15, 7-29

Charlton, W. (1970) *Aristotle: Physics I and II*, Clarendon Aristotle Series (Oxford)

Diels, H., and Kranz, W. (1951[6]) *Die Fragmente der Vorsokratiker*, 3 vols (Berlin)

Dillon, J.M. (1973) *Iamblichi Chalcidensis in Platonis Dialogos Commentariorum Fragmenta* (Leiden)

Drossaart Lulofs, H. (1965) *Nicolaus Damascenus: On the Philosophy of Aristotle* (Leiden)

Frantz, A. (1975) 'Pagan philosophers in Christian Athens', *Proceedings of the American Philological Society* 119, 29-38

Glucker, J. (1978) *Antiochus and the Late Academy* (*Hypomnemata* 56) (Göttingen)

Guthrie, W.K.C. (1936) *Aristotle: On the Heavens*, Loeb Classical Library (London/Cambridge MA)

Haase, W. and Temporini, H. (eds) *Aufstieg und Niedergang der römischen Welt* [*ANRW*] (Berlin/New York)

Hadot, I. (1969) 'Die Widerlegung des Manichäismus im Epiktetkommentar des Simplikios', *Archiv für Geschichte der Philosophie* 50, 46

Hadot, I. (1990) 'The life and works of Simplicius in Greek and Arabic sources', in Sorabji, 1990

Hadot, I. (ed.) (1987) *Simplicius – sa vie, son oeuvre, sa survie*, Peripatoi vol. 15 (Berlin)

Hankinson, R.J. and Matthen, M. (forthcoming) *Aristotle: On the Heavens I*, Clarendon Aristotle Series (Oxford)

Heiberg, I.L. (1894) *Simplicii in Aristotelis de Caelo Commentaria* (Berlin), *Commentaria in Aristotelem Graeca* [*CAG*], vol. VII

Hoffmann, P. (1987) 'Simplicius' polemics', in Sorabji, 1987

Isnardi Parente, M. (1982) *Senocrate – Ermodoro: Frammenti* (Naples)

King, H.R. (1956) 'Aristotle without *prima materia*', *Journal of the History of Ideas* 17, 370-89

Larsen, D.G. (1972) *Jamblique de Chalcis, Exégète et Philosophe* (Aarhus)

Lejeune, A. (1989[2]) *L' Optique de Claude Ptolémée* (Leiden, repr. of Louvain 1956)

Matthen, M. and Hankinson, R.J. (1993) 'Aristotle on the form of the Universe', *Synthese* 96.3, 417-35

Moraux, P. (1965) *Aristote: Du Ciel,* Budé (Paris)
Moraux, P. (1984) *Der Aristotelismus bei den Griechen*, vol. 2 (Berlin)
Sorabji, R.R.K. (1982) *Time, Creation and the Continuum* (London)
Sorabji, R.R.K. (ed.) (1987) *Philoponus and the Rejection of Aristotelian Science* (London)
Sorabji, R.R.K. (1988) *Matter, Space and Motion* (London)
Sorabji, R.R.K. (ed.) (1990) *Aristotle Transformed* (London)
Tardieu, M. (1986) 'Témoins orientaux du *Premier Alcibiade* à Harrân et à Nag 'Hammâdi', *Journal Asiatique* 127
Tardieu, M. (1986) 'Sâbiens coraniques et "Sâbiens" de Harrân', *Journal Asiatique* 274, 1-44
Tardieu, M. (1987) 'Les calendriers en usage à Harrân d'après les sources arabes et le commentaire de Simplicius à la *Physique* d'Aristote', in Hadot, 1987
Verrycken, K. 'The development of Philoponus' thought and its chronology', in Sorabji, 1990
Wildberg, C. (1987) *Philoponus: Against Aristotle on the Eternity of the World* (London/Ithaca NY)
Wildberg, C. (1988) *John Philoponus' Criticism of Aristotle's Theory of Ether* (Berlin/New York)
Williams, C.J.F. (1982) *Aristotle: On Generation and Corruption*, Clarendon Aristotle Series (Oxford)
Wolff, M. (1988) 'Philoponus and the rise of pre-classical dynamics', in Sorabji, 1988

Appendix
The Commentators*

The 15,000 pages of the Ancient Greek Commentaries on Aristotle are the largest corpus of Ancient Greek philosophy that has not been translated into English or other European languages. The standard edition (*Commentaria in Aristotelem Graeca*, or *CAG*) was produced by Hermann Diels as general editor under the auspices of the Prussian Academy in Berlin. Arrangements have been made to translate at least a large proportion of this corpus, along with some other Greek and Latin commentaries not included in the Berlin edition, and some closely related non-commentary works by the commentators.

The works are not just commentaries on Aristotle, although they are invaluable in that capacity too. One of the ways of doing philosophy between A.D. 200 and 600, when the most important items were produced, was by writing commentaries. The works therefore represent the thought of the Peripatetic and Neoplatonist schools, as well as expounding Aristotle. Furthermore, they embed fragments from all periods of Ancient Greek philosophical thought: this is how many of the Presocratic fragments were assembled, for example. Thus they provide a panorama of every period of Ancient Greek philosophy.

The philosophy of the period from A.D. 200 to 600 has not yet been intensively explored by philosophers in English-speaking countries, yet it is full of interest for physics, metaphysics, logic, psychology, ethics and religion. The contrast with the study of the Presocratics is striking. Initially the incomplete Presocratic fragments might well have seemed less promising, but their interest is now widely known, thanks to the philological and philosophical effort that has been concentrated upon them. The incomparably vaster corpus which preserved so many of those fragments offers at least as much interest, but is still relatively little known.

The commentaries represent a missing link in the history of philosophy: the Latin-speaking Middle Ages obtained their knowledge of Aristotle at least partly through the medium of the commentaries. Without an appreciation of this, mediaeval interpretations of Aristotle will not be understood. Again, the ancient commentaries are the unsuspected source of ideas which have been thought, wrongly, to originate in the later mediaeval period. It has been supposed, for example, that Bonaventure in the thirteenth century invented the ingenious arguments based on the concept of infinity which attempt to prove the Christian view that the universe had a beginning. In fact, Bonaventure is merely repeating arguments devised

* Reprinted from the Editor's General Introduction to the series in Christian Wildberg, *Philoponus Against Aristotle on the Eternity of the World*, London and Ithaca, N.Y., 1987.

by the commentator Philoponus 700 years earlier and preserved in the meantime by the Arabs. Bonaventure even uses Philoponus' original examples. Again, the introduction of impetus theory into dynamics, which has been called a scientific revolution, has been held to be an independent invention of the Latin West, even if it was earlier discovered by the Arabs or their predecessors. But recent work has traced a plausible route by which it could have passed from Philoponus, via the Arabs, to the West.

The new availability of the commentaries in the sixteenth century, thanks to printing and to fresh Latin translations, helped to fuel the Renaissance break from Aristotelian science. For the commentators record not only Aristotle's theories, but also rival ones, while Philoponus as a Christian devises rival theories of his own and accordingly is mentioned in Galileo's early works more frequently than Plato.[1]

It is not only for their philosophy that the works are of interest. Historians will find information about the history of schools, their methods of teaching and writing and the practices of an oral tradition.[2] Linguists will find the indexes and translations an aid for studying the development of word meanings, almost wholly uncharted in Liddell and Scott's *Lexicon*, and for checking shifts in grammatical usage.

Given the wide range of interests to which the volumes will appeal, the aim is to produce readable translations, and to avoid so far as possible presupposing any knowledge of Greek. Notes will explain points of meaning, give cross-references to other works, and suggest alternative interpretations of the text where the translator does not have a clear preference. The introduction to each volume will include an explanation why the work was chosen for translation: none will be chosen simply because it is there. Two of the Greek texts are currently being re-edited – those of Simplicius *in Physica* and *in de Caelo* – and new readings will be exploited by

1. See Fritz Zimmermann, 'Philoponus' impetus theory in the Arabic tradition'; Charles Schmitt, 'Philoponus' commentary on Aristotle's *Physics* in the sixteenth century', and Richard Sorabji, 'John Philoponus', in Richard Sorabji (ed.), *Philoponus and the Rejection of Aristotelian Science* (London and Ithaca, N.Y. 1987).

2. See e.g. Karl Praechter, 'Die griechischen Aristoteleskommentare', *Byzantinische Zeitschrift* 18 (1909), 516-38 (translated into English in R. Sorabji (ed.), *Aristotle Transformed: the ancient commentators and their influence* (London and Ithaca, N.Y. 1990); M. Plezia, *de Commentariis Isagogicis* (Cracow 1947); M. Richard, '*Apo Phônês*', *Byzantion* 20 (1950), 191-222; É. Evrard, *L'Ecole d'Olympiodore et la composition du commentaire à la physique de Jean Philopon*, Diss. (Liège 1957); L.G. Westerink, *Anonymous Prolegomena to Platonic Philosophy* (Amsterdam 1962) (new revised edition, translated into French, Collection Budé; part of the revised introduction, in English, is included in *Aristotle Transformed*); A.-J. Festugière, 'Modes de composition des commentaires de Proclus', *Museum Helveticum* 20 (1963), 77-100, repr. in his *Études* (1971), 551-74; P. Hadot, 'Les divisions des parties de la philosophie dans l'antiquité', *Museum Helveticum* 36 (1979), 201-23; I. Hadot, 'La division néoplatonicienne des écrits d'Aristote', in J. Wiesner (ed.), *Aristoteles Werk und Wirkung* (Paul Moraux gewidmet), vol. 2 (Berlin 1986); I. Hadot, 'Les introductions aux commentaires exégétiques chez les auteurs néoplatoniciens et les auteurs chrétiens', in M. Tardieu (ed.), *Les règles de l'interprétation* (Paris 1987), 99-119. These topics are treated, and a bibliography supplied, in *Aristotle Transformed*.

translators as they become available. Each volume will also contain a list of proposed emendations to the standard text. Indexes will be of more uniform extent as between volumes than is the case with the Berlin edition, and there will be at least three of them: an English-Greek glossary, a Greek-English index, and a subject index.

The commentaries fall into three main groups. The first group is by authors in the Aristotelian tradition up to the fourth century A.D. This includes the earliest extant commentary, that by Aspasius in the first half of the second century A.D. on the *Nicomachean Ethics*. The anonymous commentary on Books 2, 3, 4 and 5 of the *Nicomachean Ethics*, in *CAG* vol. 20, is derived from Adrastus, a generation later.[3] The commentaries by Alexander of Aphrodisias (appointed to his chair between A.D. 198 and 209) represent the fullest flowering of the Aristotelian tradition. To his successors Alexander was The Commentator *par excellence*. To give but one example (not from a commentary) of his skill at defending and elaborating Aristotle's views, one might refer to his defence of Aristotle's claim that space is finite against the objection that an edge of space is conceptually problematic.[4] Themistius (*fl.* late 340s to 384 or 385) saw himself as the inventor of paraphrase, wrongly thinking that the job of commentary was completed.[5] In fact, the Neoplatonists were to introduce new dimensions into commentary. Themistius' own relation to the Neoplatonist as opposed to the Aristotelian tradition is a matter of controversy,[6] but it would be agreed that his commentaries show far less bias than the full-blown Neoplatonist ones. They are also far more informative than the designation 'paraphrase' might suggest, and it has been estimated that Philoponus' *Physics* commentary draws silently on Themistius six hundred times.[7] The pseudo-Alexandrian commentary on *Metaphysics* 6-14, of unknown

3. Anthony Kenny, *The Aristotelian Ethics* (Oxford 1978), 37, n.3: Paul Moraux, *Der Aristotelismus bei den Griechen*, vol. 2 (Berlin 1984), 323-30.

4. Alexander, *Quaestiones* 3.12, discussed in my *Matter, Space and Motion* (London and Ithaca, N.Y. 1988). For Alexander see R.W. Sharples, 'Alexander of Aphrodisias: scholasticism and innovation', in W. Haase (ed.), *Aufstieg und Niedergang der römischen Welt*, part 2 *Principat*, vol. 36.2, *Philosophie und Wissenschaften* (1987).

5. Themistius *in An. Post.* 1,2-12. See H.J. Blumenthal, 'Photius on Themistius (Cod. 74): did Themistius write commentaries on Aristotle?', *Hermes* 107 (1979), 168-82.

6. For different views, see H.J. Blumenthal, 'Themistius, the last Peripatetic commentator on Aristotle?', in Glen W. Bowersock, Walter Burkert, Michael C.J. Putnam, *Arktouros*, Hellenic Studies Presented to Bernard M.W. Knox (Berlin and N.Y., 1979), 391-400; E.P. Mahoney, 'Themistius and the agent intellect in James of Viterbo and other thirteenth-century philosophers: (Saint Thomas Aquinas, Siger of Brabant and Henry Bate)', *Augustiniana* 23 (1973), 422-67, at 428-31; id., 'Neoplatonism, the Greek commentators and Renaissance Aristotelianism', in D.J. O'Meara (ed.), *Neoplatonism and Christian Thought* (Albany N.Y. 1982), 169-77 and 264-82, esp. n. 1, 264-6; Robert Todd, introduction to translation of Themistius *in DA* 3.4-8, in *Two Greek Aristotelian Commentators on the Intellect*, trans. Frederick M. Schroeder and Robert B. Todd (Toronto 1990).

7. H. Vitelli, *CAG* 17, p. 992, s.v. Themistius.

authorship, has been placed by some in the same group of commentaries as being earlier than the fifth century.[8]

By far the largest group of extant commentaries is that of the Neoplatonists up to the sixth century A.D. Nearly all the major Neoplatonists, apart from Plotinus (the founder of Neoplatonism), wrote commentaries on Aristotle, although those of Iamblichus (*c.* 250–*c.* 325) survive only in fragments, and those of three Athenians, Plutarchus (died 432), his pupil Proclus (410–485) and the Athenian Damascius (*c.* 462–after 538), are lost.[9] As a result of these losses, most of the extant Neoplatonist commentaries come from the late fifth and the sixth centuries and a good proportion from Alexandria. There are commentaries by Plotinus' disciple and editor Porphyry (232–309), by Iamblichus' pupil Dexippus (*c.* 330), by Proclus' teacher Syrianus (died *c.* 437), by Proclus' pupil Ammonius (435/445–517/526), by Ammonius' three pupils Philoponus (*c.* 490 to 570s), Simplicius (wrote after 532, probably after 538) and Asclepius (sixth century), by Ammonius' next but one successor Olympiodorus (495/505–after 565), by Elias (*fl.* 541?), by David (second half of the sixth century, or beginning of the seventh) and by Stephanus (took the chair in Constantinople *c.* 610). Further, a commentary on the *Nicomachean Ethics* has been ascribed to Heliodorus of Prusa, an unknown pre-fourteenth-century figure, and there is a commentary by Simplicius' colleague Priscian of Lydia on Aristotle's successor Theophrastus. Of these commentators some of the last were Christians (Philoponus, Elias, David and Stephanus), but they were Christians writing in the Neoplatonist tradition, as was also Boethius who produced a number of commentaries in Latin before his death in 525 or 526.

The third group comes from a much later period in Byzantium. The Berlin edition includes only three out of more than a dozen commentators described in Hunger's *Byzantinisches Handbuch*.[10] The two most important are Eustratius (1050/1060–*c.*1120), and Michael of Ephesus. It has been suggested that these two belong to a circle organised by the princess

8. The similarities to Syrianus (died *c.* 437) have suggested to some that it predates Syrianus (most recently Leonardo Tarán, review of Paul Moraux, *Der Aristotelismus*, vol.1 in *Gnomon* 46 (1981), 721-50 at 750), to others that it draws on him (most recently P. Thillet, in the Budé edition of Alexander *de Fato*, p. lvii). Praechter ascribed it to Michael of Ephesus (eleventh or twelfth century), in his review of *CAG* 22.2, in *Göttingische Gelehrte Anzeiger* 168 (1906), 861-907.

9. The Iamblichus fragments are collected in Greek by Bent Dalsgaard Larsen, *Jamblique de Chalcis, Exégète et Philosophe* (Aarhus 1972), vol. 2. Most are taken from Simplicius, and will accordingly be translated in due course. The evidence on Damascius' commentaries is given in L.G. Westerink, *The Greek Commentaries on Plato's Phaedo*, vol. 2, Damascius (Amsterdam 1977), 11-12; on Proclus' in L.G. Westerink, *Anonymous Prolegomena to Platonic Philosophy* (Amsterdam 1962), xii, n. 22; on Plutarchus' in H.M. Blumenthal, 'Neoplatonic elements in the de Anima commentaries', *Phronesis* 21 (1976), 75.

10. Herbert Hunger, *Die hochsprachliche profane Literatur der Byzantiner*, vol. 1 (= *Byzantinisches Handbuch*, part 5, vol. 1) (Munich 1978), 25-41. See also B.N. Tatakis, *La Philosophie Byzantine* (Paris 1949).

Anna Comnena in the twelfth century, and accordingly the completion of Michael's commentaries has been redated from 1040 to 1138.[11] His commentaries include areas where gaps had been left. Not all of these gap-fillers are extant, but we have commentaries on the neglected biological works, on the *Sophistici Elenchi*, and a small fragment of one on the *Politics*. The lost *Rhetoric* commentary had a few antecedents, but the *Rhetoric* too had been comparatively neglected. Another product of this period may have been the composite commentary on the *Nicomachean Ethics* (*CAG* 20) by various hands, including Eustratius and Michael, along with some earlier commentators, and an improvisation for Book 7. Whereas Michael follows Alexander and the conventional Aristotelian tradition, Eustratius' commentary introduces Platonist, Christian and anti-Islamic elements.[12]

The composite commentary was to be translated into Latin in the next century by Robert Grosseteste in England. But Latin translations of various logical commentaries were made from the Greek still earlier by James of Venice (*fl. c.* 1130), a contemporary of Michael of Ephesus, who may have known him in Constantinople. And later in that century other commentaries and works by commentators were being translated from Arabic versions by Gerard of Cremona (died 1187).[13] So the twelfth century resumed the transmission which had been interrupted at Boethius' death in the sixth century.

The Neoplatonist commentaries of the main group were initiated by Porphyry. His master Plotinus had discussed Aristotle, but in a very independent way, devoting three whole treatises (*Enneads* 6.1-3) to attacking Aristotle's classification of the things in the universe into categories. These categories took no account of Plato's world of Ideas, were inferior to Plato's classifications in the *Sophist* and could anyhow be collapsed, some

11. R. Browning, 'An unpublished funeral oration on Anna Comnena', *Proceedings of the Cambridge Philological Society* n.s. 8 (1962), 1-12, esp. 6-7.

12. R. Browning, op. cit. H.D.P. Mercken, *The Greek Commentaries of the Nicomachean Ethics of Aristotle in the Latin Translation of Grosseteste, Corpus Latinum Commentariorum in Aristotelem Graecorum* VI 1 (Leiden 1973), ch. 1, 'The compilation of Greek commentaries on Aristotle's Nicomachean Ethics'. Sten Ebbesen, 'Anonymi Aurelianensis I Commentarium in *Sophisticos Elenchos*', *Cahiers de l'Institut Moyen Age Grecque et Latin* 34 (1979), 'Boethius, Jacobus Veneticus, Michael Ephesius and "Alexander" ', pp. v-xiii; id., *Commentators and Commentaries on Aristotle's Sophistici Elenchi*, 3 parts, *Corpus Latinum Commentariorum in Aristotelem Graecorum*, vol. 7 (Leiden 1981); A. Preus, *Aristotle and Michael of Ephesus on the Movement and Progression of Animals* (Hildesheim 1981), introduction.

13. For Grosseteste, see Mercken as in n. 12. For James of Venice, see Ebbesen as in n. 12, and L. Minio-Paluello, 'Jacobus Veneticus Grecus', *Traditio* 8 (1952), 265-304; id., 'Giacomo Veneto e l'Aristotelismo Latino', in Pertusi (ed.), *Venezia e l'Oriente fra tardo Medioevo e Rinascimento* (Florence 1966), 53-74, both reprinted in his *Opuscula* (1972). For Gerard of Cremona, see M. Steinschneider, *Die europäischen Übersetzungen aus dem arabischen bis Mitte des 17. Jahrhunderts* (repr. Graz 1956); E. Gilson, *History of Christian Philosophy in the Middle Ages* (London 1955), 235-6 and more generally 181-246. For the translators in general, see Bernard G. Dod, 'Aristoteles Latinus', in N. Kretzmann, A. Kenny, J. Pinborg (eds), *The Cambridge History of Latin Medieval Philosophy* (Cambridge 1982).

of them into others. Porphyry replied that Aristotle's categories could apply perfectly well to the world of intelligibles and he took them as in general defensible.[14] He wrote two commentaries on the *Categories*, one lost, and an introduction to it, the *Isagôgê*, as well as commentaries, now lost, on a number of other Aristotelian works. This proved decisive in making Aristotle a necessary subject for Neoplatonist lectures and commentary. Proclus, who was an exceptionally quick student, is said to have taken two years over his Aristotle studies, which were called the Lesser Mysteries, and which preceded the Greater Mysteries of Plato.[15] By the time of Ammonius, the commentaries reflect a teaching curriculum which begins with Porphyry's *Isagôgê* and Aristotle's *Categories*, and is explicitly said to have as its final goal a (mystical) ascent to the supreme Neoplatonist deity, the One.[16] The curriculum would have progressed from Aristotle to Plato, and would have culminated in Plato's *Timaeus* and *Parmenides*. The latter was read as being about the One, and both works were established in this place in the curriculum at least by the time of Iamblichus, if not earlier.[17]

Before Porphyry, it had been undecided how far a Platonist should accept Aristotle's scheme of categories. But now the proposition began to gain force that there was a harmony between Plato and Aristotle on most things.[18] Not for the only time in the history of philosophy, a perfectly crazy proposition proved philosophically fruitful. The views of Plato and of Aristotle had both to be transmuted into a new Neoplatonist philosophy in order to exhibit the supposed harmony. Iamblichus denied that Aristotle contradicted Plato on the theory of Ideas.[19] This was too much for Syrianus and his pupil Proclus. While accepting harmony in many areas,[20] they could see that there was disagreement on this issue and also on the issue of whether God was causally responsible for the existence of the ordered

14. See P. Hadot, 'L'harmonie des philosophies de Plotin et d'Aristote selon Porphyre dans le commentaire de Dexippe sur les Catégories', in *Plotino e il neoplatonismo in Oriente e in Occidente* (Rome 1974), 31-47; A.C. Lloyd, 'Neoplatonic logic and Aristotelian logic', *Phronesis* 1 (1955-6), 58-79 and 146-60.

15. Marinus, *Life of Proclus* ch. 13, 157,41 (Boissonade).

16. The introductions to the *Isagôgê* by Ammonius, Elias and David, and to the *Categories* by Ammonius, Simplicius, Philoponus, Olympiodorus and Elias are discussed by L.G. Westerink, *Anonymous Prolegomena* and I. Hadot, 'Les Introductions', see n. 2 above.

17. Proclus in *Alcibiadem 1* p. 11 (Creuzer); Westerink, *Anonymous Prolegomena*, ch. 26, 12f. For the Neoplatonist curriculum see Westerink, Festugière, P. Hadot and I. Hadot in n. 2.

18. See e.g. P. Hadot (1974), as in n. 14 above; H.J. Blumenthal, 'Neoplatonic elements in the de Anima commentaries', *Phronesis* 21 (1976), 64-87; H.A. Davidson, 'The principle that a finite body can contain only finite power', in S. Stein and R. Loewe (eds), *Studies in Jewish Religious and Intellectual History presented to A. Altmann* (Alabama 1979), 75-92; Carlos Steel, 'Proclus et Aristotle', Proceedings of the Congrès Proclus held in Paris 1985, J. Pépin and H.D. Saffrey (eds), *Proclus, lecteur et interprète des anciens* (Paris 1987), 213-25; Koenraad Verrycken, *God en Wereld in de Wijsbegeerte van Ioannes Philoponus*, Ph.D. Diss. (Louvain 1985).

19. Iamblichus ap. Elian *in Cat.* 123,1-3.

20. Syrianus *in Metaph.* 80,4-7; Proclus *in Tim.* 1.6,21-7,16.

physical cosmos, which Aristotle denied. But even on these issues, Proclus' pupil Ammonius was to claim harmony, and, though the debate was not clear cut,[21] his claim was on the whole to prevail. Aristotle, he maintained, accepted Plato's Ideas,[22] at least in the form of principles (*logoi*) in the divine intellect, and these principles were in turn causally responsible for the beginningless existence of the physical universe. Ammonius wrote a whole book to show that Aristotle's God was thus an efficent cause, and though the book is lost, some of its principal arguments are preserved by Simplicius.[23] This tradition helped to make it possible for Aquinas to claim Aristotle's God as a Creator, albeit not in the sense of giving the universe a beginning, but in the sense of being causally responsible for its beginningless existence.[24] Thus what started as a desire to harmonise Aristotle with Plato finished by making Aristotle safe for Christianity. In Simplicius, who goes further than anyone,[25] it is a formally stated duty of the commentator to display the harmony of Plato and Aristotle in most things.[26] Philoponus, who with his independent mind had thought better of his earlier belief in harmony, is castigated by Simplicius for neglecting this duty.[27]

The idea of harmony was extended beyond Plato and Aristotle to Plato and the Presocratics. Plato's pupils Speusippus and Xenocrates saw Plato as being in the Pythagorean tradition.[28] From the third to first centuries B.C., pseudo-Pythagorean writings present Platonic and Aristotelian doctrines as if they were the ideas of Pythagoras and his pupils,[29] and these forgeries were later taken by the Neoplatonists as genuine. Plotinus saw the Presocratics as precursors of his own views,[30] but Iamblichus went far beyond him by writing ten volumes on Pythagorean philosophy.[31] Thereafter Proclus sought to unify the whole of Greek

21. Asclepius sometimes accepts Syranius' interpretation (*in Metaph.* 433,9-436,6); which is, however, qualified, since Syrianus thinks Aristotle is realy committed willy-nilly to much of Plato's view (*in Metaph.* 117,25-118,11; ap. Asclepium *in Metaph.* 433,16; 450,22); Philoponus repents of his early claim that Plato is not the target of Aristotle's attack, and accepts that Plato is rightly attacked for treating ideas as independent entities outside the divine Intellect (*in DA* 37,18-31; *in Phys.* 225,4-226,11; *contra Procl.* 26,24-32,13; *in An. Post.* 242,14-243,25).

22. Asclepius *in Metaph.* from the voice of (i.e. from the lectures of) Ammonius 69,17-21; 71,28; cf. Zacharias *Ammonius, Patrologia Graeca* vol. 85 col. 952 (Colonna).

23. Simplicius *in Phys.* 1361,11-1363,12. See H.A. Davidson; Carlos Steel; Koenraad Verrycken in n. 18 above.

24. See Richard Sorabji, *Matter, Space and Motion* (London and Ithaca, N.Y. 1988), ch. 15.

25. See e.g. H.J. Blumenthal in n. 18 above.

26. Simplicius *in Cat.* 7,23-32.

27. Simplicius *in Cael.* 84,11-14; 159,2-9. On Philoponus' *volte face* see n. 21 above.

28. See e.g. Walter Burkert, *Weisheit und Wissenschaft* (Nürnberg 1962), translated as *Lore and Science in Ancient Pythagoreanism* (Cambridge Mass. 1972), 83-96.

29. See Holger Thesleff, *An Introduction to the Pythagorean Writings of the Hellenistic Period* (Åbo 1961); Thomas Alexander Szlezák, *Pseudo-Archytas über die Kategorien*, Peripatoi vol. 4 (Berlin and New York 1972).

30. Plotinus e.g. 4.8.1; 5.1.8 (10-27); 5.1.9.

31. See Dominic O'Meara, *Pythagoras Revived: Mathematics and Philosophy in Late Antiquity* (Oxford 1989).

philosophy by presenting it as a continuous clarification of divine revelation[32] and Simplicius argued for the same general unity in order to rebut Christian charges of contradictions in pagan philosophy.[33]

Later Neoplatonist commentaries tend to reflect their origin in a teaching curriculum:[34] from the time of Philoponus, the discussion is often divided up into lectures, which are subdivided into studies of doctrine and of text. A general account of Aristotle's philosophy is prefixed to the *Categories* commentaries and divided, according to a formula of Proclus,[35] into ten questions. It is here that commentators explain the eventual purpose of studying Aristotle (ascent to the One) and state (if they do) the requirement of displaying the harmony of Plato and Aristotle. After the ten-point introduction to Aristotle, the *Categories* is given a six-point introduction, whose antecedents go back earlier than Neoplatonism, and which requires the commentator to find a unitary theme or scope (*skopos*) for the treatise. The arrangements for late commentaries on Plato are similar. Since the Plato commentaries form part of a single curriculum they should be studied alongside those on Aristotle. Here the situation is easier, not only because the extant corpus is very much smaller, but also because it has been comparatively well served by French and English translators.[36]

Given the theological motive of the curriculum and the pressure to harmonise Plato with Aristotle, it can be seen how these commentaries are a major source for Neoplatonist ideas. This in turn means that it is not safe to extract from them the fragments of the Presocratics, or of other authors, without making allowance for the Neoplatonist background against which the fragments were originally selected for discussion. For different reasons, analogous warnings apply to fragments preserved by the pre-Neoplatonist commentator Alexander.[37] It will be another advantage of the present translations that they will make it easier to check the distorting effect of a commentator's background.

Although the Neoplatonist commentators conflate the views of Aristotle

32. See Christian Guérard, 'Parménide d'Elée selon les Néoplatoniciens', in P. Aubenque (ed.), *Etudes sur Parménide*, vol. 2 (Paris 1987).

33. Simplicius *in Phys.* 28,32-29,5; 640,12-18. Such thinkers as Epicurus and the Sceptics, however, were not subject to harmonisation.

34. See the literature in n. 2 above.

35. ap. Elian *in Cat.* 107,24-6.

36. English: Calcidius *in Tim.* (parts by van Winden; den Boeft); Iamblichus fragments (Dillon); Proclus *in Tim.* (Thomas Taylor); Proclus *in Parm.* (Dillon); Proclus *in Parm.*, end of 7th book, from the Latin (Klibansky, Labowsky, Anscombe); Proclus *in Alcib. 1* (O'Neill); Olympiodorus and Damascius *in Phaedonem* (Westerink); Damascius *in Philebum* (Westerink); *Anonymous Prolegomena to Platonic Philosophy* (Westerink). See also extracts in Thomas Taylor, *The Works of Plato*, 5 vols. (1804). French: Proclus *in Tim.* and *in Rempublicam* (Festugière); *in Parm.* (Chaignet); Anon. *in Parm* (P. Hadot); Damascius *in Parm.* (Chaignet).

37. For Alexander's treatment of the Stoics, see Robert B. Todd, *Alexander of Aphrodisias on Stoic Physics* (Leiden 1976), 24-9.

with those of Neoplatonism, Philoponus alludes to a certain convention when he quotes Plutarchus expressing disapproval of Alexander for expounding his own philosophical doctrines in a commentary on Aristotle.[38] But this does not stop Philoponus from later inserting into his own commentaries on the *Physics* and *Meteorology* his arguments in favour of the Christian view of Creation. Of course, the commentators also wrote independent works of their own, in which their views are expressed independently of the exegesis of Aristotle. Some of these independent works will be included in the present series of translations.

The distorting Neoplatonist context does not prevent the commentaries from being incomparable guides to Aristotle. The introductions to Aristotle's philosophy insist that commentators must have a minutely detailed knowledge of the entire Aristotelian corpus, and this they certainly have. Commentators are also enjoined neither to accept nor reject what Aristotle says too readily, but to consider it in depth and without partiality. The commentaries draw one's attention to hundreds of phrases, sentences and ideas in Aristotle, which one could easily have passed over, however often one read him. The scholar who makes the right allowance for the distorting context will learn far more about Aristotle than he would be likely to on his own.

The relations of Neoplatonist commentators to the Christians were subtle. Porphyry wrote a treatise explicitly against the Christians in 15 books, but an order to burn it was issued in 448, and later Neoplatonists were more circumspect. Among the last commentators in the main group, we have noted several Christians. Of these the most important were Boethius and Philoponus. It was Boethius' programme to transmit Greek learning to Latin-speakers. By the time of his premature death by execution, he had provided Latin translations of Aristotle's logical works, together with commentaries in Latin but in the Neoplatonist style on Porphyry's *Isagôgê* and on Aristotle's *Categories* and *de Interpretatione*, and interpretations of the *Prior* and *Posterior Analytics*, *Topics* and *Sophistici Elenchi*. The interruption of his work meant that knowledge of Aristotle among Latin-speakers was confined for many centuries to the logical works. Philoponus is important both for his proofs of the Creation and for his progressive replacement of Aristotelian science with rival theories, which were taken up at first by the Arabs and came fully into their own in the West only in the sixteenth century.

Recent work has rejected the idea that in Alexandria the Neoplatonists compromised with Christian monotheism by collapsing the distinction between their two highest deities, the One and the Intellect. Simplicius (who left Alexandria for Athens) and the Alexandrians Ammonius and

38. Philoponus *in DA* 21,20-3.

Asclepius appear to have acknowledged their beliefs quite openly, as later did the Alexandrian Olympiodorus, despite the presence of Christian students in their classes.[39]

The teaching of Simplicius in Athens and that of the whole pagan Neoplatonist school there was stopped by the Christian Emperor Justinian in 529. This was the very year in which the Christian Philoponus in Alexandria issued his proofs of Creation against the earlier Athenian Neoplatonist Proclus. Archaeological evidence has been offered that, after their temporary stay in Ctesiphon (in present-day Iraq), the Athenian Neoplatonists did not return to their house in Athens, and further evidence has been offered that Simplicius went to Harrān (Carrhae), in present-day Turkey near the Iraq border.[40] Wherever he went, his commentaries are a treasurehouse of information about the preceding thousand years of Greek philosophy, information which he painstakingly recorded after the closure in Athens, and which would otherwise have been lost. He had every reason to feel bitter about Christianity, and in fact he sees it and Philoponus, its representative, as irreverent. They deny the divinity of the heavens and prefer the physical relics of dead martyrs.[41] His own commentaries by contrast culminate in devout prayers.

Two collections of articles by various hands have been published, to make the work of the commentators better known. The first is devoted to Philoponus;[42] the second is about the commentators in general, and goes into greater detail on some of the issues briefly mentioned here.[43]

39. For Simplicius, see I. Hadot, *Le Problème du Néoplatonisme Alexandrin: Hiéroclès et Simplicius* (Paris 1978); for Ammonius and Asclepius, Koenraad Verrycken, *God en wereld in de Wijsbegeerte van Ioannes Philoponus*, Ph.D. Diss. (Louvain 1985); for Olympiodorus, L.G. Westerink, *Anonymous Prolegomena to Platonic Philosophy* (Amsterdam 1962).

40. Alison Frantz, 'Pagan philosophers in Christian Athens', *Proceedings of the American Philosophical Society* 119 (1975), 29-38; M. Tardieu, 'Témoins orientaux du *Premier Alcibiade* à Harrān et à Nag 'Hammādi', *Journal Asiatique* 274 (1986); id., 'Les calendriers en usage à Harrān d'après les sources arabes et le commentaire de Simplicius à la *Physique* d'Aristote', in I. Hadot (ed.), *Simplicius, sa vie, son oeuvre, sa survie* (Berlin 1987), 40-57; id., *Coutumes nautiques mésopotamiennes chez Simplicius*, in preparation. The opposing view that Simplicius returned to Athens is most fully argued by Alan Cameron, 'The last day of the Academy at Athens', *Proceedings of the Cambridge Philological Society* 195, n.s. 15 (1969), 7-29. P. Foulkes, 'Where was Simplicius', *JHS* 112 (1992), 143. R. Thiel, 'Simplikios und das Ende der neuplatonischen Schule in Athen', Akademie der Wissenschaften und der Literatur Mainz: *Abhandlungen der geistes- und sozialwissenschaftlichen Klasse*, no. 8, 1999.

41. Simplicius *in Cael.* 26,4-7; 70,16-18; 90,1-18; 370,29-371,4. See on his whole attitude Philippe Hoffmann, 'Simplicius' polemics', in Richard Sorabji (ed.), *Philoponus and the Rejection of Aristotelian Science* (London and Ithaca, N.Y. 1987).

42. Richard Sorabji (ed.), *Philoponus and the Rejection of Aristotelian Science* (London and Ithaca, N.Y. 1987).

43. Richard Sorabji (ed.), *Aristotle Transformed: the ancient commentators and their influence* (London and Ithaca, N.Y. 1990). The lists of texts and previous translations of the commentaries included in Wildberg, *Philoponus Against Aristotle on the Eternity of the World* (pp. 12ff.) are not included here. The list of translations should be augmented by: F.L.S. Bridgman, Heliodorus (?) in *Ethica Nicomachea*, London 1807.

I am grateful for comments to Henry Blumenthal, Victor Caston, I. Hadot, Paul Mercken, Alain Segonds, Robert Sharples, Robert Todd, L.G. Westerink and Christian Wildberg.

English-Greek Glossary

action: *energeia*
activity: *energeia*
actuality: *energeia*
actuality: *entelekheia*
adduce: *epagein*
additional premiss: *proslêpsis*
affection: *pathos*
affinity: *koinônia*
air: *aer*
all: *pan*
alteration: *alloiôsis*
animal: *zôion*
animate: *empsukhos*
arc: *periphereia*
argue: *sullogizein*
argument: *logos*
argument: *sullogismos*
authoritative: *kurios*
axiom: *axiôma*

balance: *summetria*
be generated: *gignesthai*
body: *sôma*
by force: *biai*

capacity: *dunamis*
cause: *aitia*, *aition*
centre: *kentron*
change: *metabolê*
circular motion: *kukloi kinêsis*
circumference: *periphereia*
cold: *psukhros*
coldness: *psukhrotês*
coldness: *psuxis*
come to be: *gignesthai*
come to rest: *êremein*
complete: *teleios*
composite: *sunthetos*
compound: *sunthetos*
concave: *koilos*
conclude: *sullogizein*
conclusion: *sumperasma*
conditional: *sunêmmenon*
configuration: *skhêmatismos*
confirmation: *pistis*
conjecture: *huponoia*
continuance: *paratasis*
continuous: *sunekhes*
contraposition: *antistrophê*
contrary: *enantion*
conversion: *antistrophê*
convert: *antistrephein*
convex: *kurtos*
conviction: *pistis*
corporeal: *sômatikos*
cosmos: *kosmos*
Creator: *dêmiourgos*

deficiency: *elleipsis*
define: *horizein*
definition: *horismos*
delimit: *horizein*
demonstrate: *apodeiknumi*
demonstration: *apodeixis*
destructible: *phthartos*
destruction: *phthora*
difficulty: *aporia*
dimension: *diastasis*
dimensional: *diastatos*
diminution: *meiôsis*
directly: *kuriôs* (adv.)
discussion: *logos*
disposition: *diathesis*
dissoluble: *lutos*
distance: *apokhê*
divine body: *theion sôma*
divisible: *diaretos*
doing: *drasis*
dry: *xêros*
dryness: *xêrotês*

earth: *gê*
earthy: *geôdes*
effectively: *dunamei*
elements: *stoikheia*
end: *telos*

Greek-English Index

References are to the page and line numbers of Heiberg's *CAG* edition of 1893, which appear in the margin of the translation.

Subject Index

References are to the page numbers of this book.